Vocational Guidance in Europe

Clinton Enoch • Christoph Krause •
Rebeca Garcia-Murias • Jane Porath
Editors

Vocational Guidance in Europe

Challenges, Needs, Solutions, and Development Perspectives

Springer

Editors
Clinton Enoch
University of Applied Labor Studies
Schwerin, Germany

Christoph Krause
University of Applied Labor Studies
Schwerin, Germany

Rebeca Garcia-Murias
University of Applied Labor Studies
Mannheim, Germany

Jane Porath
University of Applied Labor Studies
Schwerin, Germany

ISBN 978-3-031-06591-0 ISBN 978-3-031-06592-7 (eBook)
https://doi.org/10.1007/978-3-031-06592-7

This Springer imprint is published by the registered company Springer Nature Switzerland AG
The registered company address is: Gewerbestrasse 11, 6330 Cham, Switzerland

Foreword

Creating a genuine European knowledge society which benefits all learners, educators and institutions is one of the key concerns of European integration.

Sustainable economic growth and the inclusion of all individuals regardless of gender, socio-economic status or qualifications require the creation of future-oriented education and training systems in Europe, systems which encourage lifelong learning. Lifelong learning guidance and career counselling is of increasing importance; however, the situation for guidance practitioners is becoming increasingly complex.

The consequences of the Corona pandemic, a looming climate crisis, uncertain economic prospects, the demands for highly skilled employees which jobseekers face and rapidly changing professional profiles, demographic change, digitalization and migration have a serious impact on existing challenges and create new ones for career counsellors. Enhanced collaboration between guidance providers is essential. Systematic multinational programmes such as Academia, the EU-project that promotes the exchange between career counsellors and guidance practitioners within Europe, gain in importance.

The objective of the Erasmus funded Academia+ programme, highlighted in this anthology, has been to provide innovative training materials for participating counsellors.

A total of three online training modules for European career counsellors on the topics of "Counselling Migrants and Refugees", "Future Jobs" and "Demographic change" were successfully developed and implemented by the Academia+ partners from Germany, Lithuania, Luxembourg, Portugal and the United Kingdom. The modules have been independently evaluated.

Besides providing a comprehensive overview of the project, this anthology focuses on the challenges of the European labour markets from the perspective of career counsellors. Each partner's contribution describes their country's specific challenges, lists the support needs of counsellors and offers conceivable strategic avenues. These contributions aim at facilitating practice-oriented discussions among guidance practitioners, on possible ways forward.

I am particularly proud that Luxembourg has been involved in the Academia exchange programme for over 20 years and that the partner from Luxembourg has actively contributed to the development of the learning modules described in this anthology. Guidance and career counselling are particularly important to me and the fact that the International Association for Educational and Vocational Guidance chose to register as a legal entity in Luxembourg emphasises this position.

I am convinced that the modules described in this anthology will serve as a very valuable reference to guidance and career counsellors in Europe and enable them to progress in their reflections and practices.

I wish this publication the success it deserves.

Minister of Education, Children and Youth, Luxembourg Claude Meisch

Preface

At the beginning of the twenty-first century, the European labour market is in transition and Europe's societies face a number of substantial employment and social challenges. These challenges include a changing world of work, demographic change, climate change, but also topics such as Industry 4.0, digitalisation, migration and globalisation. These result in different requirements, preconditions, social structures, design options and approaches to solutions at national and international level. As an example, the impact of demographic change is becoming more apparent, migrants and refugees as well as skilled workers from non-EU countries need to get integrated in the EU countries labour markets. Also, the labour markets are becoming more international, work is becoming more mobile, more flexible and volatile. Two examples to illustrate this:

(a) Demographic change and growing employment in recent years have drawn increased attention to the skilled labour situation in Germany. Employers are signalling that it is becoming increasingly difficult to fill vacancies. From these signals from employers in Germany, for example, an "assessment of bottleneck indicators" can be made. This refers to a range of indicators such as unemployment, registered job vacancies, demand and the training situation. Last but not least, forecasts of retirement also play an important role. If we take a look at the assessment for these indicators for Germany, we can identify various professions that will suffer particularly from the shortage of skilled workers in the coming years. It is notable, for example, that in Germany in the coming years, especially nursing professions and professions from the manufacturing trades will also have a very high shortage of skilled workers (Bundesagentur für Arbeit, 2022). This can have different reasons, for one thing there are very many advertised vacancies, there is very little demand for this profession, there are no new or very few trainees, or more people will leave the profession than enter it in the coming years.

(b) Finally, the Covid-19 pandemic and the resulting effects also play an important role. While the number of employees subject to social security contributions in

> Germany has increased steadily in recent years and (seasonally adjusted) was over 33,800,000 in January 2020, the number of employees fell by almost 400,000 in March 2020 due to the pandemic (Ragnitz, 2020). The metal and electrical industry (–150,000) and the hotel and restaurant industry (–72,000) were particularly affected (Ragnitz, 2020). Although the labour market in Germany has since recovered, the pandemic has also increased existing challenges. At the same time, some long-term effects, such as on the training market, are not yet fully foreseeable. The direct effects (such as the development of employment figures) can be predicted, but the Corona pandemic also has effects in other places: For example, the pandemic led to a massive increase in mobile remote workplaces, with different numbers of people working in home offices depending on the sector. If, at the same time, schools remained closed (homeschooling), the working day had to be adapted much more flexibly to the circumstances.

Counsellors play a central role in actively managing this change and in better cushioning temporary effects (such as the Corona pandemic). On a national level, guidance practitioners and employment services play a key role in addressing these challenges of national labour markets and societies. Furthermore, this is also happening at the European level.

In a European context of mobility in training and employment, guidance practitioners must ensure that everyone has the means for lifelong guidance. Such a challenge requires knowledge of the education, training and guidance systems of European countries in their socio-economic context. The importance of a European dimension to guidance, as well as the learning opportunities which exist between European countries, is often not understood as important as it is. However, in an interconnected world, this is having a detrimental effect on the quality of guidance provided. The European Semester Thematic Factsheet on Public Employment Services (PES) (2017) states that "Public Employment Services (PES) are the principal labour market institutions directly accountable to governments and set up to facilitate labour market integration of jobseekers and in some instances payment of unemployment and/or welfare benefits". The paper also states that the PES are structured differently in each country, but that "all PES help match supply and demand in the labour market through information, placement and active support services at local, national and European levels". The European Semester Thematic Factsheet on Active Labour Market Policies (EU Commission, 2017) regards counselling and job-search assistance as mostly useful measures "for short-term unemployed, but they may still play a valuable role beyond this if they form part of an individualised or 'tailor-made' approach to support for the unemployed". The paper states that "Public employment services have a crucial role to play in re-integrating the unemployed". And for functioning it needs amongst others "a sufficient number of staff, who are properly trained in aspects that improve the quality of the service".

Their tasks comprise individual career guidance and client counselling for unemployed as well as employed persons who want or need to reorient themselves, profiling, skills assessment and training delivery (Academia+ Project Working Team, 2020a). Furthermore, they match people to job profiles and offer services to employers, as well as care catering for those furthest removed from the labour market. To perform this range of tasks competently, a high-level qualification and transnational training as well as state-of-the-art information on effective concepts and approaches and networking of practitioners on a Europe-wide level is essential.

These tasks for counsellors and guidance practitioners are similarly important in the European context in almost all countries. The challenge here is that the conditions in each country can vary greatly. Depending on the national context, different challenges arise for counsellors. The transnational focus on the various challenges and tasks facing counsellors is central to this anthology. The logical structure is linked to the transnational goal of joint exchange, learning and networking. Although national circumstances are often different, these different contexts of experience can be linked. From this, multinational perspectives, concepts and ultimately approaches to action and solutions can emerge with the help of the exchange of experience.

In this context, the Academia+ project is also based on this basic assumption. This project, funded by the Erasmus+ programme, the Federal Ministry of Education and Research and Euroguidance, builds on the pillars of the Academia network. Partners from Luxembourg (Applied Vocational Psychology and Policy Research—AVOPP), Germany (Hochschule der Bundesagentur für Arbeit), Lithuania (Vsl "eMundus"), Portugal (Sociedade Portuguesa de Inovacao-Consultadoria Empresarial E Fomento Da Inovacao S.A.-SPI) and the United Kingdom (Aspire Igen Group Limited) joined forces in 2018 to facilitate, organise and support this exchange of experience and transnational learning of counsellors in Europe[1]. This project will first be presented in the second part of the anthology. To begin with, it is necessary to focus on the central challenges of the European labour markets in order to derive the project idea, the objectives and finally the implementation. This anthology is a result of the Academia+ project and, like the project, aims at the European context and the synergy effects that result from the experience reports of the individual countries on the central challenges.

After the central challenges of the European labour markets and societies have been addressed and the resulting project idea and implementation have been outlined, the second part of the anthology anchors various national perspectives on the topics of migration, demographic change and future work by means of country contributions. Each of these describes the national situation, the central challenges in the respective European country and ultimately provides information on national approaches to solutions, projects, options for action, etc. The authors of these country contributions are participants of the exchange training, which was carried out within the framework of the Academia+ project. Most of the authors are themselves practitioners in the field of counselling and guidance and thus bring an important perspective to this publication. The authors of the country contributions

[1] For more information, please visit: https://academiaplus.eu/

were responsible for setting the focus, so in addition to outlining the typical situation in the country, the focus is primarily on concrete practical references to their own work or to the national way of dealing with the central challenges. The central question, which is also important for the logic of this anthology, is: *What are main current and upcoming challenges and how can counsellors and guidance practitioners, with a focus on the transnational European perspective, master these in their respective national contexts?*

Schwerin, Germany Clinton Enoch
Schwerin, Germany Christoph Krause
Mannheim, Germany Rebeca Garcia Murias
Schwerin, Germany Jane Porath

References

Bundesagentur für Arbeit. (2022). *Engpassanalyse 2020*. Link: https://statistik.arbeitsagentur.de/DE/Navigation/Statistiken/Interaktive-Statistiken/Fachkraeftebedarf/Engpassanalyse-Nav.html;jsessionid=DD602AB7716E0732D5A02AF444F32EDA

Ragnitz, J. (2020). *Auswirkungen der Coronapandemie auf die regionalen Arbeitsmärkte*. IFO Forschungsbericht 6/2020. Link: https://www.ifo.de/DocDL/ifoDD_20-06_03-08_Ragnitz.pdf

Academia + Project Working Team (Eds.) (2020a). *Intellectual output 1. Counselling migrants and refugees. Didactical framework*. Link: https://academiaplus.eu/wp-content/uploads/2021/08/C-STEP_1_Counselling_migrants_and_refugees_Didactical_Framework.pdf

Contents

Editors and Contributors

Clinton Enoch University of Applied Labor Studies, Schwerin, Germany

Tanja Hutterer Berlin, Germany

Glykeria Kalamata Center for Social Innovation, Nicosia, Cyprus

Christoph Krause University of Applied Labor Studies, Schwerin, Germany

Katharina Kurianowski Hannover, Germany

Kalliopi Marioli Athens Solidarity Centre, Solidarity Now, Athens, Greece

Liepa Mikulevičiūtė St. Brendan's Sixth Form College, Bristol, UK

Rebeca Garcia Murias University of Applied Labor Studies, Mannheim, Germany
University of Santiago de Compostela, Santiago, Spain

Jane Porath University of Applied Labor Studies, Schwerin, Germany
Hochschule der Bundesagentur für Arbeit, Mannheim, Germany

Anu Raudasoja Häme University of Applied Science, Hämeenlinna, Finland

Soili Rinne Häme University of Applied Science, Hämeenlinna, Finland

Jean-Jacques Ruppert Applied Vocational Psychology and Policy Research Unit, Belvaux, Luxembourg

Dimitrios Sannas Athens Solidarity Centre, Solidarity Now, Athens, Greece

Annette Schorp Stuttgart, Germany

Susan Scott Dublin, Ireland

Evangelia Tsilimigkra Athens Solidarity Centre, Solidarity Now, Athens, Greece

List of Figures

List of Tables

Part I
Academia+

Academia+

Clinton Enoch, Christoph Krause, Rebeca Garcia Murias, and Jane Porath

1 How to Deal with Substantial Employment and Social Challenges?: Basic Considerations for the Academia+ Project

What are main current and upcoming challenges and how can counsellors and guidance practitioners, with a focus on the transnational European perspective, master these in their respective national contexts?

This central question, which was already introduced and pointedly outlined in the previous chapter, is one of the central basic considerations of the Academia+ project. In order to outline the basic considerations of the Academia+ project in more detail, it is first worth taking a look at the organisational embedding of the project as well as its theoretical foundation.

In terms of its organisational foundation, the Academia+ project is linked to the previous network structures and considerations of the Academia Network. While on the level of policymaking several professional networks and close cooperation in Europe exist (e.g. Euroguidance), so far the Academia Network is the only network

C. Enoch · C. Krause (✉) · J. Porath
University of Applied Labor Studies, Schwerin, Germany

Hochschule der Bundesagentur für Arbeit, Mannheim, Germany
e-mail: clinton.enoch@hdba.de; Christoph.krause@arbeitsagentur.de; jane.porath@hdba.de

R. G. Murias
University of Applied Labor Studies, Mannheim, Germany

University of Santiago de Compostela, Santiago, Spain
e-mail: rebeca.garcia.murias@usc.es

C. Enoch et al. (eds.), *Vocational Guidance in Europe*,
https://doi.org/10.1007/978-3-031-06592-7_1

from guidance practitioners for guidance practitioners. The Academia Network was set up in the year 1992 and funded by the Petra programme of the European Commission. By frequently relying on expert counsellors who inhabit the worlds of both practice and research, Academia has managed to bridge the gap that all too often exists between practice and theory. In addition, the Academia Network offers the opportunity to exchange ideas in various contexts. In 2022, for example, the Academia Network will offer 15 partner countries where counsellors and career guidance practitioners can exchange with colleagues from their respective countries. For this purpose, there are recurring events in these different countries that are designed to facilitate multinational learning and networking (Euroguidance, 2022).[1] The Academia Network is therefore already a first starting point for understanding guidance in a transnational communication and exchange process. This perspective already enables hundreds of European guidance practitioners to go on exchange in other countries in Europe every year, to get to know the national guidance structures, institutions and challenges there or to learn together. This idea of a transnational exchange is also the guiding idea of the Academia+ project. It turns out that the existing Academia structures already offer good practice in transnational exchange, but more on a one-to-one and institutional/individual basis. There are sufficient opportunities for counsellors to go to other countries and gain national experience in the counselling system and also to take advantage of learning opportunities and training nuggets on various topics. Overall, however, the Academia+ project is oriented towards a potential that has not yet been fully tapped. This synergy effect, which takes place again and again through transnational cooperation and the lively exchange between the practice of guidance, must be made permanent and moderated organisationally. The knowledge generated by the exchange and the experience gained by travelling to another country are so important for the practice of counselling that it is immensely important to make them permanent in order to exploit the potential.

In addition, the Academia+ project focuses on another level: it is not only about an organised and moderated continuation of the exchange between the counsellors of individual countries, but it is also the aim to make this concrete knowledge, which is generated in such exchange and learning processes, on the one hand, concretely usable for the practice of counselling, but on the other hand, to constantly reflect on it in a theory-practice exchange. The experience and knowledge generated in such exchange processes and programmes is first and foremost an advantage for the counsellor, who gets to know the existing counselling structures in another country for his own further training and works together with practical counsellors there. In addition, this external perspective also has advantages for the counsellor in the respective country, because new perspectives on the existing national guidance system are brought in. One's own work context and concrete practice are repeatedly exchanged, questioned and expanded by a further (trans-)national perspective in

[1]If you want to have a closer look on the counsellor exchange program, please visit: https://www.euroguidance.eu/international-mobility/academia

these contexts. This invaluable process of reflection and exchange also constitutes invaluable knowledge on a particular topic. This generated (exchange-) knowledge is initially limited to the participating groups of people, but has the potential to be of great relevance for many more groups of people. For this reason, the Academia+ project has set itself the goal of systematically channelling this knowledge and thus, on the one hand, making it permanent, but on the other hand, at the same time, also making it usable on a large scale for more advisors throughout Europe. Ultimately, this also results in learning contexts in which the theoretical foundation of these experience and learning processes can be constantly used or reflected upon. In this way, existing themes can be theoretically founded and discussed transnationally, and the knowledge generated in these experiential situations can be systematically consolidated and made usable for European guidance.

Academia+ brings together two perspectives:

- To support and consolidate the exchange and transnational training of counsellors in Europe.
- To focus on the development of training programmes to address current key challenges in labour market and counselling.

The first perspective focuses, consolidates and moderates the transnational exchange idea. This valuable knowledge, which is embedded in the respective national contexts, holds a whole new dimension of learning potential on a transnational level. However, these learning potentials must be pedagogically prepared and, above all, moderated. To this end, systematic training programmes must be created that a) facilitate the exchange situations and b) theoretically substantiate and at the same time consolidate the knowledge generated in them. Ultimately, it is only to a limited extent that the existing national contexts offer a common ground here. There is no doubt that the potentials of the different guidance systems and organisations are very large, but above all it is clear that within Europe (and beyond) there are different clusters of issues that have to be dealt with in the most diverse national contexts. These topics can be clustered as central key challenges; they show which topics with a direct impact on the practical work of guidance practitioners in Europe are/will be particularly challenging at present and in the coming years. In this way, they point to the potential needs of European counsellors and thus enable a practice-oriented basis for joint learning and further training offers.

Three central topics were to be transcendent for the focus in the Academia+ project: the counselling of refugees and migrants, demographic change and ultimately the future of work. These three main topics are without doubt three of the greatest challenges for the European labour market in general (transnational), but also for the individual labour markets of the individual countries (national). In the following, these three thematic areas will be briefly theorised in a systematic way. This also serves as a basis for the individual country contributions, in which the subsequent transnational focal points are then described again on a national level by way of example.

2 Challenge 1: Counselling Refugees and Migrants

The target group of migrants and refugees is a very complex and heterogeneous one with regard to home countries, cultural contexts, languages and language levels, reasons for migration or space (see also Academia + Project Working Team, 2020b; CMinaR project team, 2019). Therefore, migrants and refugees face numerous tasks and challenges once they arrive in their host countries and attempt to integrate into mainstream society and the labour market (Yakushko et al., 2008). They have to apply for asylum status and potentially seek reunification with their families, learn the language and culture of their host countries and find work to support themselves and potential dependents (Fleay et al., 2013).

Refugees often experience the transition from an agrarian or industrial society in a developing country to a post-industrial Western and developed country as very challenging (Abkhezr & McMahon, 2017). At the same time, governments in the host countries have to develop policies, practices and procedures to support the integration of refugees into mainstream society and the labour market. Education and employment are central mechanisms to achieve this goal, but it often takes time until refugees are (formally) able to work in their host countries (Gericke et al., 2017). For example, in Germany, only refugees who are officially granted asylum are allowed to work, and they have to pass an integration course that entails 600 hours of German lessons and 100 hours of civics (The Economist, 2017). However, these efforts seem to pay off; research shows that stable employment not only reduces welfare dependency and facilitates integration of refugees into the host society but also improves educational and health-related outcomes of children of refugee families (Pernice & Brook, 1996).

As Zacher (2018) points out, vocational or career counselling interventions for migrants and refugees, and career guidance education particularly when designed for younger refugees, can play an important role for refugees' feelings of belonging, adaptation, acculturation, mental wellbeing and long-term resettlement success. Career guidance and counselling is particularly important given that most refugees have experienced traumatic events in their home countries and many experience their new situations in the host countries as challenging (Moehling, 2008). Effective career guidance education has the potential to offer the same educational, social and economic benefits to refugee youth as for general student populations.

The varied circumstances in which migrants navigate their way into and through labour markets indicate how different groups will require different levels and types of career guidance and counselling support that take account of context.

In addition, careers counsellors work within a multicultural framework and provide migrant clients with the support and encouragement necessary to develop coping strategies—such as career adaptability—by counselling them and providing guidance in a proactive way, touching on social justice and advocating the integration of minority groups calls for career guidance and counselling professionals to espouse, proactively, a social justice approach, requiring advocacy.

3 Challenge 2: Futures Jobs

Industry 4.0, Economy 4.0, the fourth industrial revolution, the future of work, etc.; the conceptual alternatives are endless, but fundamentally all these phenomena speak the same language: a transition of our working environment and the way we work driven by technological innovations that have profound effects on both production systems and business models. Although not a brand-new technology, the concept of Industry 4.0, or "Smart" technology. These changes are based on various central international phenomena of the last 15–20 years. On the one hand, there is a steadily increasing international interdependence of economic relations in a globalised world. On the other hand, digitalisation processes in particular are having a significant impact on the economy and the way in which goods are produced. Certain jobs and activities can be completely automated; other jobs require a rethink in the organisation of work, away from stationary assembly line work towards more and more networked and holistic production. In addition, there are social issues such as demographic change, which has been given its own focus in its subject matter, and other topics of social and economic transformation in Europe (at the transnational level) as well as the European states (at the national level). Overall, however, it can be constituted: "The world of work is shaped by increasing international exchange processes, combined with the mobility of goods and services, people and capital" (Freiling et al., 2020, p v). This change is creating ever-increasing challenges for companies in all European countries at different levels. Which professions or activities will still be needed in the future? Which of these activities can be completely automated? What skills do my employees need to make their jobs fit for the future? These and other questions show technological change targets all levels of national and international labour markets. On the side of necessary technological transformation, it shows new technologies associated with digitisation are increasingly in demand in the business context. Cloud computing, for example, increased the frequency of use of companies in Germany by 5% to 78% from 2017 to 2019, the Internet of the DInge from 17% to 23% (Bitkom, 2019, p.25) and 8 percent more companies used 3D printing processes in 2019, and in terms of virtual reality usage also rose by 8 percent. New to the survey but already actively used are drones; in 2019, 15% of the companies surveyed were already using drones for their specific field of work (Bitkom, 2019, p.25). Even though the trend increasingly reveals that digital technologies are finding their way into businesses, most businesses still face key hurdles and challenges. One of the greatest challenges that UK companies are facing when it comes to Industry 4.0 is that they are unsure of how they can implement these changes. Many are aware of the benefits that Industry 4.0 technologies will have on their businesses, but being able to incorporate them is a different matter. Once Industry 4.0 technologies have been incorporated, businesses will need to hire more skilled workers that can operate smart equipment and maintain factories. What skills and what kind of skilled workers will be needed for this in the future can be predicted above all, but not definitively estimated for all companies. And this is equally one of the biggest challenges for counsellors and career guidance practitioners; they do not know the landscape of the future labour market. As a result, it can be difficult to offer careers advice when the labour market is changing in such a fundamental way to include jobs, we are not yet aware of, to reduce the needs for jobs we currently have and to change current jobs in unforeseeable ways. This may mean that careers practitioners will need to focus more of their time on learning about current labour market trends, for example, which areas are growing and why, which areas are shrinking and why, etc. In addition, as the future labour market is unpredictable, there may be a need for an increased focus on informing clients that their careers may not be linear, as many careers have historically been.

4 Challenge 3: Demographic Change

These rapid transformation processes on the European labour markets and the unpredictable shaping of future work are particularly intensified in Europe by one effect: demographic change. This demographic change is evident in two places: on the one hand, there are more and more older people; on the other hand, the number of newborns is falling sharply, especially in the last 20 years. A trend reversal, at least as far as births are concerned, has only become apparent in some European countries in the last 5 years. In 2019, 20.3% of the EU population was aged over 65, an increase from 17.8% in 2012, and in 2019, 26.2% of the population was aged 0–24, down from 27.4% in 2012.

Looking at the potential target group of counsellors and career guidance practitioners, five different generations stand out, all of which in turn have very specific needs. A main target even for businesses and counsellors and career guidance practitioners is the need of creating a workforce that comprises these generations. Another main target is re-skilling, up-skilling and retiring processes. Let us have a short look on these five generations and their special needs:

- First of all, we have *Traditionalists*, who are born before 1945. Although the majority of those aged over 75 are retired, there are those who are still in work. In general, this generation has preferred to stay with the same employer throughout their career, and therefore they are very knowledgeable about their specific area as well as the company as a whole. So, on the one hand, it is about constructive retirement management, which above all preserves the existing know-how and experience of these employees in the company. On the other hand, it is also about keeping these employees in the company as long and successfully as possible.
- *Baby boomers* were born between 1946 and 1964 (so aged 56–74). Unlike Traditionalists, this generation tended to change careers when they were younger, but as they got older chose to stick to one employer for stability. Therefore, they are also a valuable source of knowledge. Although they have worked with computers in their career, this generation, just like the previous one, has experienced a completely different pace of transformation in the companies and in digitalisation. In physical professions, long-term health management can also

prevent the "wear and tear" of employees' physical abilities, which in turn has a positive impact on the health of the workforce.

- *The Generation X*, born between 1965 and 1980, often values a work–life balance, so while they are still dedicated to their work like the previous generations, they also understand the importance of taking breaks, and having a rich personal life. This generation saw the rise in technology, so they prefer to communicate via email and other online sources.
- *Millennials* grew up with a totally different level of technology. Born between 1981 and 1996, they not just have a different perspective of technologies but also of work. Work–life balance is very important, and they value collaborative, team-based working instead of more traditional hierarchical company structures, and prefer to receive frequent feedback on their work. They also prefer to complete learning online through videos or online courses, and prefer to change organisations multiple times to progress their careers.
- Born from 1997 onwards, *Generation Z* experiences digital transformation from a particularly exciting angle. Although they are often denied a view of previous forms of work or technological changes, they grow up with this fast-moving transformation at the same time, are often much better able to adapt, etc.

Generation alpha (born after 2010) is the latest generation to enter the labour market in the coming years. Their needs and preconditions differ again in many places from the previous generations, but even with the previous five generations it becomes clear that dealing with different generations is always dealing with heterogeneous needs, preconditions and competences. For counsellors and career guidance practitioners, this has implications in two places: it is necessary to provide tailored career counselling, guidance and advice particularly for older people. Their skills are still important to companies and they can help to cushion the shortage of skilled workers somewhat. Getting back into work and receiving training is a hard challenge for these skilled people. Also, it can be difficult to retrain them, especially on digital technologies.

5 Counsellors' Study and Training Exchange Programme for Key Challenges of European Labour Markets and Societies

The aim of facilitating the exchange of experiences on these three topics was the central task of the Academia+ project. For this purpose, the project had to design and implement a training series on each topic. On this basis, the Academia+ project partners developed, piloted and evaluate 3 research-based online "Counsellors Study and Training Exchange Programs" (C-STEPs) for qualified counsellors that reflect a transnational European perspective and meet the needs of the target group. Each of these C-STEPs focused on a current key challenge and combined theory, research and practice of guidance on counselling migrants and refugees, future jobs and demographic change. As part of the Erasmus+ KA2 Strategic Partnerships for Higher Education, the idea of the project brings together the perspectives as mentioned earlier: one main target was to support and consolidate the exchange and transnational training of counsellors in Europe. The other main target was to focus on the development of training programmes and the world of work, as well as between different jobs and political issues. The project unites a core group of partners from the Academia Network (extended by a new partner from Portugal) and developed innovative concepts, resources and a new IT infrastructure including digital resources and e-learning services.

The following section will describe how the project achieved these two goals and what perspectives resulted from them. After the project was launched in 2018, the first task was to explore the specific thematic priorities. The central challenges of the European labour markets in the coming years result in the three main topics for the respective training courses.

All these main topics (counselling migrants and refugees; demographic change and future work) are united by a common system. All of them can be found on a national level in the European countries, so the topic offers an ideal abstraction surface to bundle and exchange different perspectives from different countries. This goes hand in hand with the transnational focus, because although the three main themes have been identified as central challenges in the European labour markets and societies, considerable differences are evident at the national level. The aim of these C-STEPs was therefore twofold:

- On the one hand, the aim was to design, implement and evaluate demand-oriented continuing education programmes on these three topics.
- At the same time, the focus was to be on the exchange between the nations and their nation-specific perspectives.

5.1 The Procedure

Once the main topics had been analysed and defined in a needs-oriented manner, the task was to design a pedagogical training programme based on the needs of the counsellors in Europe. On the basis of national research dossiers and the combination of these into a transnational dossier, recommendations for selection, material and resources for the individual training units could be worked out. This transnational synthesis on the three aforementioned topics includes the current research and theory landscape of the respective national contributions (from Germany, the UK, Luxembourg and Portugal). Furthermore, it focuses on concrete demand perspectives of the respective national labour markets and societies. The following questions, which explored the material, were at the centre of attention:

- What is the current uptake in the UK, Luxembourg, Germany and Portugal of the related topic?

- What are key challenges for businesses/counsellors, career guidance practitioners and societies?
- Are there any programs, supportive measures or programs regarding these topics?
- Which skills/competences are most needed and requested?
- What are challenges and knowledge gaps that career practitioners face when dealing with these topics?

These questions were each supplemented by topic-specific focuses, but the basic system is often similar.[2] Finally, this system aims to prepare the central national research and theoretical resources in order to provide a theoretical foundation for the respective topics. At the same time, the material was processed in a problem- and needs-centred manner. What concrete needs arise for national and transnational labour markets in relation to and societies, and to what extent are there already specific measures aimed at these topics? This serves above all as a theoretical basis for the learning offer to be designed and the identification of topics. At this point, for example, national measures that are already underway or functioning well in the national context and that address a sub-area of the topic are very useful. This in turn provides a basis for deciding whether such national measures should be presented/ processed in different didactic settings and made usable in the transnational context. In addition, the question then naturally arises as to how far the topic relation recurs to "new" or "changed" competences. Central to this is the following assumption: all three topics (counselling migrants and refugees, demographic change and future jobs) are to a certain extent transformational new topics. This means that they require a fundamental adaptation of coping strategies. In some cases, even a new portfolio of coping and action strategies becomes necessary. This means that the challenge of facing these issues requires a certain process of acquiring new areas of knowledge, new skills and ultimately new competences. This is fundamentally true: in the area of Industry 4.0/future jobs, digitalisation and automation play a major role. These require a completely new portfolio of competences (digitalisation competences in some national contexts) in order to master the requirements arising from digitalisation. This applies to companies as well as to their employees. However, it also applies in a double sense to counsellors and career guidance practitioners. On the one hand, they themselves have to adapt this competence portfolio to a certain extent, because their field of work is also affected by the three chosen topics. At the same time, the need for guidance on these very topics and the possibilities to acquire these competences is also increasing. It is therefore indispensable at this point for all three subject areas to ask what new or changed competence requirements there are in this area and how these competence requirements can be met. From this demand to cope with existing or new competence requirements, the demand and challenge for counsellors and career guidance practitioners arises to provide proactive and

[2] If you want to have a closer look on these questions or the transnational synthesis, please visit: https://academiaplus.eu/outputs/. There you can find all outcomes from the project, organised by topic.

successful counselling in this regard. For this it is necessary that the knowledge gaps of the counsellors are also worked out.

The last step in particular requires a further methodological step in addition to the theoretically grounded work (in the national reports and the transnational synthesis). In the follow-up to this work, the theoretical foundation was supplemented by a direct reference to practice. The concrete needs of counsellors and the competence requirements that result from them can only be mapped to a limited extent via the research landscape. In this regard, it was the aim of the Academia+ project to specifically ask these practitioners about the concrete needs and competence requirements for counsellors and career guidance practitioners. For this purpose, a qualitative questionnaire was developed which collected the concrete needs and competence requirements of the practitioners. The questionnaire also asked about other concrete topics that are of particular importance for counsellors and career guidance practitioners in relation to the topics "counselling refugees and migrants", "demographic change" and "future jobs". For this purpose, experts from all over Europe were interviewed qualitatively on the one hand, and counsellors and career guidance practitioners from different European countries were interviewed on the other hand. This methodological step offered the project team the opportunity to supplement the theoretically sound level on the topic areas with the concrete needs and focal points of the practitioners from these areas. The conclusion of these two steps results in concrete thematic areas, which in turn serve as the basis (or needs) for content to be designed. A subsequent analysis of the empirically ascertained concrete needs of counsellors and career guidance practitioners and the theoretically oriented presentation of the national and transnational research landscape offered the possibility in the next project step to cluster concrete contents for the respective subject areas and for the training programmes to be designed. This resulted in a concrete template in which the thematic fields were first systematically elaborated in order to ultimately be able to determine concrete contents. These concrete contents were to be filled in the following: for this purpose, various experts were consulted with a focus on transnational expertise. The advantage here is the precise combination of national expertise on different thematic fields within these clusters and the transnational focus in relation to the adaptation of the thematic fields. In addition, there is a didactic level, the main goal of which was a varied offer that enables and moderates joint learning and transnational exchange on different channels.[3] The different learning units found in the clusters of the survey of experts and consultants and the theoretical research reports thus provided a rough structure for the training programme in general. Furthermore, important needs, competence requirements, gaps of knowledge, etc., could be concentrated within these learning units. Based on these guidelines, learning units had to be developed for the requested experts.

[3] As a result of such a template, you will find here an exemplary fact sheet that builds up the thematic and didactic framework: https://academiaplus.eu/wp-content/uploads/2021/11/C-STEP-1-unit1_Counselling-migrants-and-refugees-FACT-SHEETS-FOR-LECTURERS.pdf

Further fact sheets on the other thematic areas and units can be found here: https://academiaplus.eu/outputs/

This concrete design of the individual thematic focal points and units was made in close consultation with the respective experts and lecturers and the project team, taking into account the previously surveyed needs, and is subsequently presented as a result in a "didactical framework". In addition to a thematic derivation, this didactical framework also contains the individual contents of the units, the structure plan for the respective unit. Furthermore, the didactical principles and courses of action are listed, followed by concrete learning objectives. Finally, organisational aspects and notes are also included. In the following, the didactical frameworks of the individual subject areas will be briefly outlined.[4] The basic structure of the didactical frameworks is the same in all subject areas.

5.2 *Intellectual Output: Didactical Framework I: Counselling Migrants and Refugees*

The main objective of the Academia+ project "+ is to support the provision of better services and guidance on competencies and qualifications by focusing on the development of training programmes that address urgent issues and current key challenges in the European labour market and career counselling" (Academia+ Project Working Team, 2020a, p 4). For this objective, a separate "Counsellors' Study and Training Exchange Programme for Key Challenges of European Labour Markets and Societies", or C-STEP for short, was developed for each of the three thematic focal points. This C-Step contains a learning offer and a training programme on the respective thematic focus and is usually divided into 4 units with central areas of need for the counsellors and career guidance practitioners interviewed.

For the first C-STEP, the results of a previous Erasmus+ project were also available. The project "CMinaR" had dealt with qualitative and demand-oriented seminars for counsellors in public employment service in the field of "Counselling refugees and migrants". A training programme was also developed there. In this C-STEP, the Academia+ "strongly refers in these didactical guidelines to the EU project CMinR (C-STEP 1 builds on outcomes and products having been developed in this previous EU-foundet project)" (Academia + Project Working Team, 2021e, p 4).[5] Based on these central outcomes from the CMinaR project, the first contents could be developed in the Academia+ project and supplemented by the further perspectives.

Migrants and refugees are particularly a specific target group for guidance. They often have a long journey behind them, in many cases involving flight and danger. Then the question of the prospects of staying arises, both on the state side (can

[4] You can find all didactic frameworks in detail on: https://academiaplus.eu/outputs/

[5] For more information about the EU-fundet project "CMinaR", please visit: https://www.cminar.eu/

people stay in the country?) and on the subjective side (do these people want to stay here or return to their home country?) (Academia + Project Working Team, 2020a). Furthermore, the target group is very heterogeneous in its language and cultural family, and the questions of life planning are also particularly specific. Finally, there is also the question of integration; often people are highly qualified in their home countries; there is the question of recognition of qualifications, etc. In short, the special needs of this target group are heterogeneous in many respects and require a very special sensitivity in counselling.

In this context, counsellors are particularly challenged when it comes to social skills and a feeling for cultural differences. This intercultural awareness is particularly important as a topic and can be specifically trained and sensitised with various methods. For this reason, it makes sense to dedicate the first unit to this topic. With regard to this unit, the didactical framework not only names the central needs of the target group and the counsellors, but it also formulates concrete learning objectives with which these competence requirements for counsellors in dealing with the target group can be trained or mastered (Academia+ Project Working Team, 2020a). An example of the concrete learning objectives for Unit 1: intercultural awareness, the concrete learning objectives for the entire units and thus also the concrete learning objectives for the entire C-STEP can be found in the so-called fact sheets.[6]

"By focusing on the above-mentioned contents Unit 1 aims to meet the following **learning outcomes:**

- Analyse challenges arising for access to and designing and handling of supportive measures and labour market schemes.
- Promote the language acquisition in supportive measures and labour market schemes.
- To know training measures for the adaptation of vocational skills for refugees and migrants.
- Find out about legal aspects of support measures" (Academia + Project Working Team, 2020a, p 7).

The other units in C-STEP 1 are generally structured in a similar way within the didactical framework; after a thematic derivation and the connection of the concrete need and competence requirements, concrete learning objectives are found. Thematically, the topic "Recognition and access to the labour market" was chosen for Unit 2, as there are considerable needs regarding the recognition and counselling of refugees and migrants with regard to their qualifications and competences and the recognition and placement processes in the respective countries (Academia + Project Working Team, 2020a).

How can the mostly well-educated and highly qualified people in the respective countries of arrival best be integrated into the labour market and what challenges

[6] The product of the fact sheets will be explained even more in the didactical framework for C-STEP 3 as a building block in the further course; furthermore you can find the fact sheets here: https://academiaplus.eu/outputs/

arise in recognition processes? These are just two of the questions addressed by this unit. This also ties in with the third unit from this C-STEP, which aims at the "analysis of client potential and empowerment". If formal qualification recognition and comparisons are not possible or cause problems, the analysis of the client's potential is very important for counsellors. In order to not only recognise this potential, but also to promote it, there are various methods and tools, a selection of which can be found in Unit 3 (Academia + Project Working Team, 2020a) Finally, the C-STEP also aims at specific supporting measures (Unit 4), which already exist in various European countries. In addition, it is also important to know which challenges can arise when you as a counsellor want to design, implement or accompany such supportive measures.

After the respective units have been built up within the didactical framework and formulated into concrete learning objectives, the next step is to find a concrete structural plan. The aim of this structure plan is the consistent listing and structuring of the individual didactic methods, inputs, group work, individual work, etc. The structure plan is based on the didactical framework.[7] The structure plan breaks down the individual main topics once again and forms individual learning units within the topic block. For example, the structure plan of the unit "intercultural awareness" consists of 9 individual didactic and content-related building blocks that deal specifically with the topic and aim at the different learning objectives (mentioned above) (Academia + Project Working Team, 2020b). Building on the structure plan, some didactic principles for procedure of learning units follow. The aim here is a didactically meaningful change of methods, which not only covers the needs of the counsellors in terms of classical knowledge transfer (input), but also includes the specific needs, skills and experience of their complete range of work (Academia + Project Working Team, 2020b). Two basic didactic principles are important at this point: firstly, remembering the project logic, not only international or national inputs are given, but rather the aim is to fill the thematic field of "Counselling refugees and migrants" with content using national examples, while always maintaining the transnational focus. It is therefore important not only to provide input but always to consider the context: what this example from another country means a) for me and my own work as a counsellor in another country and b) what transnational synergy effects arise from this. At the same time, the participants should reflect on these examples and relate them to their own context. The basic didactic orientation here therefore moves away from pure knowledge transfer to a strong focus on processes of experience and reflection (Academia + Project Working Team, 2020a).

In addition, each didactical framework also contains a section with support and implementation and design tips on organisational and didactical points. The aim of this didactical framework is, amongst other things, to make the developed topics also usable for further trainings, e.g. in-house in individual institutions. For this purpose, it is particularly important to share organisational guidelines. The training

[7] An example of how the respective structural plans look in the Academia+ project can be found in the description of the didactical framework of C-STEP two on the topic of future work.

programme on "counselling refugees and migrants" took place exclusively online due to the Corona pandemic. The Zoom and Microsoft Teams platforms appeared to be the most suitable for this, although the size of the group and the level of activity always play an important role (Academia + Project Working Team, 2020a). At the same time, it is important to provide the material for the participants. It is not only a matter of sending out the presentation in advance, but also of preparing the material according to the target group. How this was implemented in C-STEP 1 can be found in the didactical framework of the C-STEP and will be shown below as an example.

In the case of the Academia+ project, the Moodle platform was used not only to send the materials to the participants, but also to actively prepare them for them. Most countries from which potential participants or counsellors and career guidance practitioners come have perfect access to Moodle. In the didactical framework, a short section explains the basic use of Moodle. While this is not a substitute for a Moodle beginners' course where you learn to work with the platform, the didactical framework offers useful tips on how to use the platform. Above all, it is important to create the greatest possible usability:

> The provided documents are always available as PDF files to ensure a usage on most devices. Videos are inserted as a stream directly from the Moodle page so one does not need a separate flash or media player. Sometimes it is added a YouTube link on the page or on the additional material. In most cases, when the speakers have shown a video on their session, can be found this on the video (recording of the session) was prepared on Moodle (Academia + Project Working Team, 2020a, p 16).

This is accompanied by a mix of methods of presentation, different didactic methods and channels that have been or can be used. The following table lists examples of the various documents used in the Academia+ project (in the overall structure of the training programmes, but here explicitly for the C-STEP "counselling refugees and migrants") and made available to the participants on Moodle (cf. Table 1).

This provision of different forms of learning and materials has an enormous didactic benefit, which, however, also requires a certain amount of preparation. The last part of the didactical framework contains information on what needs to be prepared in advance for this unit on counselling refugees and migrants. "It is important for a good start to the training, whether it takes place in presence or online, that there is enough time for getting to know each other" (Academia + Project Working Team, 2020a, p 17). Getting to know each other in the actual event, but also perhaps familiarising oneself with the material in advance, requires specific preparation. For this reason, the various materials should be available on the platform one or two days in advance so that the participants can familiarise themselves with the structure. Furthermore, communicative "arriving" and "getting to know each other" is immensely important in events (Academia + Project Working Team, 2020a). For this, some discussion and conversation rules are needed right at the beginning, also with regard to questions in input sessions. The larger the number of participants, the more important it is to prepare a clear communication system. For example, should all microphones be muted or is there a system for asking questions (in the online setting via virtual hand or asking questions in the chat). In small groups, it is also worthwhile to queue up the video signal of the participants. Again, the larger the

Table 1 Documents on Moodle for C-STEP 1: Counselling refugees and migrants (Academia + Project Working Team, 2020a, p 16)

	Moodle learning platform of Academia + project
Videos	Each session has at least one video that consists of the recording of the online training day. As these are made available directly on Moodle, every participant/ interested party can access the videos directly on the platform. No extra software or similar is necessary, so that easy access can be guaranteed
Presentations	On every session can be found the presentation used by the speakers in the online training. Depending on whether it is a coherent input presentation or a working session with smaller input presentations, can be found one document with the whole presentation or a split presentation. These include a smaller input session from the speaker or preparations for a group work or an exercise. These documents are always named with "presentation" and the specific name of this short session
Exercises	In different sessions, the speakers prepared some exercises and group work. These documents are named with "exercise" and the specific name of this exercise and they contain two different didactic levels. On the one hand, they are prepared for participants and interested people who want to work through the material for themselves. For those there is a small introduction into the exercise and the numbered tasks one has to do. Furthermore, there is also a note how one needs to save/ share or send the outcome of this exercise. Depending on the situation one can share his/her screen or present his/her outcome or result on Padlet, sticky notes, etc. on the other hand can be found a didactic level prepared for potential trainers, speakers or lecturer who want to host further education/ training, maybe in their own institution or company. For those people and for such use of the material can be found italic additional information in the exercises which are marked with "editorial note". These notes includes hints, tips and instructions only for lecturer or teacher. For the most part, these are didactic hints or assistance, which software can be used for the presentation of the work results, etc. these notes also contain information on what needs to be prepared in advance of the session/ training. As an example if one as a trainer want his/her participants to share their work results on a whiteboard or with sticky notes, can be found a recommendation about the software we and the speakers used in the online training
Sample solutions	Safeguarding of work results is extremely important for the success of a further education session/ training. When your participants come from different countries, backgrounds or at least cities/ companies, etc. you will receive a huge mass of productive work results and outcome. In addition to the exercises we provide a specific sample solution. On one side the sample solution provided on the Moodle platform are the main work results of our participants from the online training. According to privacy policy it is needed to blur all personal data, etc. on the other side, these sample solutions are only intended as additional information. They are not all-encompassing or to be seen as the only solution of the exercise

(continued)

Table 1 (continued)

	Moodle learning platform of Academia + project
Additional material (links, texts, handouts etc.)	According to the respective session of the speakers, it is provided additional material like links, additional texts or handouts. If additional material be available for the specific session, it will be referred to at the respective place in the video or presentation

group, the more likely it may be necessary to turn off the participants' video signal (Academia + Project Working Team, 2020a). In such contexts, it is even more important to plan smaller groups, e.g. for group work, so that the participants there have the opportunity to turn on the video signal, see each other and have lively discussions with each other.

The individual units in the Academia+ project are structured on the basis of this didactic framework. Finally, the sources used and further links follow, which are also of great importance for interested participants or even other external lecturers. Fundamentally, however, the aim of the Academia+ project in developing and ultimately providing these didactical frameworks is, on the one side, to have a structured and systematic framework for the conception of learning content. On the other hand, it offers other interested participants or lecturers a structuring aid, regardless of whether they want to use this material for their own training programme or whether they generally want to design something new, but want to orient themselves structurally.

5.3 Intellectual Output: Didactical Framework II: Future Works

The basic system and structure of the respective didactical frameworks for the individual topics is almost the same, so for C-STEP two with the topic "future jobs", in addition to the content-related explanations, the further process of the creation of the offer is to be reflected and worked through.

> As a reminder: So far, the concrete needs and competence requirements for the three topics "counselling migrants and refugees", "future work" and "demographic change" have been developed on the basis of the national research

(continued)

landscape and the theoretical foundations on the one hand and the empirically surveyed needs of the counsellors and experts on the other. For this purpose, the national reports were combined into a transnational synthesis with a multinational perspective and a qualitative questionnaire was developed which was made available to various counsellors and career guidance practitioners in order to find out their concrete needs. These needs were bundled and clustered into thematic areas, which could then be filled with needs and competence requirements and thus provide initial indications of concrete learning needs and contents for a training programme. This training programme is to be designed, offered and evaluated in three "Counsellors' Study and Training Exchange Programmes for Key Challenges of European Labour Markets and Societies" (C-STEPs). From these thematic clusters, a first structure could be worked out, which was continuously differentiated in a template. The concrete requirements for action and competence and the respective key challenges were thematically elaborated. In consultation with various experts and lecturers, blocks of topics were subsumed and then filled with content by international lecturers in cooperation with the Academia+ project. A systematisation structure was created for this content, in which the didactical framework offers two possibilities: In the Academia+ project process, it served as a template for the further development of the content, and in the follow-up to the project, it now serves as a framework for the learning content and units actually offered, which can still be used for training programmes.

In the following part, the central results of the didactical framework on the topic of "future jobs" will be presented and at the same time the further process within the project period will be described.

As already described under Challenge 2: Future jobs (LINK), one of the central challenges for counsellors and career guidance practitioners in this thematic field is the necessity to take into account a certain constant of uncertainty with regard to future professions, competences, etc.

> One of the major challenges that career practitioners face is that they don't know the landscape of the future labour market. As a result, it can be difficult to offer careers advice when the labour market is changing in such a fundamental way to include jobs, we aren't yet aware of, reduce the needs for jobs we currently have and to change current jobs in unforeseeable ways. This may mean that careers practitioners will need to focus more of their time on learning about current labour market trends, for example, which areas are growing and why, which areas are shrinking a why etc. In addition, as the future labour market is unpredictable, there may need to be increased focus on informing clients that their careers may not be linear, as many careers have historically been. (Academia + Project Working Team, 2021a, p 2)

In many areas, automation, digitalisation and transformation processes are changing both the professions and the activities that take place in them (Academia + Project Working Team, 2021b). It is difficult to predict, for example, whether an occupation can be completely automated. What is already certain at this point, however, is a transformation of "work" as it has developed so far. Employees will be confronted with fewer physical activities and burdens, but rather with complex production processes, agile teams, flexible and mobile work. This means that the requirements profile for employees will also change, new skills will be needed and others will have to be developed further (Academia + Project Working Team, 2021c). In addition, there is the issue of demographic change, which generally intensifies the effect of the shortage of skilled workers in different countries and different sectors.

These new competency requirements for employees in companies naturally also have a strong impact on the activities of counsellors and career guidance practitioners (Academia + Project Working Team, 2021c). They make a fundamental contribution as an advisory interface to the various educational offers, which in turn can cover these needs for new and changed competences with the help of educational offers and training. In this role, however, guidance practitioners are of course subject to exactly the same uncertainty factors of not knowing what impact Industry 4.0 and digitisation will ultimately have on the European but above all on the national labour markets. In this context, the introduction to the didactical framework on the topic of "future jobs" again serves the thematic derivation and the presentation of central needs and research objects (Academia + Project Working Team, 2021a).

This orientation, which was primarily thematic clusters (concrete needs and competence requirements) and a systematisation aid (the didactical framework), was also carried out in the further logic of the project. After the didactical frameworks were developed according to the thematic clusters and the concrete needs of the counsellors and career guidance practitioners, concrete thematic areas (units) could be derived from them and learning objectives could be formulated in these. Based on these concrete learning objectives and initial specifications regarding the content, lecturers were then sought from various countries who are experts from different scientific professions on the designated topics. These lecturers then worked with the Academia+ project team on the concrete design of the individual learning modules within a unit. The aim of the Academia+ team was to generate as many different experts as possible for a unit in order to be able to serve the different learning objectives on the one hand and to be able to serve the different didactic settings on the other. Different didactic methods should also be used within the individual modules (Academia + Project Working Team, 2021c). The development of the individual learning contents was the responsibility of the experts from the different countries and institutions in close consultation with the Academia+ team, in order to remain very close to the needs of the participants on the one hand, and on the other hand, above all, to be able to create connection and reference possibilities between the individual learning modules. The concrete design was also oriented towards the didactical framework, which could be a help for the different experts in structuring the unit. In the next step of the project planning, the aim was to record and systematise the concrete design of the individual sessions or modules in a unit structure plan.

On the following pages there is such a unit structure plan as an example for Unit 2 "challenges and opportunities for companies within Industry 4.0" from the second

C-STEP on the topic "future work". This table can also be used to illustrate the further procedure within the project. The table is essentially structured as follows: in order to combine as many experts as possible with different specialisations from different countries and to be able to use the resulting synergy effects, the lecturers are requested for specific timeslots. This made it possible to moderate the different methods even during the process of developing the concrete contents. The example shows, amongst other things, five content sessions (in addition to the greeting and farewell as well as the necessary breaks). For this unit, 4 lecturers from different European countries and institutions could be found for this day (Academia + Project Working Team, 2021c). These lecturers worked out the different learning objectives in advance, taking into account the didactic framework, which should be the goal of their respective session. In the following column, the topics of the lecturers are roughly presented. In this unit, as in C-STEP 2 in general, the challenges for companies and their employees with regard to the required competences for Industry 4.0 played a major role (Academia + Project Working Team, 2021c). This orientation was paired with the idea of critically uncovering and reflecting on these challenges and possible barriers in the individual countries.

The third and fourth columns of the table essentially contain the two central aspects that were also of great importance in the design process. In connection with the possible outcomes, which were defined for each session and linked to the previously developed learning objectives, the concrete design of the individual sessions was to go through a two-stage review process after the conception phase, which reflected on the learning content and sessions, especially with regard to the fourth column. For this purpose, the submitted sessions were first assessed in an internal review process. This review process was essentially aimed at the following review schemes:

- Is the overall structure recognisable and logical?
- Are the envisaged thematic focal points consistent in their structure and selection; which necessary thematic fields can be focused on more strongly?
- How do the planned methods and content ensure that the learning objectives and anticipated outcomes are achieved?
- Is the planning of structure, time and methods coherent; can this session be conducted online?

These review questions should once again put a stringent focus on the needs identified and the learning objectives developed from them (Academia + Project Working Team, 2021b). For this purpose, all project partners prepared such an internal review for each unit. This review procedure was supplemented by a second stage in which independent external experts were acquired to complete the same questions once with regard to the individual units and thus provide an external expert review. This review process was bundled and summarised after the expert feedback and finally reflected back to the individual lecturers in their respective units. The review process was supervised in both directions: on the one hand, the sessions designed by the lecturers and experts had to be reviewed in terms of content and didactics and checked against the learning goals and needs of the participants. This coverage analysis of the learning objectives had another advantage: at the same time, the main outcomes could be refined and linked even more precisely to the respective learning objectives. In the end, a "summary of main outcomes" was created, which in turn was integrated into the didactical framework and thus provided additional quality. In this review process, the didactical methodology was assessed in addition to the coverage of the session learning objectives with the needs and learning objectives from the didactical framework. The aim of the Academia project was to work with different methods as far as possible and, remembering the major project goal at the beginning of the article, to predominantly promote transnational exchange. This can always be best combined in training sessions with active participation by the learners. In this respect, the natural aim was to give the participants many pedagogically moderated opportunities to actively accept and implement this reflection and exchange. This was to be achieved in the various sessions through different materials, methods and media. The example of Structure Plan shows the diversity of the different channels. Starting with a direct impulse video showing a possible "future of jobs and companies" and a subsequent plenum discussion, the participants should enter into a transnational exchange right at the beginning.

In order to facilitate reflection processes and transnational exchange on the topic, it is also possible to conduct small opinion polls using an online tool, which can then be processed in the plenary. The fine-tuned goal of this session was to introduce the participants with a short impulse to a discussion and reflection phase about their own concern and about specific barriers in relation to upcoming challenges, but also to work towards their solution. This activation phase can be extended in an input phase to include various theoretic aspects, thematically oriented above all to various challenges for companies and their employees. Basically, this system runs through the entire unit and also through the other sessions. The aim is always to get into an exchange as close to practice as possible (Academia + Project Working Team, 2021b) (cf. Table 2).

5.4 *Intellectual Output: Didactical Framework III: Demographic Change*

After the individual project steps have been presented in the two previous didactical frameworks and connected with the content-related and didactical considerations and designs, this didactical framework will deal with the presentation of the last project steps on the basis of the third C-STEP with the topic "demographic change". For this purpose, it may be useful to summarise and structure the two didactical frameworks of the previous C-STEPs.

Table 2 example: structure plan from C-STEP 2 Unit 2 challenges and opportunities for companies within Industry 4.0 (Academia + Project Working Team, 2021b)

Time	Topic	Method, media and material	Outcome	Comments
10.00	Introduction	Plenary session	Introduction speakers and agenda	Presentation of the agenda for the day, give a small talk about the last day and tell the days and topics of the other days
10.20	Challenges: Change and resilience to it	Video Plenum discussion Fable Mentimeter	Participants discuss some possible barriers to change and resilience to it. Some barriers refer to the barriers to women's workforce (the industry gender gap) whose participation varies by industry and often reflects different industry cultures in addition to overarching economic and societal factors such as the dual burden of caregiving and breadwinning, unconscious biases, traditional organisational practices in the workplace, a lack of role models, confidence, etc.	Participants watch the video about jobs of the future from the cognizant Centre for the future of work (6 min.) https://www.cognizant.com/futureofwork/whitepaper/21-more-jobs-of-the-future-a-guide-to-getting-and-staying-employed-through-2029 Moderation (1 min.): It seems that the Corona pandemic is pushing existing trends forward, trends seem to speed up especially in terms of digitalisation The following ted talk covers different aspects of change in an overview (e.g. workplace/companies, health, universities) Participants watch the ted talk with ben Pring from cognizant Centre for the future of jobs (18 min.): https://www.ted.com/talks/ben_pring_the_new_jobs_of_the_future_and_other_insights_on_the_changing_workforce Moderation (2 min.): Quintessence: Re-invent existing models in the different areas *(hint to the website https://www.cognizant.com/future-of-work especially the jobs of the future index - link in chat)* Participants answer the question via Mentimeter, speaker sums up the main results of the wordcloud (10 min.) *link and code in the chat* *https://www.menti.com/* *Code XXX* 1. What barriers to change might advice-seeking people have?

(continued)

Table 2 (continued)

Time	Topic	Method, media and material	Outcome	Comments
				2. What barriers to change might companies have? After focusing on change it is time to focus on resilience to change Speaker is telling the participants the fable of the oak and the reeds (3 min.) Plenum discussion about the question: 3. What does this tell us about resilience and its components? (10 min.) Speaker gives short input about the results of Diane Coutu research about the 3 components of resilience: Facing down reality, the search for meaning, ritualised ingenuity (10 min.) Plenum discussion about the question (10 min.): How can these components help to overcome the barriers to change?
11.30	Short break			
11.45	Challenges: Staff and structure of the company • Investing in a skilled workforce • Keeping pace with new technologies • Competing for a skilled workforce • Training and retraining • Gap between skills needs and supply • Inequality of skill / employment access	PPT presentation	Participants get an overview of the segment of enterprises in industry 4.0—Industry profiles. They discuss some challenges for the staff and the structure of the company such as invest in a skilled workforce, training and retraining, lifelong learning, motivation of employees, etc.	Lecturer gives an input to selected topics from this list via ppt presentation Speaker will frequently ask for questions during the presentation

(continued)

Table 2 (continued)

Time	Topic	Method, media and material	Outcome	Comments
	• Mental and physical health of the worker • Financial and legal aspects for companies • Update equipment and accessories • Motivation of employees to follow the development • Prevention of social exclusion Labour mobility			
12.30	Challenges: Competition Main challenges and ways in which career practitioners can help overcome them	Article reading Plenum discussion	Participants know how to be prepared/get an idea towards competitive labour markets and how practitioners can help to overcome them	Participants read the introduction and the conclusion of the article (5 pages) (15 min.): http://www.oecd.org/daf/competition/competition-in-labour-markets-2020.pdf *Link in the chat* Afterwards they discuss what career guidance practitioners should keep in mind about competitive labour markets when they counsel potential employees and the possible ways career practitioners can help to overcome them (10 min.) At the end of the session the participants share their thoughts about all the challenges discussed during the morning sessions (5 min.)
13:00	Lunch break			
14:00	Opportunities: New businesses/business models and new products/services	Article reading, followed by group work, presentation of the results and	Participants know some opportunities for companies within industry 4.0, they learn	5 minutes for introduction and explanation of the activity (participants divided into 8 groups) 25 minutes for the participants to fulfil their activity

(continued)

Table 2 (continued)

Time	Topic	Method, media and material	Outcome	Comments
	• New specialisations leading to the creation of more and new professions • Sustainability of digitalised production and work Efficiency of production by technological rationalisation of workflow and improvements in productivity	plenum discussing	new business models that will emerge in this landscape: New professions and professional profiles, digitised production and work, etc. Participants discuss other possibilities for the companies within the industry 4.0 and discuss new products and services as current challenges	(https://www.pwc.com/gx/en/services/people-organisation/workforce-of-the-future/workforce-of-the-future-the-competing-forces-shaping-2030-pwc.pdf) Yellow world: https://drive.google.com/file/d/1X1xXSks-H5igl6XZNiQfwwjmZohjlMp5/view?usp=sharing Red world: https://drive.google.com/file/d/1-r2rIrwREjNs6uw11FDlqd6MEXUXTrhw/view?usp=sharing Green world: https://drive.google.com/file/d/12DIpuGIy4xuYesna-jAwCDekQ7PYr_MU/view?usp=sharing Blue world: https://drive.google.com/file/d/1BQM2O7FwhU1L6ExFribP4cFPgs04J4fb/view?usp=sharing 15 minutes for the participants to join in groups of their colour and share the ideas for new businesses and products 20 minutes to present the results to the other groups 10 minutes for final discussion
15:15	Short break			
15:30	Opportunities: Organisation of work • Gap between skills needs and labour market supply and gap between skills needs and interest of potential applicants (future workforce) Emergence of new fields of activity, qualifications, professions;	PPT presentation	Participants learn new ways of organising work, seen as opportunities for change. They discuss new fields of activity, qualifications and professions which implies a transformation of traditional jobs and jobs profiles in the current labour market	Speaker gives input via ppt presentation (40 min.) Why are they doing what they doing? What are they doing? Who is using what we are doing and how? (examples of customers on a global scale) What topics regarding organisation of work do they cover with their services (job rotation, job shadowing, job matching, working circles) Strategic thought behind their work Q&A (20 min.) (directly asked by participants)

(continued)

Table 2 (continued)

Time	Topic	Method, media and material	Outcome	Comments
	transformation of traditional jobs/job profiles into modern jobs/job profiles and qualification in high demand			
16:30	Opportunities: Thoughts of the participants	Plenum discussion	The afternoon session ends with a discussion made by participants in order to know their thoughts and view concerning these sets of opportunities described for companies in the frame of the fourth industrial revolution	Participants share their thoughts about the presented opportunities in the afternoon sessions
16:45	Wrap-up and final discussion		Summary and sharing	
17:00	End of day			

Several people and professionals support in the design and development of the training sessions, amongst others: Guest speakers/lectures (those who do the whole presentations, in charge to provide the training input/contents); moderator/s (usually support with the introduction by the speaker, the interventions, the closure of the sessions and sometimes, with certain technical aspects…); a person who is taking care to make notes and support participants by the email (academia.info@gmail.com) and help with phone numbers; a personal technician who is in charge of recording the sessions and to split/distribute the groups in breakout rooms for the group work, etc.; a person responsible for providing links on the chat and/or other additional material, taking care of checking and answering the chat.

As a reminder: So far, the concrete needs and competence requirements for the three topics "counselling migrants and refugees", "future work" and "demographic change" have been developed on the basis of the national research landscape and the theoretical foundations on the one hand and the empirically surveyed needs of the counsellors and experts on the other. For this purpose,

(continued)

the national reports were combined into a transnational synthesis with a multinational perspective and a qualitative questionnaire was developed which was made available to various counsellors and career guidance practitioners in order to find out their concrete needs. These needs were bundled and clustered into thematic areas, which could then be filled with needs and competence requirements and thus provide initial indications of concrete learning needs and contents for a training programme. This training programme is to be designed, offered and evaluated in three "Counsellors' Study and Training Exchange Programmes for Key Challenges of European Labour Markets and Societies" (C-STEPs). From these thematic clusters, a first structure could be worked out, which was continuously differentiated in a template. The concrete requirements for action and competence and the respective key challenges were thematically elaborated. In consultation with various experts and lecturers, blocks of topics were subsumed and then filled with content by international lecturers in cooperation with the Academia+ project. A systematisation structure was created for this content, in which the didactical framework offers two possibilities: in the Academia+ project process, it served as a template for the further development of the content, and in the follow-up to the project, it now serves as a framework for the learning content and units actually offered, which can still be used for training programmes. With these learning objectives in mind, the Academia+ project was now looking for qualified experts from different European countries who would like to contribute or give a session on the topic. In close consultation with the Academia+ Project, these lecturers then designed their respective offers. The central focus here was on the learning objectives and main outcomes that had been worked out in advance. In addition, the lecturers also oriented themselves to the central needs of the interviewed counsellors and career guidance practitioners. Innovative concepts for different types of sessions were developed. Classical input sessions were represented as well as discussion rounds, moderated group work phases, short impulse presentations with subsequent transnational exchange, smaller exercises, etc. The most important thing was to be able to generate and offer a good mix of methods, media and materials. The resulting range of different sessions within the units aimed above all at diversity in terms of content and methodology. At the same time, the transnational exchange and the elaborated learning goals were always a priority. Under these conditions, the conceptualised offer for the respective thematic sessions was to be reviewed again precisely with regard to the learning goals, the needs of the counsellors and career guidance practitioners and ultimately also the methodological-didactic diversity. For this purpose, a qualitative questionnaire was developed, which primarily referred to the coverage analysis of the learning objectives issued and the session contents designed by the experts. This review process was carried out internally with all

(continued)

partners, and external experts were also acquired to review the designed sessions. The feedback from the double review process was reflected back to the lecturers and, at the same time, their own learning objectives were reflected again for additions. In the end, this resulted in a detailed structure plan as a basis for the concrete implementation of the training programme in addition to the numerous materials, which we focus again later in this section.

In the first two sections on the intellectual outputs, the topics "counselling migrants and refugees" and "future work" were discussed and their respective didactical frameworks were used to exemplify the implementation of the project. The third C-STEP now deals with a phenomenon that is already interwoven in the second thematic block: demographic change. At this point, two central structures emerge for advisors: on the one hand, the population of the European countries is becoming increasingly older. At the same time, fewer children are born than old people die in many European countries. Basically, two processes are taking precedence: there is a decline in population figures in the EU countries and at the same time this population is getting older and older. On the other hand, this trend is particularly noticeable with regard to the national labour markets. On top of that, the population is not only getting older. Much stronger is the effect that more and more older people are close to or already on the threshold of retirement. This trend will intensify in the coming years as the baby boomer generation, which was very strong in its birth cohorts, gradually retires (Academia + Project Working Team, 2021d). The influence of this upcoming trend on counsellors and career guidance practitioners was also the topic of the last C-STEP and is thus also the topic of the last two project steps, which have always been included here in the course of the contribution.

After the expert lecturers were able to incorporate the feedback into their own concepts in a final revision, there were essentially two steps left in the course of the project: the implementation of these online training weeks and the evaluation. The implementation of these C-STEPs (and by this we mean all three) will be explained below using the material results that emerged from this implementation as an example. First, however, something about the formalities: the first C-STEP on the topic of refugees and migrants took place online from 28 May to 9 June 2020 (with 80 registrations) due to the Corona crisis. The advantage of offering this training week online can be seen in different places. Amongst other things, the setting was designed in such a way that the materials could be used as quickly as possible in further training measures (e.g. planned and implemented by people who could not participate in the training or even by people who participated and want to disseminate the topic in their own institution). Another advantage of this online setting was that many more people from different countries could participate in this training week. There were significantly more registrations than in an anticipated face-to-face setting, especially because the travel hassle was eliminated. This meant that even some non-European participants were able to take part in the C-STEP, for example from Georgia, Azerbaijan or even India. Finally, the second and third training weeks were also moved to an online setting, which again led to a strong heterogeneity in the nationalities of the participants. The second C-STEP on the topic of "future jobs" also took place in 4 day units from 09.03.2021 to 18.03.2021 (with >100 registrations) and the third C-STEP on the topic of "demographic change" then took place from 10.05.2021 to 20.05.2021 (with 100 registrations). As already mentioned in the intellectual outcomes for the first C-STEP, the necessary materials and additional materials provided by the lecturers or the Academia+ project were published on the Moodle platform in advance of the respective events. The provision of material in the Academia+ project pursued two goals. On the one hand, Moodle was used directly as a platform for exchange and material for the events taking place. The links to the group rooms but also to the "lecture hall" were stored there, as was all the material. This was set up systematically according to the structure plan. The most accurate and systematic presentation and provision of the material was closely linked to the second goal: The C-STEPs were not developed exclusively for one week of training, but should rather offer the possibility of permanent on-demand learning. The objective is basically explained as follows: in addition to the conception and implementation of three one-week practical Counsellors' Study and Training Exchange Programmes (C-STEPs), the material conceived within the project was also to be made available on a technical infrastructure (Moodle). All resources and material will be made available through national as well as target-group oriented sections of the project web portal.

Specifically, however, the material is not only made available for the personal use of new participants or counsellors. It also serves as a collection of material that has been prepared in such a way that counsellors and career guidance practitioners or other lecturers from guidance institutions can use this material to offer online training on the three offered topics in their working groups. This is expressed in the provision of the material as follows: in addition to the classic output materials, which have arisen from the lecturers' presentations, from the exercises or the group work assignments, the didactically prepared templates can also be found on the Moodle platform. The material is therefore always designed for the use of future participants and interested consultants (for their own context of use), but at the same time as a complete didactic-methodical package for interested lecturers. For example, fact sheets were developed in two forms. On the one hand, for potential users who would like to further educate themselves on this topic, etc., and on the other hand, for the teachers themselves. On the other hand, there is always an offer for interested lecturers in a separate fact sheet. This also contains all the materials, all the structure plans and all the media, for example, with the help of instructions on how to set up such an online session or how best to use Moodle for which groups (see intellectual outcome I, where we reported on the instructions for using Moodle). The following are excerpts from the fact sheet for lecturers from C-STEP 3 "demographic change" and Unit 2 "retraining in later life". The fact sheets for the different units in the three C-STEPs are basically structured in the same systematic way. The main objectives of the C-STEP are explained once again and finally the concrete learning contents for this unit are defined (cf. Fig. 1).

IO3 C-STEP 3 'Demographic change'

Fact sheet for lecturers: Unit 2 "Retraining in later life"

Objectives and learning contents

C-STEP 3 deals with the challenge of demographic change on the labour market; in particular the impact of an ageing population and how the labour market will need to adapt to better incorporate these workers as people live longer, retire later and the number of older workers increases. Currently employment amongst older workers is quite low, and there are large differences in their employment rate across the European countries. As a result there is a lot of work to do across Europe to increase the employment rate of older workers and change attitudes held amongst the general population in relation to older workers. Careers guidance professionals are integral to this process as they can help older workers realise and receive training, as well as market the value of older employees. This course unit will focus on retraining, in particular the benefits of retraining in later life, both for individuals as well as companies, and how to promote and find retraining options suitable for each client.

Overview of the **learning contents** in Unit 2:

1. challenges arising from skills mismatches and a reluctance to retrain
2. how to make training attractive for older people
3. work-based learning for the older generation
4. mentor training
5. digital training (the digital divide)

Fig. 1 IO3 C-STEP 3 fact sheet for lecturer (Academia + Project Working Team, 2021e)

On the basis of these learning contents, which structured the respective unit and gave thematic suggestions, as they also took place in C-STEP 3, the concrete learning outcomes were then worked out, so that any interested lecturers would have the opportunity to follow them up in detail. The objectives and learning outcomes for Unit 2, with the theme "retraining in later life", focused on the following learning outcomes:

- Learn about employability as a challenge in times of demographic change.
- Learn about participation rates in training for older adults—age as risk for exclusion from training and employment.
- Share and discuss examples for current policies—national and European perspectives.
- Present strategies to support employability.
- Discuss how older employees can be supported near the workplace and identify challenges and chances.
- Awareness about the challenge of activating older employees.
- Describe factors for "successful qualification" of older employees and counselling and mentoring as an instrument for good qualification.
- Discuss and compare needed knowledge and competence, counsellors and mentors should have (Academia + Project Working Team, 2021e).

A list of all collected and prepared materials follows in each fact sheet. Here, the lecturers (and the participants in their version, of course) can access the respective materials with a direct link. These can always be accessed via Moodle using a guest account. The following graphic shows an example of the material prepared and presented for the unit "retraining in later" life (cf. Fig. 2):

In addition, the didactic level mentioned above can be found as an add-on in the respective fact sheet for the lecturer. In this example of Unit 2, the didactic information that lecturers need in advance of the course is included. For example, information is given that comes directly from the lecturers' experience during the training week. Valuable tips can be given, for example, on technical feasibility or the exact preparation time. The following is an example of the instructions for the unit "retraining in later life":

5.5 *Preparation Work*

It is recommended to consider the following preparation steps for a successful unit:

- To do a technical test with participants and lecturers in advance is highly recommend.
- To have enough time for getting to know each other (participants and lecturer/s).
    - To start the training with a brief introduction by the lecturer about him or her professional profile, institution, lines of research, etc., in order to get closer to the group.

Material for use

- Didactical framework, Unit descriptions and List of additional material and resources (OUTPUTS – Academiaplus)
- List of learning material and resources (all materials can be found on Academia+ Moodle platform)
- >>> AGENDA 12th May, 2021

Speaker 1

- 1. Presentation: "Retraining in later life. Perspectives from training and guidance for older employees"
- 2. Results of the working groups: Flinga and Mentimeter results
- 3. Reading (session 2): "Designing Effective Training for Older Workers"
- 4. Reading (session 3): "Promoting an Age-Inclusive Workforce: Living, Learning and Earning Longer"

Speaker 2

- 1. Presentation (session 4): "Late-Career Learning for Work (and Life)"
- 2. Results of the working group: Mentimeter results u2 s4 "Thinking about older workers as learners"
- 3. Presentation (sessions 5&6): "When retraining in later life is the only option: chronic illness, disability and vocational rehabilitation"
- 4. Readings (session 5): Reading groups
- 5. Practices (session 6): Case studies/tasks

Additional material

Fig. 2 IO3 C-STEP 3 material for use (Academia + Project Working Team, 2021e)

  - To ask for volunteers/participants to introduce themselves (name, institution and what they would like to learn) depending on the size of the group.
- Lecturer explains the agenda for the day and get a first overview about the schedule for the session.
- Lecturer presents a few brief indications and establishes some rules for the session (especially for an online training with many participants, some specific rules of conduct can structure the session and thus contribute to the success):
  - It is recommended to mute/turn off all the microphones while the speaker is talking (otherwise, the connection will deteriorate, background noise and any interference will cause anxiety and poor understanding).
  - Depending on the number of participants, it is also necessary to turn off the video signal while the speaker is presenting. More video signals mean more data consumption, which may affect the quality of the conference. In small groups or for group work and discussions in several groups it is useful to switch on the video signal.
  - While using the meeting platform there are two different options for asking questions while an input session. On the one hand, it is possible to use the chat. It is very helpful to collect and channel the questions during a longer input

> session. The questions asked in the chat can then be answered in special Q&A sessions. On the other hand, Zoom and MS Teams provide different actions for participants who want to say or ask something. Participants can raise their hand symbol when they have a question or want to say something. The little hand will then pop up at the speakers desktop so he or she knows that someone wants to say something. (Academia + Project Working Team, 2021e).

The fact sheets of all units of the 3 S-STEPs contain links to all presentations, video recordings, group work assignments, work results, discussion and chat protocols and further materials of the online learning platform Moodle. Analogous to the fact sheets for lecturers, there are fact sheets for participants. In summary, the idea of this methodology is explained once again and supplemented by the last step of the project. The online training sessions presented in the individual units on various topics from the areas of "migrants and refugees", "future work" and "demographic change" were evaluated directly by the participants afterwards. This evaluation also aims at different levels. Basically, of course, it serves to evaluate the offer that has been created. On another level, the results are particularly useful in that they deal with the usability of the individual materials, the online media library (Moodle) and its use and ultimately also the processed materials. This process is important overall, especially from the point of view that the use of the online platform, easy access for the materials provided, etc. has a direct influence on the further use and usability of the platform beyond the training week. The evaluation showed a very good usability of the materials, an extremely intuitive access and an equally intuitive use of the Moodle course room. Ultimately, the aim of this evaluation was to have the material critically assessed once again by the target group that should ideally work with it in the further course: counsellors and career guidance practitioners. The high degree of congruence between the materials and sessions offered and the wishes and needs of the participants once again shows how important it is to synthesise the theoretical foundation and the concrete needs of the practically oriented target group already in the basic work. The content and the 3 C-STEPs, which are available in their entirety and at a high quality level on the online learning platform, can be used for further training measures quickly and in a resource-saving way due to the online character and the topics.

The potential and synergy effects of further utilisation or further focusing of these transnational exchanges is bearing fruit in many different places. On the one hand, there is lively participation in further discussions on the topics mentioned, but also on other topics on different platforms. On the other hand, it is also the basic idea of this anthology. At this point, the goal of creating a transnational exchange goes beyond the project duration of the Academia+ project, which ended in August 2021. However, it will continue to develop, be it in further offers from the Academia and Euroguidance family, in possible uses of the prepared material or ultimately in the individual contributions that now follow. These individual contributions will take up the national perspective on the topics "counselling migrants and refugees", "future of work" and "demographic" change, and report on the central challenges and the current status from the respective countries. In the last part of the anthology, this will then be transferred into a transnational exchange including an outlook.

References

Abkhezr, P., & McMahon, M. (2017). Narrative career counselling for people with refugee backgrounds. *International Journal for the Advancement of Counselling, 39*, 99–111.

Academia + Project Working Team (Eds.) (2020a). *Intellectual output 1. Counselling migrants and refugees. Didactical framework.* Link: https://academiaplus.eu/wp-content/uploads/2021/08/C-STEP_1_Counselling_migrants_and_refugees_Didactical_Framework.pdf.

Academia + Project Working Team (Eds.) (2020b). *Intellectual output 1. Counselling migrants and refugees. Unit 1: Intercultural awareness.* Link: https://academiaplus.eu/wp-content/uploads/2021/08/C-STEP_1_Unit_1_Intercultural-awareness.pdf.

Academia + Project Working Team (Eds.) (2021a). *Intellectual output 2. Transnational report. Future jobs: Impact, needs and challenges.* Link: https://academiaplus.eu/wp-content/uploads/2021/07/IO2_Transnational_Synthesis.pdf.

Academia + Project Working Team. (Eds.) (2021b). *Intellectual Output 2. Future jobs. Recommendation for selection of content, material and resources for the media centre (O4).* Link: https://academiaplus.eu/wp-content/uploads/2021/07/IO2_Recommendation-for-selection-of-content-material-and-resources-for-the-media-centre-O2.pdf.

Academia + Project Working Team. (Eds.) (2021c). *Intellectual output 2. Future jobs. Unit 2: Challenges and opportunities for companies within industry 4.0.* Link: https://academiaplus.eu/wp-content/uploads/2021/08/C-STEP_2_Unit_2_Challenges_and_opportunities_for_companies_within_Industry_4.0.pdf.

Academia + Project Working Team. (Eds.) (2021d). *Intellectual output 3. Transnational report. Demographic change: Impact, needs and challenges.* URL: https://academiaplus.eu/wp-content/uploads/2021/07/IO3-Transnational-Report.pdf.

Academia + Project Working Team. (Eds.) (2021e). *IO3 C-STEP 3 'Demographic change'. Fact sheet for lecturers: Unit 3 "Realigning the expectations of the labour market"*. URL: https://academiaplus.eu/wp-content/uploads/2021/08/Unit-3-C-STEP-3-%E2%80%98Realigning-the-expectations-of-the-labour-market-FACT-SHEETS-FOR-LECTURERS.pdf.

Bitkom. (2019). *Trendstudie Digitalisierung 2019.* Link: https://www.bitkom-research.de/de/Trendstudie-Digitalisierung-19

CMINAR Project Team (eds. Karl-Heinz P. Kohn) (2019). *Counselling refugees means modernising counselling.* Link: https://www.cminar.eu/upload/files/Book_CMinaR_project-outputs-and-evaluation%281%29.pdf

Euroguidance. (2022). *Academia network.* Link: https://www.euroguidance.eu/academia-network

Fleay, C., et al. (2013). Refugees and asylum seekers living in the Australian community: The importance of work rights and employment support. *Australian Journal of Social Issues, 48*, 473–493.

Freiling, T., Conrads, R., Müller-Osten, A., & Porath, J. (2020). *Zukünftige Arbeitswelten. Facetten guter Arbeit, beruflicher Qualifizierung und sozialer Sicherung*. Springer.

Gericke, D., Pundt, L., & Deller, J. (2017). *Wie aus Geflüchteten Kolleg/innen werden*! [How refugees become colleagues!]. In-Mind Magazin, 3. Link: http://de.inmind.org/article/wie-aus-gefluechteten-kolleg-innen-werden

Moehling, K. K. (2008). *Career guidance education: Helping resettled refugees plan their future*. Unpublished thesis, University of Pittsburgh.

Pernice, R., & Brook, J. (1996). Refugees' and immigrants' mental health: Association of demographic and post-immigration factors. *The Journal of Social Psychology, 136*, 511519.

The Economist. (2017). *How Germany is integrating its refugees.* Link: https://www.economist.com/news/europe/21728992-it-seems-be-managing-how

Yakushko, O., et al. (2008). Career development concerns of recent immigrants and refugees. *Journal of Career Development, 34*, 362–396.

Zacher, H. (2018). Career development of refugees. In J. A. Athanasou & H. N. Perera (Eds.), *International handbook of career guidance* (2nd ed.). Leipzig University/Springer.

Part II
Vocational Guidance in Europe: Challenges, Needs, Solutions and Development Perspectives

Cyprus: Migrants' Inclusion in the Labour Market, Education and Society of Cyprus: Current Needs and Perspectives for Change

Glykeria Kalamata

1 Current Status of Migrant Population in Cyprus

Cyprus is a small country which, due to its strategic geographical position, has been conquered by many different empires, civilisations and cultures, from ancient times until recent decades. Given the fact that the country gained its liberty and independence in 1960 and experienced a Turkish invasion in 1974, which brought many fluctuations to the composition of its recently liberated population, it comes as no surprise that it is characterised by many inequalities and injustices. In particular, for many decades women's activities were limited to the household and child raising, while thousands of women were engaged in non-paid work in the fields of agriculture and stock raising (Papaeracleous, 2003). Apart from that, the recent financial crisis in 2013 and the dramatic increase in the flow of migrants and refugees have affected the local economy, labour market and the educational system.

Currently, Cyprus' foreign population is the second largest after Luxembourg in the European Union in percentage terms, as foreign residents comprise 15.7% of its population. The last 30 years have brought a dramatic increase of immigration to the country, with 21,306 new arrivals of long-term immigrants in 2017 compared to only 246 in 1981. Except for the years 2012–2015 when Cyprus' economy was in deep recession, net migration has been positive (Eurostat, 2018).

In general, Cyprus is receiving a relatively low number of asylum applications and has a small number of recognised refugees despite the proximity of Cyprus to Syria. In 2017, there were 4582 asylum applications out of which 142 gained refugee statuses with Syria, India, Vietnam, Bangladesh, Egypt, Pakistan, Sri Lanka, Somalia, Cameroon and the Philippines as the top countries of origin. Almost 6 in 10 applications for asylum are rejected. In the last three years, asylum applications

G. Kalamata (✉)
Center for Social Innovation, Nicosia, Cyprus
e-mail: glykeria.kalamata@csicy.com

C. Enoch et al. (eds.), *Vocational Guidance in Europe*,
https://doi.org/10.1007/978-3-031-06592-7_2

have doubled, even though in the years 2008–2013 they were decreasing. The low number of asylum applications can be partly explained by the fact that Cyprus, even though it is a member state of the European Union, is not in the free movement area of Schengen (Ministry of Labour, Welfare and Social Insurance, 2021).

2 Status of Migrants' Integration in the Educational System

The number of foreign-born students in primary and secondary education is consistent with the general immigration statistics, comprising around 15% of the student body. Regarding tertiary education though, almost half of the students studying in Cyprus are foreign born. The vast majority of foreign students come from Greece, Southeast Asia and North Africa (Cyprus Ministry of Education and Culture, 2021).

The Cyprus Ministry of Education and Culture is running intensive Greek language programmes for foreign children to enable their smooth integration in the public educational system, and exempts from evaluation migrant children not fluent in Greek in subjects such as modern, ancient Greek, religious studies and French. Regarding adult education, a large number of Greek language classes run throughout the year, organised by the Ministry of Education, universities or local municipalities, free or at a low cost. The majority of the classes though do not go beyond teaching elementary Greek (UNHCR, 2021).

Apart from language courses, the government implements vocational training courses for specialised manual labour in sectors such as plumbing, automation and car repairs, but they are mostly provided in Greek, which is a barrier to entry for migrants. A few NGOs and local municipalities offer VET in English, but in the absence of a national policy on the integration of migrants, these programs are sparse.

3 Status of Migrants' Integration in the Labour Market

Migrants in Cyprus, especially from non-EU countries, face low levels of unemployment in absolute terms. In 2017, 3324 third-country nationals (TCNs) were unemployed, compared to 5476 EU nationals and 38,366 Cypriots. The main sectors in which third country and EU nationals are employed in Cyprus are activities of households (domestic workers), agriculture, construction, wholesale, HORECA (hotel, restaurant, catering), administration and financial services (Eurostat, 2018) (cf. Table 1).

EU nationals enjoy the same rights to enter, live and work in Cyprus, under the same conditions as Cypriots, as well as the same rights on social insurance, health and unemployment benefits. Non-EU nationals who wish to be employed in Cyprus must hold a long stay work visa, in predefined positions and for definite amounts of time. As shown in the table above, almost half of non-EU nationals in Cyprus are

Table 1 Main sectors of employment of EU and non-EU nationals in Cyprus (Eurostat, 2018)

Sector	Cypriots	EU nationals	Non-EU nationals
Total	**304,750**	**46,747**	**28,125**
Agricultures, forestry and fishing	7233	504	1859
Manufacturing	22,772	3762	642
Construction	22,119	6670	2399
Wholesale and retail trade, repair of motor vehicles and motorcycles	54,502	12,412	2184
Transportation and storage	14,778	2019	332
Accommodation and food service activities	22,831	9526	2224
Financial and insurance activities	18,311	1582	978
Professional, scientific and technical activities	24,138	1617	1116
Administrative and support service activities	7143	1896	1039
Education	25,927	1100	414
Human health and social work activities	19,754	1210	297
Arts, entertainment and recreation	5341	989	454
Other service activities	10,452	946	805
Activities of households	332	104	12,300

employed in households, mostly as domestic workers. They are also required to have a private health insurance (Eurostat, 2018).

All migrants and refugees in Cyprus, both from the European Union and Third Country Nationals that hold a long-term residence permit, can access the Guaranteed Minimum Income Benefit, under the same income criteria (including immovable property ownership and bank deposits) as Cypriots. The benefit aims to ensure a socially acceptable minimum standard of living to people that cannot satisfy their basic financial needs on their own, and is granted in the form of financial support or services. In order to access the benefit, migrants must have been residing in Cyprus for 5 years and continue to stay in Cyprus while receiving the benefit.

Students that come from non-EU countries can seek employment in Cyprus if they study full-time in a recognised institution of higher education in Cyprus and have completed 6 months of study in Cyprus and their working hours are outside school hours. They are only allowed to work in low-skilled professions such as food delivery drivers, petrol station attendants, workers and caregivers (Ministry of Labour, Welfare and Social Insurance, 2021).

Finally, while refugees have equal access to employment as Cypriots, asylum seekers are not allowed to work during the first six months from the date when they submit their asylum application. After that period and until their application is processed, they are only allowed to work as unskilled or low-skilled labour in specific sectors such as agriculture, farming, manufacture and waste management. According to NGOs working with asylum seekers and refugees, these legal restrictions in employment, along with the rent allowances that are much below the market rate, have brought increasing numbers of asylum seekers to sleep in the open and cannot satisfy their basic needs (Cyprus Refugee Council, 2021).

4 Legislation

In the past two decades, there has been a systematic effort from government members and EU representatives to settle a legal framework for migrant and gender inclusion policies at different levels.

4.1 Higher Education Qualifications

Higher education qualifications are recognised in Cyprus by the Council of Recognition of Higher Qualifications, called KYSATS, which was established in 1996. For a degree or title of studies obtained from private universities in Cyprus and universities abroad to be recognised, it must be evaluated against the same degrees issued by the public universities of Cyprus in the same discipline and same title. It should be noted, however, that the above processes last for approximately 6 months and costs around 120 euros for each title recognised, thus being unapproachable to the majority of migrants, who face a lot of financial difficulties (KYSATS, 2021).

4.2 Laws Regarding the Recognition of Working Skills

Several laws have been established for the recognition of working skills of people who do not have a Cypriot citizenship, like the above:

- Laws concerning the free movement of people.
- Law 121 (I) / 2003—The Second General System for the Recognition of Qualifications Law—(in Greek only).
- The General System for the Recognition of Professional Qualifications Law 179 (I) 2002 and the General System for the Recognition of Professional Qualifications Law-modifying (in Greek only).
- The third system on the Recognition of Qualifications Law of 2004—(in Greek only).
- Law 31(I)/2008—The Recognition of Professional Qualifications Law (in Greek only).
- P.I. 87/2007—The Combating of Trafficking and Exploitation of Persons and Victims Protection Law of 2007 (in Greek only).

For regulated professions such as doctors, architects, lawyers, taxi drivers, managers, etc., interested applicants must contact the Department of Labour of the

Ministry of Labour and Social insurance in order to apply for recognition of their working skills and enrol in the corresponding associations.

When it comes to gender equality, in 2002 the Law on Equal Treatment of Men and Women in Professional Plans and Social Insurances (L. 133(I)/2002) was put into effect. The law provides the following:

- It intends to embed in the national framework of professional social insurance plans the principles of equality and non-discrimination between men and women. It addresses both direct and indirect discriminatory provisions and actions.
- It forbids discriminatory actions in relation to the admissibility criteria in a professional plan, the calculation of benefits, the additional benefit that might arise in light of dependents as well as a number of other detailed provisions related to admissible and non-admissible actions in a professional plan.
- The law sets forth two possible ways of addressing potential violations, either through judicial means (such as the Supreme Court, through article 146 of the Constitution) or through submitting a complaint before the Commissioner for Administration and Human Rights (Ombudsman) as an independent out-of-court means of resolving conflicts.

An additional legislative instrument was put into effect in 2002, the Law on Equal Treatment of Men and Women in Employment and Vocational Training (L. 205(I)/2002). This is particularly important for people with a migratory background, and especially women who are either pregnant or who have children. The law provides and regulates the following:

- The aim of the law is to provide equal treatment of men and women in relation to accessing professional orientation, training, access to employment and career development, but also the criteria for being laid off and participation in employee – employer bodies and organisation.
- The law indicates that the provisions apply equally to both direct and indirect form of discrimination, though the latter needs to be further substantiated and justified.
- Issues such as direct and indirect discrimination towards women for reasons pertaining to pregnancy, leave of absence or sick leave related to pregnancy and breastfeeding as covered in the law.
- The provisions of the law are directly related and involve issues covered in the legislative instrument regulating maternity/paternity leave, and parental leave as a result of force majeure.
- The law lays down a very specific framework of action in cases of harassment and sexual harassment in the work environment. The provisions lay upon the employers the burden of taking positive action to address such incidents and/or implement a framework that would protect employees from harassment or sexual harassment.
- The means of addressing violations of the provisions of the law are, as indicated in the law, through judicial proceedings before the national courts, or through other administrative bodies such as the Labour Relations unit of the Ministry of

Labour, Welfare and Social Insurances and/or the Commissioner for Administration and Human Rights (Ombudsman).
- The law also provides for ongoing dialogue and communication with civil society organisations (CSOs) active in the promotion of equality between men and women.

More specifically, in 2014 the President of the Republic of Cyprus appointed the Committee for Gender Equality in Employment and Vocational Training, in order to oversee legislation and policies related to gender and make relevant suggestions. The Committee is in constant cooperation with the following bodies and organisations, attempting to improve the everyday life of men and women, especially of those with a migratory background:

The National Machinery for Women's Rights (NMWR) advises the Committee on policies, programmes and laws promoting women's rights, monitors, coordinates and evaluates the implementation and effectiveness of these programmes and laws, carries out information, education and training programmes on relevant issues, contributes to the mobilisation and sensitisation of the public sector on equality issues and serves as a cooperation channel between the Government and women's organisations and NGOs working on gender equality and women's rights (NMWR, 2021).

The Cyprus Gender Research Centre (EKIF) is a non-governmental, non-profit organisation, which cooperates with the Committee in order to promote equality and equal opportunities between men and women and reconciliation between work and private life, encourage respect and co-operation between citizens irrespective of gender, ethnicity, race and religion, carry out research on issues of gender and equality in order to underline the need for change and more democratic values and citizenship, organise activities and functions which will help to transform long-held perceptions on gender and eliminate discrimination in the social, cultural, educational and political spheres. The Centre has been active in organising events, research projects and interventions, which aim at highlighting and combating gender discrimination and promoting women's empowerment (EKIF, 2021).

The Mediterranean Institute of Gender Studies (MIGS) is a non-profit organisation which works with the Committee to promote and contribute to projects of social, political and economic themes relating to gender, with an emphasis on the Mediterranean region. The Institute recognises the multi-layered levels of discrimination against women and accepts that this discrimination takes different forms. It is committed to the elimination of this discrimination using a combination of research, advocacy and lobbying, as well as training courses, conferences and other activities (MIGS, 2021).

Thus, it could be said that some systematic attempts are being made in order to address the needs of females with a migratory background in Cyprus and facilitate their integration in the Cypriot labour market, education and society.

5 The Field of VET in Cyprus

VET is considered to be an important and prominent part of the Cyprus lifelong learning strategy referred to as CyLLS. In the education and training system of Cyprus, there are VET qualifications that can be obtained and certified (CEDEFOP, 2016). They are legitimised by the Council of Ministers and/or Acts, approved by the House of Representatives. Upper secondary level at the technical schools, including the evening technical schools, is considered to be the earliest level at which VET is available in Cyprus. In both the theoretical direction and the practical direction, the VET programmes are offered free of charge by the MoEC (Ministry of Education and Culture). The certificate acquired after completion has the same status legally as the certificate acquired by the upper secondary general education, unified lyceum and mainstream technical schools. VET is also available through the apprenticeship system, which accepts students who leave formal education between grades eight and ten. According to the VET in Europe report in Cyprus (2016), vocational training is widely available for people who are unemployed and employed, for other groups that are in risk of exclusion from the labour market and for adults in general. Public and private provision such as colleges, training institutions, consultancy firms and enterprises can provide training to these people. The Department of STVE of the MoEC offers three-year programmes that are provided in the setting of afternoon and evening classes in technical schools. They are at limited fees and help employed and unemployed adults re-integrate in areas in the workforce where there is a lack of skilled workers. They also help them to respond more efficiently to the contemporary demands of the labour market.

Unfortunately, there are no specific formal VET courses in Cyprus related to professionals or social workers working with people with migrant backgrounds.

VET programmes in Cyprus which do not lead to formal qualifications but to professional development and help adults improve their competences and get better in specific skills are the following (CEDEFOP, 2016):

- Training for the employed: The main bodies that are endorsing training provision for the employed are the Human Resource Development Authority of Cyprus (HRDA), the Ministry of Education and Culture (MoEC) and the Ministry of Labour, Welfare and Social Insurance (MLWSI).
- Training for the unemployed: The main bodies that are promoting training provision for the unemployed are the HRDA in cooperation with the MLWSI and the MoEC.
- Training for other groups at risk of exclusion from the labour market: Groups at risk of exclusion from the labour market are considered to be asylum seekers, women who are inactive, single parents, recipients of public assistance, early school leavers and people with disabilities. The main bodies that are promoting training provision for these groups are MLWSI, the MoEC, the HRDA and other ministries. In relation to the legal immigrants, the Ministry of Interior aims to integrate them into the society under conditions of increased social cohesion.

Some of the actions that the ministry takes is in areas such as education, health, learning of the Greek language and vocational training and information.

- Training for adults in general: A broad range of courses are offered to this group of people by the adult education centres of the MoEC. The aim of these courses is to assist holistically in the development of each adult's personality and the cultural, financial and social development of the society and its citizens.

However, a gap in the educational system of Cyprus is that there are limited opportunities for VET for professionals on higher education level offered by universities. In the past few years, some efforts have been done to bridge this gap, such as the educational technology sector, which promotes innovation related to the utilisation of digital technologies in adult learning as a means of enhancing the effectiveness of teaching and learning. It also implements programs of continuous professional development, explores and suggests new applications through European, research and intervention programmes (Pedagogical Institute, 2021). It is also a member of the Digital Competence Framework for Educators (DigCompEdu), which provides a general reference frame to support the development of educator-specific digital competences in Europe. DigCompEdu is directed towards educators at all levels of education, from early childhood to higher and adult education, including general and vocational education and training, special needs education and non-formal learning contexts (DigCompEdu, 2021).

6 Existing Policies and Practices Regarding Migrants' Integration

Apart from the laws mentioned above, there are many organisations and associations which take initiatives and work on making Cyprus a more inclusive society.

First of all, the Commissioner for Administration and Human Rights (Ombudsman) is a senior independent state officer. The institution of the ombudsman constitutes the most prevalent institution of extrajudicial control of the administration and protection of human rights. The main pivots of the mission of the Commissioner for Administration and Human Rights are to ensure legality, to promote good governance, to combat maladministration and to protect citizens' rights and human rights in general. The Commissioner for Administration and Human Rights operates as a guarantor of legality, keeps equal distances between the citizen and the administration and defines the limits of his or her competences and powers by adhering to the law and to the institutions of the state. For the citizens in particular, the Commissioner for Administration constitutes perhaps the most powerful means of safeguarding their rights and of supporting their claims, as the Commissioner's activity is turned against any arbitrary act and abuse of power by organs of the state and the services exercising public administration (Ombudsman, 2021).

Secondly, the Committee for Gender Equality in Employment and Vocational Training monitors the application of Law by the concerning Service of Labour

Ministry and Social Insurances (the Department of Labour) and has an advisory role in regard to:

- The formation or the revision of national policy regarding its scope of field.
- The import or revision of relative legislation.
- The adoption of measures and the application of programs for the promotion of gender equality in its field of competence.

The Committee also promotes the conduct of studies and researches, collects statistical values and submits reports and proposals to the Minister of Work and Social Insurances.

The Civil Registry and Migration Department of the Ministry of Interior is the competent authority on migration-related issues and policies in Cyprus, mainly regarding citizenship, residence permits, family reunification and labour disputes. A Committee on the Integration of Migrants that entered the Republic of Cyprus legally was established in 2007 and has prepared a two-year Action Plan on integration in 2010, with the participation of external experts, local government institutions, trade unions, NGOs and other relevant stakeholders. The Action Plan is not available online and has not been renewed since it ended in 2012.

However, the following programmes are currently in place that facilitate the integration of migrants and refugees through language trainings, technical vocational trainings, general skills trainings, finding a job and general orientation in Cyprus:

The upgraded Cyprus Guide is a useful orientation tool for third country nationals arriving in Cyprus to gain a basic understanding of the history, culture, economy and politics of Cyprus. The guide is tailor-made to help third-country nationals integrate in the Cyprus society, economy and labour market, providing practical information on utilities, health services, employment law and social insurance and education/training opportunities. The Guide is available in English, Arabic, Filipino, Hindi, Moldovan, Romanian, Russian, Sinhala, Tamil, Ukrainian and Vietnamese, lifting the language barrier to access this information for migrants who do not speak English or Greek. The guide has been developed by the NGO CARDET and SME Innovade, and is funded by the Asylum, Migration and Integration Fund of the EU and the Republic of Cyprus.

Epimorfotika (adult education classes), organised by the Ministry of Education and Culture, is the most widespread and popular programme for adults wanting to gain new skills or learn a trade or language. These are offered all across Cyprus and classes are based on demand with a small fee per year. Unfortunately, even though they have a big range of courses in foreign languages, creative arts, vocational skills, health, etc., they are all taught in Greek. Greek language classes for third-country nationals are offered for third-country nationals, but they only take place once a week. Thus, the language barrier is very important for migrants' integration in the Cypriot labour market, education and society at large.

State Institutes of Further Education (SIFE) of the Ministry of Education also offer Greek classes all over Cyprus, twice per week at a rate of EUR 250–400 per year, which is very high for people with a migratory background.

iLearnGreek is a programme offering free Greek language courses to third-country nationals over the age of 18, in three big cities and three villages, one of which hosts an asylum reception centre. The courses are both for beginners and those that have an intermediate knowledge of Greek.

There are also language courses offered by local municipal authorities such as Mingle and Colourful Societies that generally aim to better integrate third-country nationals in the local society, not only through language courses but also through cultural events and skills workshops.

SC-IRIE. Integrating minority, migrant and refugee children at European schools and society—ShipCon: ShipCon provides Erasmus+ courses that are created to meet the personal and professional needs of all the people who are working at Universities, teachers at primary and secondary education, trainers and VET staff. They are delivered by top-quality trainers in outstanding locations across Europe, such as Limassol (Cyprus), Palermo, Prague, Barcelona and London, amongst others.

One of the courses they provide is the course which is ideal for School principals and directors (primary and secondary), teachers (primary and secondary), educational advisors, community leaders, community workers, social workers, NGOs working with minority groups, migrants and refugees and civil organisation staff. The participants will have the opportunity through theory, practice and hands-on experience and reflection to acquire the following competences:

- Deal with cultural differences inside the classroom and make the most out of cultural diversity.
- Embrace cultural diversity and best practices for integration.
- Develop and implement desegregation policies.
- Understand the importance of national language acquisition for integration of minority groups and migrants.
- Implement best diversity policies and take affirmative actions.

However, the existing programs present gaps though, as they are mainly organised in the city or big municipalities, excluding migrants who live in smaller communities. Also, the majority of the courses are mainly for beginners and those who wish to gain advanced knowledge of Greek would need to resort to private lessons.

7 The Needs of Professionals Who Work with Migrants

The training needs of professionals who work with migrants are in line with the actual needs of migrants. Therefore, in order for effective training tools to be designed and implemented, the voices of migrants themselves should be taken into consideration.

In a study which was carried out in the framework of the Erasmus+ project "GVETS—Introducing gamification in vocational education and training for professionals and social work in the field of migrant children protection and support", the needed skills, knowledge and competences of the professionals working in migration environments were identified. According to the findings, the most common skills that professionals who work with migrants should demonstrate are (GVETS, 2021):

- Empathy
- Communication
- Acceptance/non-judging
- Critical thinking
- Intercultural sensitivity and knowledge
- Cooperation
- Sensitivity
- Non-verbal communication skills
- Non-formal education methods and techniques
- Problem-solving
- Creativity
- Conflict resolution

According to the participants, it is very important for all relevant professionals and organisations to have common approaches in relation to this particular field and to be open to cooperate with each other. To understand that they need to approach this particular area of interest in a more holistic and systemic way. It is also important for them to have the government's support by providing them formal education and training in this specific field, and a structured system that every professional can follow and rely on.

In another study, which was carried out with migrants in the framework of the Erasmus+ project "Transversal Model for Migrants", it was revealed that there are both positive and negative aspects of migrants' everyday life in Cyprus, as well as many barriers to their successful integration in education, labour market and society in general (Transversal Model for Migrants, 2021).

A main finding was that, despite the fact that most participants had a medium or higher education level and they had succeeded in the recognition process of their certificates, they had not received any professional guidance or assistance in the recognition procedure; instead, they had received encouragement from their families and friends. This implies an evident need for guidance from local agents and authorities to migrants who have secondary or tertiary education certificates, which could be utilised in the local labour market.

Another interesting finding was that many migrants believe that professionals who work with migrants should be aware of available resources, programs and counselling, so they could provide individualised, face-to-face training, support and guidance. Last but not least, it was found that most participants are in favour of online applications and learning tools for migrants, but they are not aware of any. Therefore, online tools prove to be valuable for migrants' integration and should be developed based on the country's educational system and labour market requirements.

In the same study, professionals who work with migrants—such as counsellors, psychologists, social workers and adult trainers—stated that the first step for a professional to succeed in working with such individuals and/ or groups is to realise that each person is at the crossroads of intersections among their multiple identities, such as gender, age, ethnicity, religion, socio-economic status and cultural background, as well as their individual experiences, which have shaped their personality and character. Those identities might differ from each professional's perception of migrants, as well as from their beliefs, attitudes and everyday behaviours in general.

Perhaps the most common finding was that the main obstacle in the recognition of migrants' knowledge, skills and competences is the language barrier, along with cultural and religious factors. In most cases, migrants struggle with bureaucracy, while at the same time struggling to survive and learn a foreign language, and this delays their integration in the labour market and in the local society. Therefore, the need for designing and implementing new tools and methods of recognition of migrants' transferal skills is more evident than ever.

A finding that should be taken into consideration is that, according to many professionals, although in theory there are many legal procedures which are designed to make migrants' inclusion easy and safe, in practice, bureaucracy, financial recession and lack of national resources are the main factors for delaying or preventing the whole process. Much work is done through non-profit and non-governmental organisations and is based on voluntary services, showing that there should be pressure on local authorities to take action.

In line with the above, professionals believe that spending time with migrants and being able to listen to their fears, needs and voices in general should be a main priority in the frame of their work. Apart from theoretical approaches, their training demands practical skills and tools, based on migrants' actual experiences and needs. Furthermore, a combination of offline, face-to-face and online meetings and material would broaden the professionals' horizons and assist their effort for migrants' social and cultural integration.

Taking all the above into consideration, it can be supported that adult migrants in Cyprus lack language and civic competences and therefore face serious difficulties in socialising and getting integrated in the labour market and society in general. On the other hand, professionals working with migrants lack the necessary tools and methods to provide career orientation and assist migrants in their effort to present and develop their transversal skills. For those reasons, it is highly recommended that professionals attend relevant training activities, which will help them first of all understand migrants' needs and concerns and then support and empower them in the process of self-development and capacity building.

8 Conclusion

According to the research carried out in the frame of the anthology, Cyprus has one of the largest migrant population in Europe, due to its location and its prosperity. This population is quite successfully integrated in the primary and secondary educational system, meaning that the majority of migrant children are attending school. Regarding migrant employment, however, the situation is quite different, due to the fact that the Greek language is a prerequisite in Cyprus' labour market. To be more specific, despite the fact that the percentage of unemployed migrants in Cyprus is low, the latter are either underpaid or working part-time in fields different from their expertise. This finding is explained by the fact that adult migrants who arrive in Cyprus (and therefore have not attended school in Cyprus) face difficulties in the process of their certificate's recognition, as well as the integration in the labour market, due to their low Greek language competence. As a result, they are mainly employed in households (domestic workers), agriculture and construction, while many of them apply for vocational training or studies in management and finances, aiming at finding a job in the hotel industry, which is very developed in Cyprus.

Women with a migratory background are facing additional obstacles in their effort for inclusion in education and in the labour market, due to the fact that gender equality in Cyprus is generally lower than in other countries. In the past few years, however, there have been some organised efforts to make education and labour market more accessible to women, through official laws and initiatives from NGOs, ministries etc.

In this context, the role of professionals who work with migrants—such as counsellors, social workers, psychologists and VET trainers—is crucial. For this reason, thorough training on migratory issues is essential for professionals, in order for them to develop a set of skills that will allow them to contribute to migrants' full integration in education, labour market and society at large.

References

CEDEFOP. (2016). *Vocational education and training in Europe Cyprus 2016*. Accessed October 25, 2021, from http://www.cedefop.europa.eu/en/publications-and-resources/country-reports/cyprus-vet-europe-country-report-2016

Cyprus Ministry of Education and Culture (MoEC). (2021). *The Education System of Cyprus*. http://www.highereducation.ac.cy/en/educational-system.html. Accessed October 25, 2021.

Ombudsman. (2021). https://www.ombudsman.gov.cy

Digital Competence Framework for Educators. (2021). Accessed December 10, 2021, from https://ec.europa.eu/jrc/en/digcompedu

EKIF (Cyprus Gender Research Centre). (2021). Accessed October 25, 2021, from https://www.ekif.org/

Eurostat. (2018). *Main sectors of employment of EU and non-EU nationals in Cyprus*. Accessed October 23, 2021, from https://ec.europa.eu/eurostat

GVETS. (2021). Accessed October 25, 2021, from https://gvets.eu/

KYSATS. (2021). *Recognition of title of studies*. Accessed December 10, 2021, from http://www.kysats.ac.cy/index.php/en/genikes-plirofories/anagnorisi-titlon-spoudon

MIGS (Mediterranean Institute of Gender Studies). (2021). Accessed October 25, 2021, from https://medinstgenderstudies.org/

Ministry of Labour, Welfare and Social Insurance. (2021). *Employment of Asylum Seekers*. Accessed December 10, 2021, from http://www.mlsi.gov.cy/mlsi/dl/dl.nsf/page5j_en/page5j_en?OpenDocument

NMWR (National Machinery of Women's Rights). (2021). Accessed October 25, 2021, from http://www.nmwr.gov.cy

Papaeracleous, C. (2003). *Cyprus – Financial growth 1974–2003 and membership of the European Union [in Greek]*. ATEI of Kavala Publications.

Pedagogical Institute of Cyprus. (2021). Accessed December 10, 2021, from https://tet.pi.ac.cy/

Transversal Model for Migrants. (2021). Accessed October 25, 2021, from http://www.transversalmodel.eu/

UNHCR. (2021). *Languages, sports and other programmes*. Accessed October 25, 2021, from https://help.unhcr.org/cyprus/integration-support/language-programmes/

Finland: Vocational Guidance in Finland

Soili Rinne and Anu Raudasoja

1 Introduction to Vocational Guidance in Finland

The main actors providing guidance are public education (including the education providers from basic education to universities) and employment bodies. Educational institutions are mainly responsible for the guidance of pupils and students. The Employment and Economic Development Offices provide guidance mainly for individuals who are no longer in education. One-Stop Guidance Centres are easy-access guidance centres that are run by municipalities and other organisations. These centres offer transdisciplinary guidance to young people. Private companies also provide vocational guidance, supplementing public guidance services.

In Finland, policymakers on different levels and in different disciplines support multisectoral guidance services. This makes it possible for public employment services to complement educational guidance services and vice versa (see, for example, Euroguidance, 2020; Finnish National Agency of Education, n.d.-a).

In Fig. 1, we describe the multisectoral vocational guidance system in Finland. The system consists of governmental, regional and organisational levels. The vocational guidance system consists of several service providers in order to offer multifaceted guidance services (cf. Fig. 1).

Changes like globalisation, rapid technological development and the ageing population affect the types of jobs in Finland (OECD, 2020). Digitalisation of guidance services is increasing in importance in Finland. There are many national R&D projects that aim to support vocational guidance for individuals and develop practitioners' competence in using new technologies.

In Finland, the overall trend in guidance has been to move towards holistic, lifelong and life-wide guidance. Promoting individuals' self-understanding in order

S. Rinne (✉) · A. Raudasoja
Häme University of Applied Sciences, Hämeenlinna, Finland
e-mail: soili.rinne@hamk.fi; anu.raudasoja@hamk.fi

C. Enoch et al. (eds.), *Vocational Guidance in Europe*,
https://doi.org/10.1007/978-3-031-06592-7_3

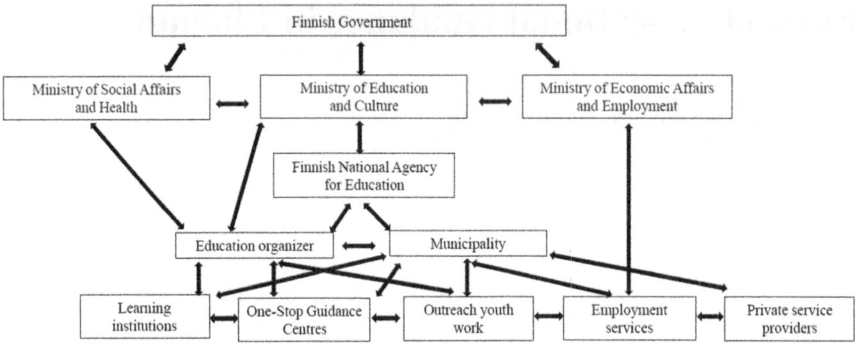

Fig. 1 Finnish vocational guidance system

to develop their competence in making plans and choices and supporting their agency is seen as an important task for vocational guidance. The accessibility of guidance services has also been emphasised during the past few years. The aim is to provide guidance services that are equally accessible to all in ways that meet a person's needs. For example, the One-Stop Guidance Centres offer a low threshold service without the need to identify oneself.

The National Strategy for Lifelong Guidance (Finnish Government, 2020) defines the strategic objectives for the development of guidance; its recommendations extend to the year 2023. The strategy aims to improve individuals' abilities to make educational and career decisions for themselves and to ensure that they receive the necessary support to recognise their competencies, to find possibilities for developing their competence and to demonstrate their understanding of their opportunities in the labour market by making meaningful decisions related to their educational and career paths.

The ongoing parliamentary reform of continuous learning is closely linked to the Strategy for Lifelong Guidance. The reform of continuous learning aims to reduce the skills gap and to improve up-skilling and re-skilling opportunities for working-age people (Ministry of Education and Culture, n.d.-a).

2 Vocational Guidance Practitioners in Finland

Guidance practitioners in Finland have a reasonably high level of education. In Finland, there are qualifications for career guidance practitioners in comprehensive and secondary education. Vocational psychologists are also defined in legislation. In addition to the required qualifications for teachers, all school guidance counsellors must have a higher level education in the form of a Certificate of Specialist Training in Guidance and Counselling (60 ECTS) or a master's degree in Guidance (300 ECTS). Their qualification requirements are amended in Asetus opetustoimen henkilöstön kelpoisuusvaatimuksista 986/1998 [Decree on Qualification

Requirements for Teaching Staff 986/ 1998]. Most of the career practitioners in Finland graduate in a work-based programme (60 ECTS) in one of the five schools of Professional Teacher Education at the universities of applied sciences (Euroguidance, 2020).

There are also two master's degree programmes (300 ECTS) available at two universities. The schools of Professional Teacher Education and the universities cooperate in offering a specialist certificate in career guidance (30 ECTS) in close collaboration with the world of work. Both universities and universities of applied sciences conduct academic and applied research in the field of vocational guidance, mainly in various development projects and national/international research cooperation (Epale, 2019).

2.1 One-Stop Guidance Centres

A European Council initiative—the Recommendation on Establishing a Youth Guarantee (European Council, 2013)—was the driving force behind the establishment of One-Stop Guidance Centres in Finland. Today, there is a network of locally and regionally operating One-Stop Guidance Centres. In 2021, there are approximately 70 One-Stop Guidance Centres in Finland (Kohtaamo, n.d.). Their main task is to provide information, advice and guidance on a walk-in and easy-access basis to all young people under 30. One-Stop Guidance Centres play an important role in vocational guidance. These centres offer personal guidance and counselling, with a focus on educational and employment transitions. At One-Stop Guidance Centres, guidance experts represent different fields of expertise and different administrative sectors. The personnel usually consists of experts in labour administration, social work, healthcare and education and training. One-Stop Guidance Centres can be described as transdisciplinary services. Collaboration between the practitioners is seen as the key to high-class services, and it takes place between organisations as well as within organisations so that the services can be tailored according to the needs of the young people. Their aim is to support young people when they are still seeking more permanent decisions, a job or a study place, or if they need other support in their lives (see e.g. Kohtaamo, n.d.; Euroguidance, 2020; Kettunen & Felt, 2020).

2.2 Outreach Youth Work

Nuorisolaki 1285/2016 [The Youth Act 1285/ 2016] regulates the outreach youth work in Finland. Outreach youth work is based on the European Council's initiative: the Recommendation on Establishing a Youth Guarantee (European Council, 2013), just like One-Stop Guidance Centres.

The main goal is to reach young people under 29 years of age who are not in education, training or work and need support to get the services they need. Outreach youth workers establish a confidential, respectful relationship with their clients, helping them to commit to a process that supports their independence, their inclusion and their ability to build a good everyday life and future. Outreach youth workers help clients to find answers to their questions and problems and assist them in finding the services they want and need. The goal is to improve their clients' readiness to find a job or to study by improving their life skills and helping them solve life's challenges. Outreach youth work also aims to help clients to create peer communities. The clients are seen as subjects who make their own life decisions with the support of professionals (Into, 2021). Outreach youth workers often cooperate very closely with One-Stop Guidance Centres, as municipalities can place outreach youth workers under different administrative sectors to support multisectoral guidance services.

2.3 Guidance at Public Employment Services

Vocational guidance is also offered at public employment services (TE Offices), usually by vocational guidance psychologists, but also by other experts according to their job profiles and competencies. TE Offices' professional guidance and career planning services help the clients to improve their skills. They also offer guidance in education-related issues, for example for decisions regarding the content of the clients' studies and options for funding studies. Experts support the clients in finding training or career solutions that are compatible with their life situation.

The employment and economic development services are mostly targeted at adults who are not in education or training. The primary aim is to support access and integration into the labour market. They offer various forms of support to enhance individuals' employability. Activities offered can be work tryouts, training courses, rehabilitation, language learning for migrants and so on (see, e.g. Euroguidance, 2020; TE services, n.d.). The main objective of TE services is to increase employment amongst unemployed jobseekers, to find suitable training and educational options and to find solutions that ensure the availability of competent labour.

In Finland, there are ongoing local government pilot projects relating to employment. The main aim of the pilot projects is to improve access to the labour market by developing services and service models for jobseekers, especially for the long-term unemployed and those in a vulnerable position in the labour market. The pilot project will also increase client orientation by identifying and addressing clients' individual needs, barriers for employment and competence development. These local government pilot projects in 25 areas and 118 municipalities were launched on 1 March 2021 and will end on 30 June 2023 (Ministry of Economic Affairs and Employment, n.d.).

2.4 Private Service Providers

Private service providers work mainly in job placement and career guidance tasks, as do public employment and economic development services. There are still a few private service providers in Finland, and they often cooperate with public employment services. A private service provider can be utilised when a client is thinking about his or her future in working life. Career guidance services can be implemented as group activities or individual services. The process usually consists of a few meetings with the career counsellor and possible intermediate assignments. Most commonly, career guidance services include mapping a client's current situation and future desires. These may include a personal assessment to determine their personality, way of working, career aspirations, skills and motivation towards new tasks. They may also include the identification of practical employment and training opportunities. The process often also includes job-search coaching (see, e.g., Euroguidance, 2020; TE services, n.d.).

2.5 Educational Guidance Services in Finland

Vocational guidance is being integrated into the Finnish education system because pupils and students have the legal right to guidance and study counselling services at educational institutions. The educational guidance service is provided by full-time guidance counsellors, whose qualification for the position is a master's degree and guidance counsellor studies (Ministry of Education and Culture & Finnish National Agency of Education, 2018, p. 25). Vocational guidance is strongly present in the Finnish educational system; it aims to help people to build a solid foundation for lifelong and life-wide learning. The forms and content of the guidance and the requirements for practitioners differ between levels, but the aim and the principles are the same.

Vocational guidance practitioners work in basic education, secondary education and higher education institutions in Finland. They are responsible for scheduled career training, group activities, individual guidance and cooperation with employers and stakeholders in accordance with the objectives of the curricula. Guidance counsellors work in cooperation with group tutors, who provide their own students with holistic support in their daily activities (Toni & Vuorinen, 2020).

The prevailing ideas on vocational guidance, as on education in general, in Finland emphasise that the potential of each pupil and student should be maximised. Educational guidance is therefore considered essential. The aim of guidance and counselling is to support, help and guide learners so that they perform as well as possible in their studies and can make the correct and appropriate decisions about their education and career. Guidance and counselling are seen as the work of all education staff, with guidance counsellors playing an important consulting role. Education staff treat learners as individuals and help them to progress according to their own capabilities so that they can experience success and the joy of learning. Today, all learners have the right to educational support, which may be support for the learner's special needs (Ministry of Education and Culture and Finnish National Agency of Education, 2018, p. 7).

The criteria for good guidance, drawn up by the Finnish National Agency of Education, are used to develop and ensure the quality of basic education, general upper secondary education and vocational education and training (VET) guidance. The aim of the criteria is to promote versatile guidance and to ensure the availability and equity of high-quality guidance, regardless of the learner's place of residence or other conditions (Finnish National Agency of Education, 2014).

One of the basic principles of the Finnish education system is that all people must have equal access to high-quality education and training. The same educational opportunities should be available to all citizens irrespective of their wealth, age, ethnic origin or where they live. Learners can always continue their studies at a higher level of education, regardless of the choices they make between them. The practice of recognising previously acquired competence has been developed to avoid an unnecessary overlapping of studies (Ministry of Education and Culture & Finnish National Agency of Education, 2018, pp. 6–9).

The Finnish education system (Ministry of Education and Culture & Finnish National Agency of Education, 2018) consists of:

- Early childhood education and care.
- Pre-primary education.
- Basic education.
- Upper secondary education, which is either vocational education and training or general upper secondary education.
- Higher education provided by universities of applied sciences or universities.

2.5.1 Guidance and Counselling in Basic Education Grades 7–9

The goals of the work of guidance counsellors in basic education come from legislation and the national curriculum. Guidance counsellors guide pupils in developing an ability to cope with changing life situations and the transitions in their studies and future careers. It is important at educational transition points, such as when pupils make educational transitions or make other choices concerning their studies. Topics discussed in guidance and counselling include study skills and school attendance, self-knowledge, professions and professional fields, opportunities for further studies and working life. Guidance counsellors give advice and guidance to all pupils personally or in small groups in addition to the lessons reserved for guidance and counselling if necessary. Pupils are guided by guidance counsellors in the use of different information-seeking tools and the guidance and counselling services provided by society (Finnish National Agency of Education, n. d.-b).

2.5.2 Guidance and Counselling in General Upper Secondary Education

The goals of the work of guidance counsellors in general upper secondary education come from legislation and the national curriculum. Guidance counsellors provide students with sufficient basic knowledge and skills for planning their general upper secondary and further studies and for reflecting on the direction of their career. Guidance counsellors offer personal guidance, guidance in groups, guidance in the subject and peer guidance during upper secondary general education. These forms of guidance support students in identifying their strengths and interests, in career planning and in making choices and resolving problems. Students have opportunities to discuss questions about their general upper secondary studies, career planning, choices for further education, their life situation and the future in personal one-to-one guidance and counselling with guidance counsellors. Guidance counsellors provide students with information about the employment and business sector and entrepreneurship. During their studies, students are given the opportunity to familiarise themselves with the world of work and options for further studies during their studies. These periods support students in making their own plans and choices by enabling them to compare different options for career planning and options for further studies. Guidance counsellors help students to perceive the impact of different choices on their careers and opportunities for further studies. The general upper secondary education providers must offer guidance in career planning and applying for further studies to a student who has graduated from the educational institution for one year following the student's graduation if the student has not obtained a study place (Finnish National Agency of Education, n.d.-c).

2.5.3 Guidance and Counselling in Vocational Education and Training

The purpose of guidance and counselling in VET is to support students in developing the skills they need for studying and working. VET students are entitled to guidance and counselling services provided by guidance counsellors, teachers and experts and supervisors at workplaces. Guidance is given both individually and in groups. Career counsellors support students in making choices during their studies, for example in selecting the qualification units that match their goals, and in moving on to further studies and the world of work or in progressing in their career. Each student has a personal competence development plan (PCDP). The student, teacher and the guidance counsellor (if needed) participate in planning the individual study path. The competence development plan also includes the student's career plan. The first version of the PCDP will be drawn up at the beginning of the student's studies together with the student and teacher, and the plan will be updated as their studies progress (Finnish National Agency of Education, n.d.-d).

2.5.4 Guidance and Counselling at Universities of Applied Sciences and Universities

Even though guidance and counselling are not obligatory at universities of applied sciences and universities, guidance is commonly offered by these institutions. In higher education, it is important to consider that all students have their own strengths, interests and prior learning. Guidance counsellors' work mostly consists of helping students to familiarise themselves with the curriculum and to define their goals in their personal study plan. Students are offered guidance if they need to make choices and decide what, how and when they want to study or apply for a job. Students are also guided and supported if they have special needs or the desire to develop their study skills.

2.5.5 Liberal Adult Education

Educational institutions that provide a liberal adult education include folk high schools, learning centres, sports training centres, adult education centres and summer universities. Guidance counsellors support people's versatile development and provide education and training that supports equality, the cohesion of society and active citizenship on the basis of the principle of lifelong learning. An essential aspect of liberal adult education is that everyone has the right to apply to take part in it. The organisers of liberal adult education differ from each other. Some of them have career counsellors, while others have tutors.

3 Challenges and Needs in Vocational Guidance

The diversification of the clients and their individual needs challenge vocational guidance. The demand for guidance services has increased and is growing due to education policy objectives, changes in working life and the individual needs of clients. As one result of the reforms in education policy, the compulsory school leaving age in Finland was raised to 18 in 2021. In practice this means that compulsory education ends when the student reaches the age of 18 or has completed an upper secondary qualification. Because of this reform, more guidance counsellors are needed in both primary and secondary education.

Guidance is needed in all life situations, especially during transitional phases. Services should be integrated and comprehensive. In Finland, the diversity of guidance actors and services might even make developing guidance and guidance services more difficult. In principle, individuals have access to information, advice and guidance services. In practice, all these services are not fully utilised. For example, entrepreneurs and employees mostly seek access to guidance services when they become unemployed or need to work outside their own company

(Ministry of Education and Culture, n.d.-b). Services provided can be overlapping, and there might be needs that no guidance provider fills.

There are currently problems between labour demand and supply on the Finnish labour market. There is a shortage of skilled labour in many sectors, which undermines the development potential of companies. On the other hand, unemployment lasts longer and is seen as a major challenge. The strong demand for labour is expected to result in a fall in the number of the long-term unemployed (Työ- ja elinkeinoministeriö [Ministry of Economic Affairs and Employment], 2021). Efforts are being made to support the re-entry of the long-term unemployed into the labour market through training and internships, for example.

Changes in the world of work require continuous learning opportunities for everybody. This stresses a need for building up competencies as an initial and ongoing part of the vocational biography. It is crucial that a person's skills are up-to-date and that they are able to describe their own competencies and have a knowledge of how to develop their competencies in the future. Guidance practitioners' work is affected by the diversity of their clients as well as the very individual requirements from clients, and this is a growing part of the daily work of guidance counsellors. These starting points require the competencies of guidance professionals to be updated (Euroguidance, 2020).

The essential question for vocational guidance practitioners is how to support clients in taking responsibility for their own learning and developing a passion for personal competence building. This requires cooperation between employers and educational institutions in order to enable continuous learning and vocational guidance, taking into account the needs of both the workplace and the individual employee.

Finland is currently undergoing a reform of continuous learning, which will also change the goals of the work of guidance practitioners in different organisations. In the future, adequate generic skills, and more importantly motivation, opportunities and the ability to develop one's vocational competence, will also play an important role for practitioners. The diversity of the clientele, with their individual needs and demands, is challenging vocational guidance practitioners, and these aspects should be addressed in their continuing professional development. A rising demand to increase practitioners' competence is essential due to the rapid renewal of skills needed in the future world of work.

Reforms in the world of work, society and education change the job descriptions of guidance counsellors. As a result of these changes, they will have to update their own work and competence identity. Christiansen (1999) describes competence as an identity based on one's skills and abilities. Counsellors can build their competence identity as a process, where they acquire new competencies and compensate for possible missing competencies. Competence identity develops in interaction with others, and it is linked and intertwined with work and interpretations of work (Raudasoja et al., 2021). There have been changes in the work identity of guidance counsellors towards a personal work identity instead of a collective work identity, as work tasks are often scattered, including at the organisational level. Guidance counsellors have been able to specialise in individual guidance, for example organising studies for their clients in cooperation with other educational institutions, and/or working life. The work community of guidance counsellors increasingly consists of professionals in other organisations.

Challenges in the work of guidance counsellors may include the large number of supervisors, bureaucracy, insufficient time needed for guidance, a lack of tools for digital guidance and legal obstacles to cooperation between different authorities (Zacheus et al., 2021, p. 50).

Multisectoral and transdisciplinary guidance services can sometimes increase the number of direct and indirect supervisors. There are also legal obstacles to cooperation between authorities in Finland. Information about clients cannot be exchanged, even if it would be necessary in order to offer high-quality guidance services. One guidance counsellor may have responsibility for 500 students; even the target is 200 students per guidance counsellor. As a result, the time available for guidance per student is insufficient.

The requirements for implementing digital guidance challenge guidance counsellors. Not everyone has the necessary modern tools, equipment and software at their disposal, and even if they do, some guidance counsellors do not know how to use them well enough. It is essential to create well-functioning digital vocational guidance services in order to make better use of shared information on education, the labour market and competencies needed in the future. New technological environments and solutions should support vocational guidance as the growing individual needs of the clients will also place a demand on multi-locational services.

4 Solutions and Development

As in many countries, guidance in Finland is distributed across educational institutions, the labour market and social and healthcare, under different ministries and other jurisdictions (schools, tertiary education, public employment services, social partners, the voluntary sector, the private sector, different projects). All providers of vocational guidance are facing a growing demand for guidance. Therefore, it is important to intensify current cooperation between different sectors, administrative organisations and individuals. Services should be flexible and agile in order to support everyone's individual guidance needs. One solution to this growing need is career guidance for job seekers in public employment services (TE services), where the clients' paths are tailored to working life. At the same time, more private service providers have come into being, and they are working at the interface between guidance and employment, for example with highly educated immigrants who could need coaching in Finnish working life culture and training in the Finnish language. Cross-sectoral networks in vocational guidance are one solution; they also bring more flexibility to the entity of guidance services.

Strengthening career education and guidance throughout our educational system can be one solution to meet the multifaceted needs in the future. Extended compulsory education is one way to meet this challenge. When offering young people, in particular, flexible possibilities to enter the labour market, it is also important to intensify cooperation with the world of work at all stages of studies (Finnish Government, 2021, pp. 29–30).

Vocational guidance for guidance counsellors is based on dialogue with clients. Guidance practitioners in Finland consider guidance holistically and inclusively while strengthening and building their clients' competence identity. The work of guidance professionals is going to need a more multidisciplinary network collaboration that considers the customer's personal, educational and professional needs so that the client takes responsibility for themselves and becomes a change-maker for their own professional career. At One-Stop Guidance Centres, the staff develop a shared understanding of the objectives, means and work method. Lilja et al. (2019) state that interdisciplinary career guidance needs to be regarded as a skill that can be developed.

There have been some initiatives to develop artificial intelligence to support vocational guidance. It is important to define a new competence framework for guidance professionals and support for their up-skilling and re-skilling, as guidance practitioners support the implementation of national decisions on education and labour market policy. Currently, their development is focused on fostering the role of supporting their clients' competencies and strengthening the possibilities for everybody. It is important to make the skills that will be needed in the future visible. This means different services for different target groups, strengthening career education and guidance throughout our educational system, promoting digital solutions and defining a competence framework for career professionals. In order to transform lifelong guidance services to meet rapid technological and societal changes, it is important to break down the silos to ensure the availability and competence of the labour force. Providing educational opportunities for everybody, strengthening social cohesion and equity and the objectives for an extended working life and raising the employment rate could create the conditions for lifelong learning.

5 Conclusion

In Finland, the guidance system is seen holistically. It should work well as part of the education system and support the promotion of studies as well as transitions to further education and working life. Outside the education system, young people are guided at One-Stop Guidance Centres, and TE services are available to all unemployed persons and those under threat of unemployment. The challenge in the Finnish guidance system is for people in working life who want to acquire new skills for themselves. We do not have a clear system for guiding continuous learning, so guidance can take place in the workplace (as competence management) by contacting educational institutions or TE services directly. The adult population does not have enough information about private companies that provide career guidance, as these companies are a new phenomenon in Finland and are often small companies with one or very few people. Finland is a country of long distances, so the availability of guidance is not uniform. This challenges guidance counsellors to implement guidance with more digital tools in order to make it accessible for everyone. For clients, this is an important issue to support their continuous learning.

Vocational guidance practitioners operating in the education system and TE services are highly educated, and they have a career counselling or psychology degree for the job. Other organisations providing guidance do not have similar degree requirements, although there are also highly educated practitioners working there. All persons working in guidance must regularly update their own competencies due to changes in education, working life, society and technological development. Guidance and guidance services should be holistic so that clients can receive the widest possible service with the help of one person.

References

Asetus opetustoimen henkilöstön kelpoisuusvaatimuksista 1998/986 [Decree on Qualification Requirements for Teaching Staff 1998/986. https://www.finlex.fi/fi/laki/ajantasa/1998/19980986

Christiansen, C. H. (1999). Defining lives: Occupation as identity: An essay on competence, coherence, and the creation of meaning. *American Journal of Occupational Therapy, 53*(6), 547–558. https://doi.org/10.5014/ajot.53.6.547

Epale. (2019). *Uraohjauksen erikoistumiskoulutus tuottaa uudenlaista osaamista työelämän tarpeisiin* [*Specialization training in career guidance produces a new kind of competence for the needs of working life*]. https://epale.ec.europa.eu/fi/blog/uraohjauksen-erikoistumiskoulutus-tuottaa-uudenlaista-osaamista-tyoelaman-tarpeisiin

Euroguidance. (2020). *Guidance system in Finland*. https://www.euroguidance.eu/guidance-system-in-finland

European Council. (2013). *Council recommendation of 22 April 2013 on establishing a youth guarantee*. No. 2013/C 120/1, April. Brussels, Belgium: European Council. https://eur-lex.europa.eu/legal-content/EN/TXT/PDF/?uri=CELEX:32013H0426(01)&from=EN

Finnish Government. (2020). *Strategy for lifelong guidance 2020–2023: National Lifelong Guidance Forum* (p. 34). Publications of the Finnish Government 2020. http://urn.fi/URN:ISBN:978-952-383-536-8

Finnish Government. (2021). *Education policy report of the Finnish government* (p. 64). Publications of the Finnish Government 2021. http://urn.fi/URN:ISBN:978-952-383-927-4

Finnish National Agency of Education. (2014). *Hyvän ohjauksen kriteerit* [*Criteria for good guidance*]. https://www.oph.fi/fi/tilastot-ja-julkaisut/julkaisut/hyvan-ohjauksen-kriteerit

Finnish National Agency of Education. (n.d.-a). *Information, guidance and counselling services*. https://www.oph.fi/en/services/information-guidance-and-counselling-services

Finnish National Agency of Education. (n.d.-b). *Guidance and counselling in basic education*. https://www.oph.fi/en/education-and-qualifications/guidance-and-counselling-basic-education

Finnish National Agency of Education. (n.d.-c). *Guidance and counselling in upper secondary education*. https://www.oph.fi/en/education-and-qualifications/guidance-and-counselling-upper-secondary-education

Finnish National Agency of Education. (n.d.-d). *Guidance and counselling in vocational education and training*. https://www.oph.fi/en/education-and-qualifications/guidance-and-counselling-vocational-education-and-training

Into. (2021). *Outreach youth work*. https://www.intory.fi/etsiva-nuorisotyo/in-english/

Kettunen, J., & Felt, T. (2020). One-stop guidance service centres in Finland. In E. H. Haug, T. Hooley, J. Kettunen, & R. Thomsen (Eds.), *Career and career guidance in the Nordic countries* (pp. 293–306). Brill Academic Publishers. https://doi.org/10.1163/9789004428096_020

Kohtaamo. (n.d.). *Kohtaamo, Ohjaamojen tuki ja verkko-ohjauksen kehittäjä* [*Kohtaamo, supporting One-Stop Guidance Centres and developing e-guidance*]. https://www.ely-keskus.fi/web/kohtaamo/ohjaamot

Lilja, T., Pukkila, P., Helander, J., Leppänen, A., & Mäkinen, S. (2019). A tool for assessing interdisciplinary career guidance. In Š. Grajcár & T. Šprlák (Eds.), *Conference proceedings from the 2019 conference of the International Association for Educational and Vocational Guidance (IAEVG), 11–13 September 2019, Bratislava, Slovakia* (pp. 263–270) https://iaevgconference2019.sk/wp-content/uploads/2020/03/IAEVG-Conference-Proceedings 2019_FINAL.pdf

Ministry of Economic Affairs and Employment. (n.d.). *Local government pilots on employment.* https://tem.fi/en/local-government-pilots-on-employment

Ministry of Education and Culture. (n.d.-a). *Reform of continuous learning.* https://minedu.fi/en/project?tunnus=OKM033:00/2019

Ministry of Education and Culture. (n.d.-b). *Strategy: Lifelong guidance to support people on educational and career paths.* https://minedu.fi/en/-/1410877/strategy-lifelong-guidance-to-support-people-on-educational-and-career-paths

Ministry of Education and Culture & Finnish National Agency of Education. (2018). *Finnish education in a nutshell.* https://www.oph.fi/en/statistics-and-publications/publications/finnish-education-nutshell

Nuorisolaki 1285/2016 [*The Youth Act 1285/2016*]. https://www.finlex.fi/fi/laki/alkup/2016/20161285

OECD. (2020). *Continuous learning in working life in Finland, getting skills right.* OECD Publishing. https://doi.org/10.1787/2ffcffe6-en

Raudasoja, A., Heino, S. & Rinne, S. (2021). Ohjauksella rakennetaan kestävää tulevaisuutta [Guidance builds sustainable future]. *HAMK Unlimited Journal.* http://urn.fi/URN:NBN:fi-fe202103197851

TE services. (n.d.). *Career, education and training.* https://www.te-palvelut.fi/jobseekers/career-education-training

Toni, A., & Vuorinen, R. (2020). Lifelong guidance in Finland. Key policies and practices. In E. H. Haug, T. Hooley, J. Kettunen, & R. Thomsen (Eds.), *Career and career guidance in the Nordic countries* (pp. 127–143). https://doi.org/10.1163/9789004428096_009

Työ- ja elinkeinoministeriö [Ministry of Economic Affairs and Employment. (2021). Alueelliset kehitysnäkymät syksyllä 2021 [Regional Development Prospects in Autumn 2021]. Työ- ja elinkeinoministeriön julkaisuja 2021:56 [Publications of the Ministry of Economic Affairs and Employment 2021:56]. http://urn.fi/URN:ISBN:978-952-327-963-6

Zacheus, T. & Kalalahti, M. & Varjo, J & Harjula, S. (2021). *Yhteistyö nuorten opinto- ja uraohjauksessa* [*Cooperation in the study and career guidance of young people*]. Kunnallisalan kehittämissäätiö. https://kaks.fi/julkaisut/yhteistyo-nuorten-opinto-ja-uraohjauksessa/

Germany: The Challenges of Career Counselling in Germany

Tanja Hutterer, Katharina Kurianowski, and Annette Schorp

1 Introduction

Germany is facing "the digital shift", a "fourth industrial revolution", a climate crisis and numerous political crises, to name just a few current challenges of this modern age. Megatrends have a growing impact on individual lives, whether we realise it or not. All of these circumstances shape the way we live as well as the way we work.

We would like to take a look at topics current in Germany, especially regarding migrants and refugees and future jobs, and the resulting challenges for career counselling.

The services offered by the Bundesagentur für Arbeit (Federal Employment Agency, BA) are comprehensive and specialised. Counsellors are specifically qualified to advise a certain target group. There are different teams of counsellors for university graduates, people returning to work, skilled workers from abroad, severely disabled academics and refugees—there is even a separate specialist placement service for artists. Career counsellors from the Employment Agency regularly

T. Hutterer
Jobcenter Berlin Reinickendorf, Berlin, Germany

Federal Agency of Employment in Germany, Nuremberg, Germany
e-mail: tanja.hutterer@jobenter-ge.de

K. Kurianowski
Agentur für Arbeit, Hannover, Germany

Federal Agency of Employment in Germany, Nuremberg, Germany
e-mail: katharina.kurianowski@arbeitsagentur.de

A. Schorp (✉)
Agentur für Arbeit, Stuttgart, Germany

Federal Agency of Employment in Germany, Nuremberg, Germany
e-mail: annette.schorp@arbeitsagentur.de

C. Enoch et al. (eds.), *Vocational Guidance in Europe*,
https://doi.org/10.1007/978-3-031-06592-7_4

visit general and vocational schools, and young people up to the age of 25 can find contact persons at the Jugendberufsagenturen (Youth Employment Agencies).

In order to be able to provide individualised counselling in the context of a rapidly changing labour market and an increasing shortage of skilled workers, specialisation is used in particular, as it can respond to the strengths and special features of the individual target groups and provide targeted support. However, all counselling is based on the examination of and knowledge about developments in the labour market and society.

This chapter provides an overall picture of three aspects of the situation in Germany. With the importance of focusing on the phenomena currently affecting the labour market, there is a good chance of adapting to the challenges facing the labour market in the future. The demand for skilled workers is a central challenge which this article chapter address from two perspectives: on the one hand, there are problems of fit and problematic long-term prospects for highly qualified people from abroad to stay. On the other hand, their labour is urgently needed in Germany. In addition, the problems of fit can be seen in another area, namely with regard to the country's own trainees. The chapter focuses on these aspects in three parts:

The first part looks at the general conditions we have to assume in Germany as things stand today (2021) and refers to various academic sources that can help in assessing the future development of the labour market in Germany. It addresses the problems arising from digitalisation, demographic change and the academisation of professions, and describes initiatives and programmes with which Germany is attempting to counteract the resulting shortage of skilled workers. The second part presents a report on the experiences of many years of counselling students from non-EU countries who came to Germany for their studies and possible subsequent careers. It discusses the challenges that hinder this well-educated target group, who are urgently needed in the labour market, from entering the workforce. The third part deals with the question of why there are so many open apprenticeship positions in Germany while many young people are still without training. From the perspective of a counsellor for young people from unemployed families, it describes possible reasons for the fact that many young people with a migration background in particular are more often without training and where possible solutions could be found, in addition to what has already been set in motion to make better use of this great potential.

We try to offer suggestions for how to make even better use of existing resources and support offers and also try to introduce new ideas. In addition, we come to the conclusion that successfully mastering future challenges requires effort from all parties involved. For this, we need well-informed consultants, flexible and tolerant employers and motivated applicants.

2 The Future of Jobs and the Challenges for Career Counselling in Germany

Before talking about the future of jobs and its challenges for career counselling, we must analyse the status quo and take a look at the scientific predictions for the foreseeable future. This coming chapter looks at megatrends, then in particular digitalisation and the fourth industrial revolution in Germany, as well as the academisation of professions and career paths.

2.1 Megatrends

To better understand the challenges of career counselling given the changing future of jobs, we would like to introduce the concept of megatrends as defined by the Zukunftsinstitut (Future Institute), a research and consultancy organisation around the researcher Matthias Horx and his team.[1] Megatrends specify and describe the extremely complex dynamic forces leading to change and are to be understood as a model to understand our changing world. Such megatrends are defined by the following criteria:

- Duration: They last for more than 50 years.
- Ubiquity: They have implications across different dimensions of society: economy, consumption, ethics, media, the way we live together, political systems, etc.
- Globality: They are global phenomena; though they may not be noticed everywhere with the same strength, they can eventually be observed everywhere in the world to some extent.
- Complexity: They are multi-layered, many-dimensional trends and produce specific dynamics often due to their interactions and interdependencies (Zukunftsinstitut, 2022).

Horx and his team specify 12 megatrends and a number of sub-trends (Zukunftsinstitut, 2022). These 12 megatrends are:

---

[1] The Zukunftsinstitut was founded in 1998 and has played a major role in shaping trend and future research in Germany from its inception. Today, the company is considered a leading international contact for questions on social and economic developments. In its work, the team of researchers and consultants explores the question of which changes—which trends and megatrends—shape our present and what conclusions can be drawn from them for the future of the economy and society. The primary goal is to make change comprehensible and to understand the future as an opportunity.

On the basis of trend analyses and studies as well as specially developed methods, the Zukunftsinstitut reveals potentials that result from change processes in order to help companies and decision-makers develop forward-looking strategies and innovations. For further information, visit: www.zukunftsinstitut.de/ueber-uns/

- Globalisation.
- Connectivity.
- Mobility.
- Urbanisation.
- Neo-ecology.
- Health.
- Individualisation.
- Gender shift.
- Silver society.
- Knowledge culture.
- New work.
- Security.

Because of their ubiquity, megatrends are to be understood as deep currents of change. They do not touch merely the surface of our individual and societal way of living and working. "They are multidimensional phenomena which emerge from a variety of trends and with their coming into existence also produce opposite trends which in their recursion produce new interactions" (Zukunftsinstitut, 2022; translated from the German). In section "Challenges for career counselling" we will take a closer look at the impact of these megatrends on career counselling in Germany.

2.2 *Digitalisation and the Fourth Industrial Revolution in Germany*

Two other terms that are frequently used in the discussions of future jobs, both in general and specifically in Germany, are "digitalisation" and the "fourth industrial revolution". The terms often co-occur and describe factors influencing not only the future of work but also the way we live more generally. Digitalisation can be seen as a manifestation of several megatrends.

The term digitalisation has more than one meaning and is often used synonymously with the terms "digital revolution" or "digital turning point". It means the digital translation, presentation or implication of information and communication or the modification of instruments, devices and vehicles. The digital revolution can be seen as the third industrial revolution in the twentieth century, where information technology was used for automatisation and optimisation, in modernised private households and workspaces as well as through developed computer networks, software products and enterprise resource planning systems. In the twenty-first century, we talk about the fourth industrial revolution, marked by disruptive technologies and innovative business models as well as autonomisation, flexibilisation and the individualisation of digitalisation. In this context, "Industry 4.0", "enterprise 4.0" or "work 4.0" is often used to describe the modern business world.

As a direct consequence of digitalisation, four main developments have had significant impact on the (German) labour market: (1) mechanisation of work,

Table 1 Shifts in the labour market due to digitalisation—industries in which the number of employees will increase most sharply in Germany between 2014 and 2030

Social professions, complex services	Repetitive professions, industry, administration	Forecast, data in thousands
Business-related services		425
Social services, domestic		335
Placement/leasing of workers		260
Social services, healthcare		218
Business/legal/tax consulting		168
Education/teaching		125
Data processing, etc.		75
IT services		71
	Retail trade	−70
	Manufacture of basic metals	−169
	Accommodation/hotels and restaurants	−244
	Mechanical engineering	−285
	Public administration	−372

(2) change in business models, (3) change in the organisation of work and (4) change in the required skills and competencies.

With reference to the mechanisation of work (1) and the change of required competencies and qualifications (4), Osborne and Frey conducted a famous study on the substitutability of jobs by automated and digitalised processes. Whereas Frey and Osborne (2013) predicted that 47% of all employed US Americans were at risk of losing their jobs to automatisation or digitalisation, Bonin et al. (2015) determined that 42% of employees in Germany worked in fields which Osborne and Frey considered in their study and only 12% of them were threatened by digitalisation and automatisation. Another research study by the Organisation for Economic Co-operation and Development (OECD, 2019) predicts that 18% of jobs in industry will be eliminated by 2040 in Germany. But other future projections vary from 8 to 50% regarding the elimination of jobs. The reasons for this large variation can be found in the different study settings as well as the complexity of technological change. These factors make dynamical and interdependent changes hard to predict.

Overall, most studies show a negative shift in employment rates in low- to medium-skilled work which is marked by a large amount of routine. Such work, like accounting and quality control, can easily be automated. Fields of work which require a great deal of empathy, creativity, complex problem-solving and entrepreneurial thinking, however, are on the rise (cf. Table 1).

The World Economic Forum (WEF) future of jobs report of 2018 simultaneously predicts the elimination of 75 million jobs and the development of 133 new jobs:

If we take a look at the situation in Germany, the QuBe Project predicts the following scenario for different job fields: the biggest decline of jobs is to be found in logistics and transportation, followed by the piloting of vehicles and means of transportation, cleaning services, sales, tourism and administrative jobs. The biggest

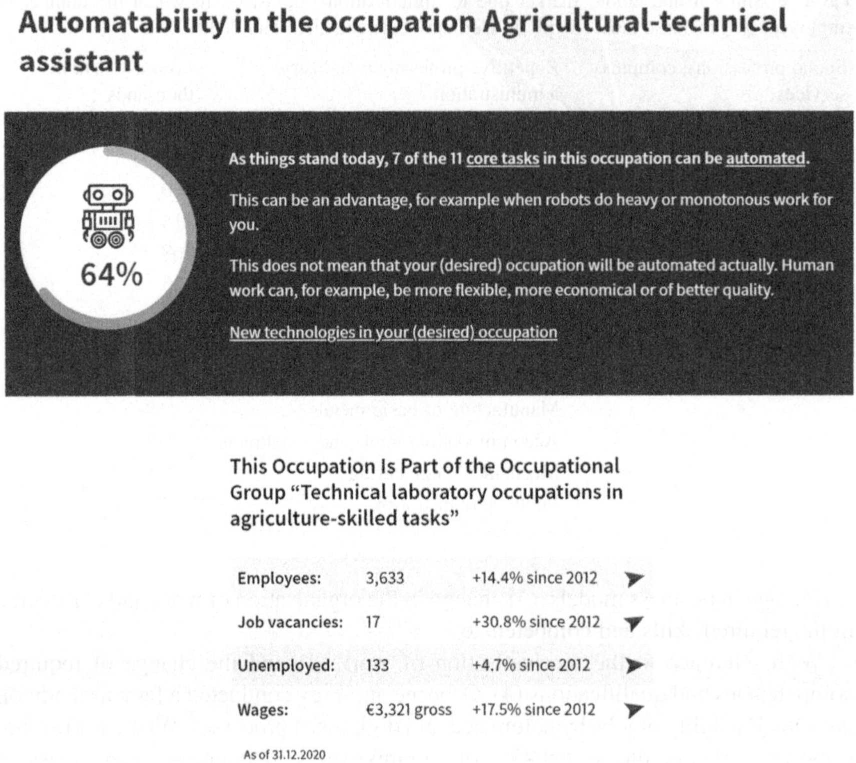

Fig. 1 Automatability in the occupation agricultural-technical assistant

increase is to be expected in informatics and technical jobs, followed by jobs in marketing, media and online business, as well as management, organisation and technical development, controlling of production and construction (Wolter et al., 2018).

The German Institut für Arbeitsmarkt- und Berufsforschung (Institute for Labour Market and Professional Research, IAB) developed a tool that allows users to assess how easily different professions can be replaced by automatisation and robotisation given the present situation. This tool, the "Job Futuromat" (roughly, "job futures machine"), offers predictions for the automatability of a profession input by the user. Due to our focus in the second part of the chapter on occupations in the field of agricultural science, we have selected an occupation from this field for the following chart, created using the IAB tool[2] (cf. Fig. 1).

Germany is not amongst the leaders in digitalisation, as shown by the 2020 DESI report, which measures the progress in digitalisation according to five main indicators (DESI, 2020, p. 2) (cf. Fig. 2).

[2]For more information, see: https://job-futuromat.iab.de/

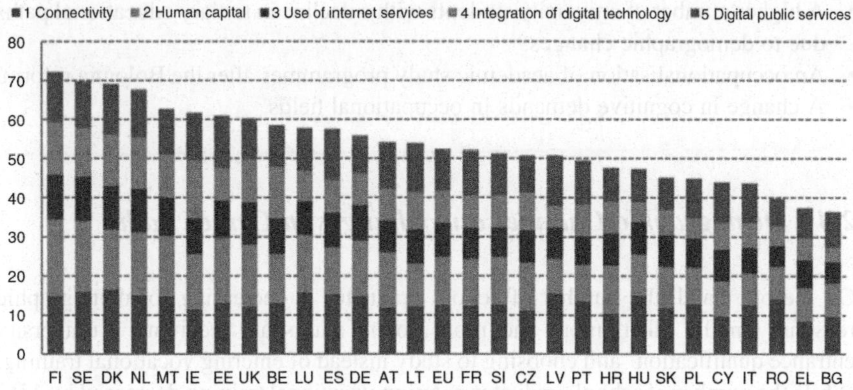

Fig. 2 Digital economy and society index 2020 (DESI) (2020, 2)

Especially when it comes to the use of Internet services, the integration of digital technologies and the digital public services, Germany has a great deal of ground to cover.

2.3 *Academisation of Professions/Career Paths*

Until the 1970s, the German educational system was marked by a clear distinction between the professional and the academic path. After four years at primary school, the first decision has to be made. The child can enter either a secondary grammar school, leading to an Abitur (A-level degree) which gives access to university education, or a secondary professional school, which gives access to professional vocational training afterwards.[3] This separation of educational paths was historically justified by the divergent demands of the labour market.

Only after a severe warning by an education specialist in the 1960s that Germany was heading towards an educational catastrophe did the educational system become more open and flexible: new ways of achieving the Abitur were established on the so-called secondary educational path (e.g. attending evening schools while working full-time or part-time) and other forms of university entrance qualifications besides the Abitur were established.

In the last few years, experts have noticed competition between the academic and vocational courses of education (Euler & Severing, 2014). There are three main reasons for this process (Schütte, 2013):

[3] Further information on the German vocational training system can be found at https://www.bmwi.de/Redaktion/EN/Downloads/duales-ausbildungsprogram.pdf?__blob=publicationFile&v=3

- A higher number of university students with a decline in tertiary educational paths due to demographic changes.
- An occupationalisation of academic study programmes after the Bologna reform.
- A change in cognitive demands in occupational fields.

2.4 Demographic Changes and Changes in Career Paths

On the one hand, the number of school graduates is decreasing for demographic reasons. On the other, more and more young adults are receiving a university entrance qualification[4] and choosing to study instead of entering vocational training. While the number of school graduates entering vocational training decreased by 15% between 2000 and 2013, the number of new university students increased by 64% in the same period. This trend is persistent. This has consequences not only for the labour market and training companies, but also for vocational training schools: their number of students decreased by 18% between 2008/2009 and 2018/2019, and consequently the number of vocational training schools decreased by 9% (Bundesministerium für Bildung und Forschung, 2020, p. 9). The government as well as the private sector has started initiatives to slow down these processes as well as to support and stabilise the vocational education sector.

2.5 Occupationalisation of Academic Study Programmes

For a long time, universities of applied sciences were perceived as extensions of vocational colleges. They were therefore attended mainly by vocational training graduates wanting further education in their respective professional fields. This perspective has changed sustainably. Nowadays, a growing number of school graduates with an Abitur enrol in universities of applied sciences, which proves both their higher social prestige and the labour market's ever-growing interest in their graduates (Pahl, 2018).

After the establishment of universities of applied sciences with their clear focus on practice and application-oriented research and teaching—in contrast to the theory—and scholarship-oriented study courses at universities, cooperative study programmes are becoming increasingly popular. They offer a combination of professional training within a company, organisation or institution and theoretical education at a university of applied sciences. While there are around 10,000 bachelor's degree programmes at universities or universities of applied sciences, there are

[4]The proportion of school students with university entrance qualifications has increased continuously from 36.4% (1995) through 44.4% (2007) up to 52.8% (2014). The percentage of male graduates (48.3%) is lower than that of female graduates (67.5%).

around 1600 cooperative study courses, mainly in the field of economics, engineering, IT, health, media and communication, social work, tourism and event management, administration and public services (Hochschulkompass, 2020).

Furthermore, once classical vocational professions in Germany, such as nursing, have become cooperative study courses, especially in the fields of health and caretaking. It remains doubtful whether this alone will help to raise their prestige and attract more students into these professional fields, which currently have the greatest lack of workers. The outlook is all the more bleak given that in other countries these professions are already academic professions and still suffer from a lack of personnel.

2.6 *Change in Cognitive Demands in Occupational Fields*

According to a number of studies, there has been a change of cognitive requirements in a number of occupational fields in the last 30+ years. On the one hand, more people are working in professions requiring mainly cognitive tasks. On the other hand, these cognitive tasks themselves have changed as well, becoming more complex and requiring higher and more specialised qualifications. Furthermore, a great deal of specialised knowledge acquired during vocational training or university education becomes outdated after only a short amount of time. This calls for lifelong learning programmes, especially but not solely in the IT sector. Companies must establish knowledge management systems which provide continuous training and learning opportunities. Figure 3 shows the growing number of people working in cognitive task groups between 1980 and 2017.

A study done by the German Bundesinstitut für Berufsbildung (Federal Institute for Vocational Education and Training, BIBB) shows a growing demand for the following competencies between 2011/2012 and 2017/2018: reading and writing competencies, collection and evaluation of complex information and data, creativity and problem-solving, service provision, IKT, management and coordination, legal matters (cf. Fig. 3).

2.7 *Public and Private Sector Initiatives*

The decreasing number of school graduates seeking vocational training as well as the shortage of specialists in many areas has led to a growing number of public and private sector initiatives aiming to attract new talents and prepare society and future generations for the challenges of Industry 4.0. In the following, some of these measures are briefly presented as examples.

Allianz für Aus- und Weiterbildung 2015–2018: At the end of 2014, Germany's Federal Government, Federal Employment Agency, the Chamber of Commerce, trade unions and federal states (Bundesländer) entered into an "Allianz für Aus- und

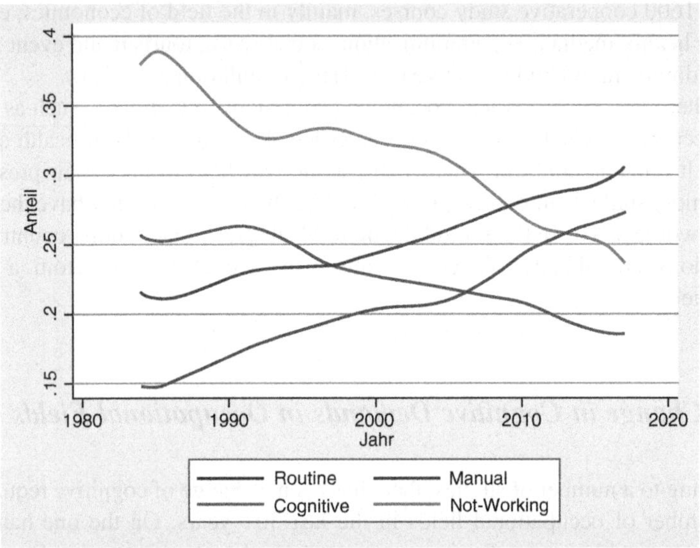

Fig. 3 Share of task groups and non-employment in working-age population 1984–2017 (Bachmann & Stepanyan, 2020)

Weiterbildung" (alliance for initial and further training) for 2015–2018. Their shared aim was to strengthen dual vocational training and to promote vocational education just as valuable as academic education. The underlying objective was to convince more young people from Germany and from amongst the refugees who have fled to Germany to train for one of the over 300 professions for which vocational training is available. In this way, and through its work, the Alliance for Initial and Further Training aims to close the skills gap in Germany.[5]

BMAS Dialogprozess Arbeiten 4.0: Germany's Bundesministerium für Arbeit und Soziales (Federal Ministry of Labour and Social Affairs, BMAS) started the "Dialogprozess Arbeiten 4.0"(dialogue process "working 4.0") in 2015 to create a space for a public as well as professional exchange about the future of work. The focus was not only on the new production processes in Industry 4.0, but also on developing guiding principles for "good work"—that is, defining the social requirements and guidelines of the future work society.

Between 2015 and 2016, conferences and expert workshops took place, workbooks were published, guidelines were developed, think tanks and experiments were initiated and a film festival took place. The dialogue concluded with the publishing of the *White Book Working 4.0* in 2016. This book summarised the key findings and discussed possible configuration and implementation options.[6]

[5]For more information, please visit http://www.aus-und-weiterbildungsallianz.de

[6]For more information, see https://www.bmas.de/DE/Service/Publikationen/a883-weissbuch.html

As another direct result of the dialogue, the Federal Ministry of Labour and Social Affairs set up an interdisciplinary, agile organisational unit, the Policy Lab Digital, Work & Society.[7] It analyses technological and social trends with a view to how society will work in 2040, assembling a strategically oriented overview of the future of all processes relevant to labour and social policy. Together with representatives from the fields of research, implementation and the social partners, it develops problem-solving approaches for the future of work in our society (BMAS, 2022a, 2022b).

Nationale Weiterbildungsstrategie: The Nationale Weiterbildungsstrategie (National Skills Strategy) was developed by the Federal Ministry of Labour and Social Affairs and the Bundesministerium für Bildung und Wissenschaft (Federal Ministry of Education and Research), together with social partners, the federal states (Bundesländer), the Chamber of Industry and Crafts and the Federal Employment Agency (BMAS, 2022a, 2022b). The National Skills Strategy was officially adopted on 12 June 2019 and is based on the Qualifizierungschancengesetz (Skills Development Opportunities Act), which already contains a binding right to counselling on continuing education and training by the Federal Employment Agency. In future, the focus will no longer be on formal qualifications alone, but also on individual skills. The aim is to help all current and future employees maintain and adapt their qualifications and skills in a changing work world and to enable their up-skilling or career mobility (Euroguidance, 2022).

Within the different sectors, there are many other regional initiatives too numerous to list within the framework of this chapter.

2.8 Challenges for Career Counselling

In principle, the German career guidance system (Euroguidance, 2022) provides access to educational and career guidance services for all citizens at any stage of their lives—whether they are in education or training, employed, unemployed or looking for continuing education.

In career guidance, a distinction is traditionally made between educational guidance and vocational guidance in the vocational training and employment sector.

Educational guidance comprises:

- School guidance and counselling.
- Guidance on educational paths.
- School psychological services.
- Vocational and careers guidance by the Federal Employment Agency (Bundesagentur für Arbeit, BA).
- Higher education counselling services.

[7] The Policy Lab Digital, Work & Society is a new organisational unit within the "Digitalisation and the Labour Market Department" at the Federal Ministry of Labour and Social Affairs; for more information please visit: https://www.denkfabrik-bmas.de/en/

Vocational guidance includes:

- Placement and counselling in the employment agencies/job centre.
- Career guidance in the BA.
- Municipal educational guidance.
- Adult education centres.
- Career guidance in the chambers (e.g. commerce or industry).
- Guidance providers.

The structure of guidance provision reflects the German education and employment system[8] with its shared responsibilities between the Federal Government, the federal states and the municipalities. A key player in the implementation of guidance provision is the Federal Employment Agency (Bundesagentur für Arbeit, BA)[9] with its more than 150 local employment agencies (Arbeitsagentur, AA) and career information centres (BIZ). In addition to federal institutions, the local municipalities play an important role by providing guidance services either themselves or through their social welfare services (cf. Fig. 4).[10]

Further, the Nationales Forum Beratung in Bildung, Beruf und Beschäftigung (National Guidance Forum for Education, Career and Employment, NFB)—an independent network of politically responsible institutions, organisations and experts—promotes the delivery of professional, high-quality guidance in the education and employment sector in Germany (NFB, 2022a, 2022b). Along with members of the Bundesministerium für Bildung und Forschung (Federal Ministry of Education and Research, BMBF), the Kultusministerkonferenz (Standing Conference of the Ministers of Education and Cultural Affairs, KMK) and the Bundesagentur für Arbeit (Federal Employment Agency, BA), it also contributes to a strategy of lifelong learning in Germany in which a coherent system of lifelong guidance is an integral component.

Finally, here are several key points that describe the situation in Germany and structure the rest of the chapter. The megatrends mentioned earlier show a major challenge, especially with regard to demographic change and the resulting shortage of skilled workers.

2.9 Demographic Change/"Silver Society"

The figure below shows the age structure in Germany in 2019 and a predicted age structure for 2060. It is clear to see that the number of people reaching an age of 80 and above will grow significantly. People will live longer and therefore work longer. For many decades, the regular retirement age was 65; it has already been

[8] For more information, please visit: https://www.arbeitsagentur.de/en/welcome

[9] For more information, please visit: https://www.arbeitsagentur.de/bildung

[10] For more information, please visit: https://www.volkshochschule.de/

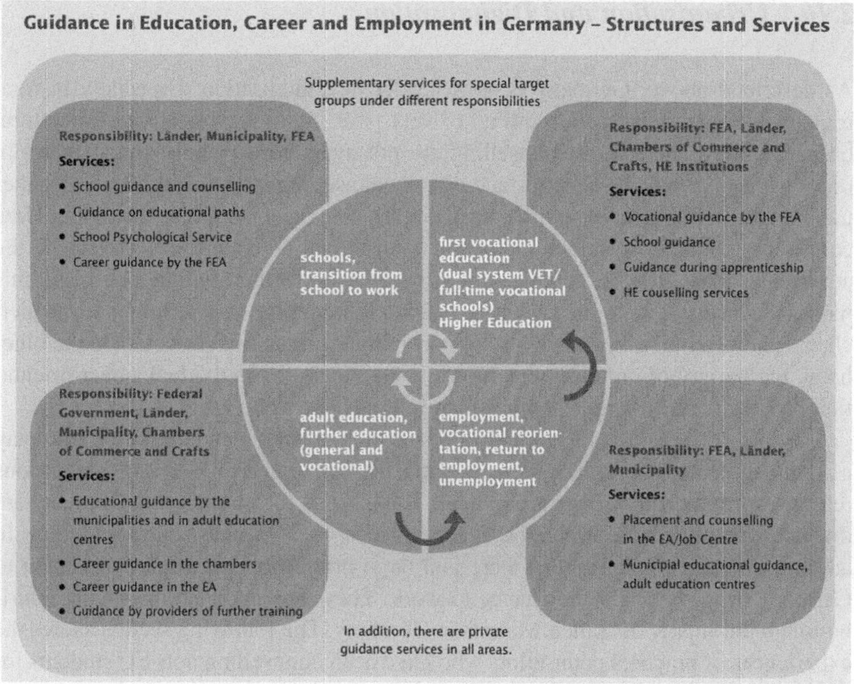

Fig. 4 Guidance in education, career and employment in Germany: structures and services (National Guidance Forum, 2022a, 2022b)

raised to 67. There are voices that demand raising the retirement age to 70 within the next decade. A greater number of older people will need further qualifications, while fewer children will attend school and therefore fewer people enter the labour market.

This trend is not new, but its consequences are becoming ever more visible. In 2019, the Federal Employment Agency introduced a programme for lifelong career guidance, starting in schools at least two years prior to graduating from the secondary education model of choice, through finding a fitting vocational training or study programme of choice and entering the labour market for the first time or after a break due to parental leave or care-taking of a family member, up to needing further professional qualification to stay in the professional field of choice or changing professions or studying/working with a handicap.

The BMAS introduced a federal programme for establishing regional further training alliances aimed at small and medium enterprises. Businesses of this size should be enabled to participate in further training programmes more often. In order to reach this goal, connections and cooperation between companies and educational and training associations and counselling organisations are supported. In cooperation with the BA, the BMAS also introduced a new online training platform "NOW" ("Nationale Online-Weiterbildungsplatform", national online continuing education platform), aiming for more transparency regarding the continuing professional training market and its various opportunities.

2.10 Urbanisation and Digitalisation

As described above, Germany is not a leader in digitalisation. Especially in rural regions, there are large areas with no or very poor Internet connectivity. Therefore, online training and online counselling are not available for those living there. In order to receive on-site, face-to-face career counselling, they would have to either travel to the next bigger city with a local employment agency office which offers free counselling or choose another type of counselling or counsellor. Given all the advantages they offer, large cities are growing even further. On the one hand, this means that schools are more crowded, making it harder for counsellors to reach their clients and offer all of the students support in their orientation process. On the other hand, the variety of organisations offering support in the individual career orientation process is much larger in cities than in the countryside.

Last but not least, the megatrends globalisation, mobility and migration also play a significant role. Particularly non-EU citizens, who come to Germany for various reasons, form a central focus group here. The reasons for migration to Germany are diverse, and the counselling these people receive is equally heterogeneous. In addition to refugee migrations, there is a large proportion of people who come to Germany to study or for the chance to work. They thus make an important contribution to the supply of skilled workers in Germany. The following section shares the experiences of practical counsellors who have been counselling non-EU students for many years.

3 The Challenges and Chances of Counselling Non-EU, Non-German-Speaking Students in Master's Degree Programmes in Germany from a Practitioner's Perspective

This chapter shares a practitioner's experiences in counselling students in English language master's degree programmes near Stuttgart, Germany. These findings are based not on empirical data but on individual counselling sessions over the past 30 years.

As the teaching and exams in such master's degree programmes are carried out entirely in English, I am concentrating on the issues relating to students with only a minimal knowledge of German. Due to the types of degrees offered for international students at the University of Stuttgart and the University of Hohenheim, the relevant courses are mostly in the following fields: agriculture, business/economics, architecture, engineering and natural sciences. In many cases, studying abroad is just an episode in someone's educational path and the graduates return to their home country on graduating. In many other cases, however, it is also a way of getting access to this country's labour market and finding a future there.

3.1 When Do I See these Students?

This is a typical email I receive:

> "Good morning,
> I have recently graduated from the M.Sc. in Computational Linguistics and I am currently looking for a job related to my area.
> I have been looking for a job for three months and I don't even get invited to interviews. That's very frustrating.
> I was wondering if you had any advice for situations like mine."

Usually, students are referred to me by their universities either well into their course, when they plan to do an internship in their field, or right at the end of their course, when they are thinking of finding employment in Germany following their course. Often they come and see me when applications do not yield positive results. I then counsel them on the CV structure and application process. However, I feel this is often too little too late. If the students have any plans to stay and find employment here, acquiring solid German language skills should start either before coming to Germany or through intensive summer courses preceding the semester. If I see them only in their third or fourth semester or when they have finished their degree, time is ticking in terms of finance and visa regulations: non-EU students who graduate in Germany can receive a so-called job-seeker's visum for a maximum period of 18 months while looking for a skilled job suited to their qualification.

3.2 What Are the Benefits for these Students of Studying in English but in Germany?

Many postgraduate students receive grants to come to Germany, and German postgraduate coursework gives them the opportunity to receive an internationally recognised qualification to further their career.[11] Although German universities do not generally rank in the world's top ten (see, e.g., Times Higher Education or QS), German universities seem to have a solid standing, tradition and reputation. At first glance, it appears that not much time needs to be "wasted" on learning German, as most prospective students already have an extremely good knowledge of English. Course fees in Germany are low in international comparison. In the state of Baden-Württemberg, non-EU students pay ca. €3000 in fees for a whole year (2021). The situation on the labour market in the Stuttgart region was very good before the

[11] For further information, see the Deutscher Akademischer Austauschdienst (German Academic Exchange Service, DAAD).

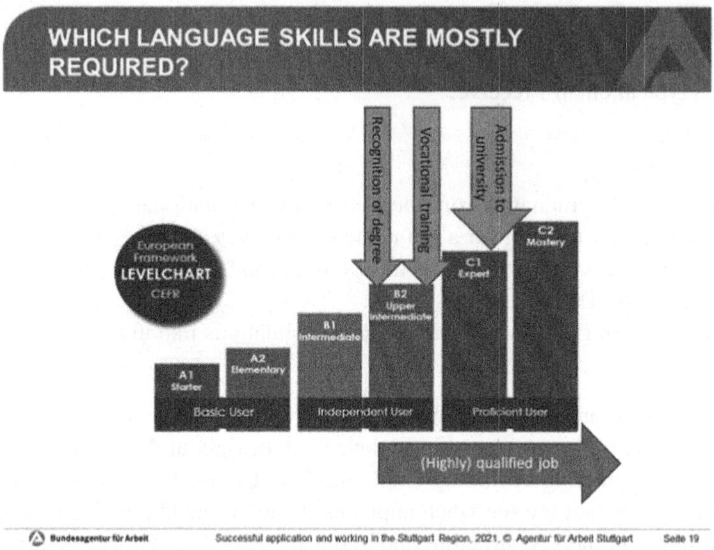

Fig. 5 Successful application and working in the Stuttgart region

COVID-19 pandemic, so students could reasonably expect to find student jobs to subsidise their costs while studying. Quite a few of Germany's big companies are based in the immediate vicinity of the city (e.g. Bosch, Daimler, Porsche), which indicates future perspectives.

Wissenschaftsladen Bonn e. V. (WILA) points out one very important factor: "communication skills are very important" (Wissenschaftsladen Bonn e. V., 2022). For non-native German speakers, this can prove quite difficult to achieve (cf. Fig. 5).

The majority of this student group achieves level B1–B2 by the end of their course when I see them. However, to fulfil the requirements for proficient/professional use of German, the level needs to be around C1–C2. (These levels are based on the Common European Framework of Reference for Languages, abbreviated CEFR.)

3.3 *What Are the Students' Issues?*

For most of the students under consideration, their life in Germany has taken place in the university setting and/or in student accommodations—in both of these settings they can operate mostly in English. However, as soon as they wish to enter the labour market in Germany the need for German language skills comes into full force, particularly at graduate job level, where communication of all kinds plays an essential role. These are very ambitious and talented young people from all over the world who have concentrated mostly on their aim to complete their master's programme and have not concentrated on learning the local language. Learning a new language requires a great deal of time and effort which can be scarce during an intensive master's programme. Some of the students had already gained several years of professional experience in their home country before embarking on a degree programme in Germany. However, none of these clients are language graduates, so learning languages is not their primary aim; without language learning, it simply proves extremely difficult to land a graduate job. Their skills and expertise lie in the areas of science, business/economics or engineering. Often they are surprised or even shocked that working life in Germany mostly takes place in German and not at all in English.

The issues often start during the application process, where most companies (some exceptions notwithstanding) require a German language CV and letter of application. But while writing the CV can still be supported by a German speaker, the interview represents a massive hurdle. Application processes can also be highly culturally specific and must be practised, particularly for graduates with no previous work experience. To give two examples:

1. An Iranian graduate in agriculture specialised in growing pistachio nuts and pomegranates during her first degree course in Iran and was extremely proud of her specialist expertise in this field during the counselling session. As an interview/application strategy in Germany, it would probably be beneficial for her to concentrate more on her good general knowledge of plant production, as these particular plants cannot be grown in our climate, and to show more of her ability to transfer her skills to agricultural produce grown in central Europe.
2. One Asian student had a five-page, far too long CV quoting every prize she had won since the age of six. It was difficult to communicate that a shorter version would make it easier for the reader/personnel manager and that it could be beneficial to concentrate on most recent achievements and those relating to the post advertised, as she clearly felt she needed to mention absolutely everything.

3.4 What Are Possible Solutions?

When students enquire about English language master's degree programmes in Germany from their home country, they should be strongly advised that German will be necessary not only for possible internships or positions in Germany following graduation but also for everyday life in their community. Students should therefore be strongly encouraged to start language classes before coming to Germany. The experience of studying in a foreign country could also be broadened by understanding the local language and venturing beyond the narrow university life. Universities offer German classes alongside the students' main courses, but students often underestimate how important these language skills may be.

Some institutions have recently reacted to these issues and have developed remedial projects:

1. In cooperation with career counsellors, the language centre of Stuttgart university in 2021 started a workshop preparing students for the labour market. This workshop includes learning how to interpret job ads, write applications, present oneself in interviews and assessment centre training and use social media, as well as getting to know local companies and working with alumni who have already secured jobs.
2. Group information on "Successful job applications in Germany" at the Stuttgart Welcome Centre is available to everyone, not only graduates.
3. The student fair "Your start in Stuttgart", organised by the city council, is aimed at newly arrived foreign students to help them settle and get to know all the necessary network partners (e.g. housing, finance, counselling, legal, residence/work permit and language classes).
4. The graduate fair "Your future in Stuttgart", organised by the city council together with all the network partners, encourages graduates to take up positions in the region after their graduation.
5. "Network Internationals": Various institutions meet up every three months to exchange experiences/issues regarding international students. Such issues may concern the Federal Employment Agency, career counsellors, health insurance, universities, student associations, grants office, residence permits, etc.
6. Some universities support the creation of so-called language tandems or buddies by putting in touch two people who meet regularly to practise each other's language and to provide support.

These are just a few examples of how students' challenges with intercultural differences and linguistic barriers could be met and how career counsellors can support graduates on their way into a job. For the future, I hope to see clients much earlier in their course so that they can integrate their language learning much earlier if they are looking for employment in Germany.

University education in English has become a global, international market. This has opened up opportunities for young people in many countries. However, this opening up should not stop there but look at the whole picture of international skills movement, including skills and requirements for securing a job.

4 Why Do Many Young People Fail to Achieve an Apprenticeship Despite a Shortage of Apprentices in Many Sectors?: Findings from Counselling Young People Mainly with a Migration Background in an SGB II Context

While we strive to integrate well-educated students from non-EU countries into the German labour market, another focus is on the large group of young people with a migration background who are first-, second- or third-generation immigrants to Germany. These last make up a growing portion of the applicants for apprenticeship, according to the "Data Report on the Vocational Education and Training Report of the BIBB": in 2016, the share of such applicants was 29%; by 2018, it had grown to 36%. The increase is due, amongst other things, to young refugees who applied for training (Bundesinstitut für Berufsbildung, 2019, p. 220).

At the same time, many applicants with a migration background are unable to find a training place—even if they grew up in Germany. In 2016, only about one in four applicants with a migration background was able to start an apprenticeship (29%). Amongst their peers without a migration background, the figure was significantly higher (47%). Compared to previous years, this has hardly changed. On the contrary, the difference has even increased since 2004 (Beicht & Walden, 2019, p. 20).

In order to provide young people with the best possible support during the transition to training and work, Germany has developed a programme of youth employment agencies. As an amalgamation of several public institutions such as job centres, the Jugendamt (Youth Welfare Office), counsellors for vocational schools and the employment agencies, the Jugendberufsagentur (Youth Employment Agency) offers a comprehensive counselling service under one roof.

Young people from families receiving unemployment benefits are assigned a personal contact person at the Youth Employment Agency as soon as they are 15 years old. This contact person keeps track of their school attendance and is supposed to accompany their vocational orientation up to the transition to training. Depending on the particular agency's catchment area, the proportion of young people with a migration background in this group can be very high. In my clientele, slightly less than half do not have German citizenship. The other half, with a few exceptions, have a migration background. The offer of early counselling, support and funding opportunities contributes to many school graduates being able to take advantage of a direct follow-up perspective. Nevertheless, there are still a large number of young people without an apprenticeship—while many companies remain unable to fill their training positions. Obviously, there is a matching problem here: those who are looking for a position do not come together with the companies that want to provide training in order to secure their future skilled labour needs.

In the following, possible reasons, solution strategies and ideas will be outlined based on the experience of counselling the above-mentioned target group, in particular young people with a migrant background.

4.1 Career Choices

On what basis do young people choose their career aspirations? Do they always correspond to the existing strengths, competencies and qualifications of the person in question? How does real interest in a profession arise?

In conversations with young people with a migrant background, it is noticeable that their families often have high expectations of their children. The children should be better off later, prove themselves in the new country and take up a respectable profession, if possible completing an academic degree. Training in the skilled crafts and trades or in the construction industry, for example, is unpopular, possibly also because many activities in this area do not require special training in many countries of origin and have a correspondingly low standing.

The young person's circle of friends also plays a major role: Which professions are recognised and popular, and how does the career choice affect one's own image? How do the others react if I train as a janitor? It is also striking that some state the same wish as their best friend or big sister. Many express a desire for a profession and can say little about it when asked: What they like about it, what the work involves, and why the profession suits them. A real confrontation with it has not taken place. Why is that? Perhaps because teachers and employment agencies constantly ask them about their professional aspirations and they need a quick answer. Or the image of a profession is more important than its tasks, and the choice of profession is therefore quickly ticked off. And certainly, at 16 or 17, one also has many other concerns and interests that are important. But to truly find out which career path offers the greatest opportunities and success, young people need to look much more closely and with more open minds at their career choices.

In my experience, this relatively superficial consideration of the choice of profession is why there is often an accumulation of certain career aspirations, such as motor vehicles technician and office management clerk. Based on the demand, however, certificates and application documents must be provided at a relatively high level.

An apprenticeship as a roofer, tiler or scaffolding builder on the other hand is not considered even after months of unsuccessful training search. Young people associate these professions with physical exertion, low income and low status. This combination is understandably off-putting. Young people often see their future selves more as a bank employee, IT specialist or in the medical field—even if school qualifications and skills do not match and a successful career is unlikely.

4.2 *More Convincing Presentation of Unpopular Professions in Counselling*

In my consultations, I try to talk with the client about the path beyond the general job description. What will it mean for this individual to take this career path, and what opportunities can arise? Of course, how the labour market and/or a specific job will develop in the future also plays a significant role. Employers can help a great deal by providing information on important questions that young people often ask:

- How are the professions developing? What will still be needed in 20 years? Will some professions actually become more attractive in the long term because they will become less strenuous with the help of new technologies?

- What career opportunities are there? Especially due to the lack of competition, less common career choices can offer much more attractive opportunities than more popular professions. These should be described vividly and practically and should show a path that seems feasible and realistic to career starters.
- How modern are the companies, for example, do they offer trainings with VR glasses and work with new technologies?
- How are employees taken along in the changing world of work? Do companies have concepts for new models of work and offers such as internal training, learning platforms or knowledge databases?

Another major aspect needs to be kept in mind: appreciation of multilingualism and cultural competences and a much more open attitude towards applicants with an Arab or Eastern European background is becoming increasingly important. If employers are open to this, many new options could emerge.

4.3 What Motivates Generation Z?

Furthermore, it helps me in my consultations to put myself in young peoples' shoes and ask: what are this generation's values, and what is particularly important to them in their professional lives?

Consultants (and companies) need an awareness of the values and goals of generation Z when it comes to starting a career. Before we give them advice on their career choices, we should know what is important to them. So it makes sense to simply ask them:

What do you expect from your career?

- Security and stability?
- More money?
- Greater meaningfulness?
- Companies with commitment to social projects or climate protection?
- Modern technology?
- Career advancement opportunities?
- More free time and flexibility?
- Part-time training?
- Flat hierarchies?

Their answers to these questions will not necessarily give us a job profile yet, but they do give us an indication of how we need to adjust to young people as well, not just they to us (or to the labour market). Companies could regularly send an employee to schools to present their profession. If students can identify with this employee, for example because he or she is still relatively young and has a similar sociocultural background, the employee could serve as an inspiring and motivating role model.

4.4 Fixed Career Aspirations but Lack of Qualifications

Young people with a migrant background often have more difficult starting conditions and therefore achieve lower school qualifications on average than their peers without a migration background (Beicht & Walden, 2019, p. 12).

Counsellors therefore often find themselves confronted with the fact that young people's career aspirations do not match their school qualifications. Especially for young people with very concrete ideas and wishes, the challenge is then to be flexible and possibly take detours, for example through another apprenticeship or the improvement of school qualifications. The path to the desired profession is extended by two to three years, which often seems very long in combination with a subsequent three-year training—especially since a relevant degree and possible career entry are only achieved at the very end.

There are already numerous programmes and instruments that start at an early point. The offers of career guidance in schools as well as school internships make an important contribution to career orientation. There are special coaching offers that can be taken up after school and are free of charge for young people who receive benefits, as well as vocational language courses to improve German language skills. The vocational schools offer a one-year vocational preparation (IBA) in previously selected occupational fields, including the opportunity to achieve a better degree. If a young person is uncertain which profession to choose, they can get to know different occupational fields and complete internships through the programme known as Berufsvorbereitende Bildung (Vocational Preparation, BvB). Higher school qualifications can be achieved via the second educational path. Most of these programmes can be supplemented by language support; the career-oriented offer Ausbildung in Sicht ("Apprenticeship in sight") is particularly suitable for this. In order to enable training even without a sufficient school degree, there is the possibility of a subsidised training position (for example through the Berliner Ausbildungsplatz-Programm and Berliner Ausbildungsmodell) or an entry-level qualification (Einstiegsqualifizierung) in the form of a paid long-term internship, which should lead to an apprenticeship. The training achieved can be accompanied by the support option Assistierte Ausbildung (assisted training/AsA) through tutoring and language support, amongst other things.

This list is far from comprehensive. But since there are still many young people without training and at the same time a shortage of skilled workers, the question still arises: what is missing? Or what works well but could be adapted even better to the needs of the target group or perhaps also to the changing external conditions?

Here are several suggestions:

4.5 Internships

The first internship takes place during school and can already provide important insights and establish contacts.

Not infrequently, young people resort to an internship at the supermarket around the corner or the business of a relative, thereby failing to make the most of the opportunity. More support could be provided here, possibly also by the employment agency. When students experience an inspiring internship, it can have a huge impact on their further career and motivation and also improve their school performance.

4.6 Sufficient Language Support in Schools (Transition from "Welcome Class" to Regular School)

After school, there are numerous opportunities to make up for language deficits, whether during vocational training or in earlier language courses. Of course, it would be better if the young people finished school with a sufficient language level. In my experience, the problem arises in the transition from the so-called welcome classes—in which newly arrived migrant students with poor or non-existent German language skills receive remedial training—to the regular school. Language support in the "welcome classes" is implemented differently in schools, and many young people finish the classes after two years with a language level of A1. In most cases, students automatically enter a regular class after two years and then often have significant problems that cannot be fixed before the end of schooling. A solid A2 language level should be a prerequisite for regular school attendance.

4.7 Mentors/Tandems

A lack of social mixing in schools means that especially young people with a migrant background are less likely to be able to take on new perspectives and are denied access to certain networks, information and also language and behaviour codes. It would be helpful for them to have a contact person who comes from outside the environment. One possibility would be to form cross-school tandems through which students from different backgrounds can exchange ideas and get to know each other. Another alternative, for example, might be to provide young people with a migration background or refugees with a mentor who is only a little older but can support them amicably with career choices and applications—here too, a good personal relationship is the most important factor.

4.8 Sponsored Long-Term Internship (Einstiegsqualifizierung, EQ)

A long-term internship of this type enables companies and young people to get to know each other and, with lower requirements, offers the chance to enter training in a profession that normally requires a higher qualification. Since the EQ also includes vocational school lessons, it can even be credited as the first year of training, if conditions permit.

Young people will not always find interesting offers in the list of internships registered with the Employment Agency. In this case, young people could approach employers of interest to them on their own initiative and ask about the possibility of an EQ. In my experience, this is extremely difficult for young people from migrant backgrounds, especially if they have to explain to the employer what an EQ is. Often the target group for an EQ are young people who speak German as a second language. In addition to efforts to offer the widest possible range of EQs, an easy-to-implement strategy could be developed for young people to approach companies themselves, e.g., with a pre-formulated cover letter and more detailed information material for the employer, as well.

4.9 *Intensive Dialogue between Companies and Vocational Schools*

Another way to achieve the desired profession with insufficient school qualification is training at a vocational school. Demand for the two-year training as a socio-pedagogical assistant has been particularly high, especially in the last two years. This course requires at least the lowest German educational qualification Berufsbildungsreife (vocational training qualification certificate, Bbr) and offers the prospect of subsequently completing training as a childcare worker. In addition, unlike vocational preparation, after two years, students acquire a vocational qualification with which they can already enter a profession. Easily accessible courses that enable a first vocational qualification and at the same time lay the foundation for further training are therefore a good alternative for many.

The selection of school training courses may not yet be optimal, and not all of them are as popular as the socio-pedagogical course. Many have higher entrance requirements, such as the Mittlerer Schulabschluss (secondary school completion certificate, MSA). Especially in the field of IT, which is growing in importance and also interests many young people, an extended offer would certainly be well received. Employers and vocational schools should be in constant dialogue about which school training courses are particularly helpful for companies and businesses with regard to new trainees and employees. In addition, the dialogue between vocational schools and companies could determine how these training courses can be further optimised, so that, for example, through the use of VR glasses and online internships, the training receives a much more practical approach and the young people enter dual training or their job at a higher, tried and tested level.

4.10 The Criteria of Application

In order to respond even better to the needs of the world of "work 4.0", the application system could be made more open, and soft skills, which will obviously play an increasingly important role, could be taken into account more strongly. On the website of Integrated Micro-Electronics, Inc. (2022), some of these soft skills are mentioned:

- Analytical thinking and innovation.
- Active learning and learning strategies.
- Resilience, stress tolerance and flexibility.
- Critical thinking and analysis.
- Creativity, originality and initiative.
- Reasoning and problem-solving.

If these competencies compensate for a lack of degrees, the rigid system in Germany, which is very focused on certificates, could be opened up and provide room for assessments and prerequisites that can be adapted to the modern workplace. This could open up more perspectives for refugees and people with a migration background. These cohorts often have lower school qualifications due for example to language barriers—but on the other hand can marshal their cultural skills and experiences in a new country to demonstrate skills such as flexibility, resilience or problem-solving.

4.11 The Application Process

In a company survey conducted by the Bertelsmann Foundation, almost three-quarters of the 412 companies surveyed stated that no young people with a migration background and adequate qualifications would apply for their training positions (Enggruber & Rützel, 2014: 9). On the other hand, a BIBB applicant survey in 2014 shows that young people with a migration background even apply significantly more frequently than those without such a background (Bundesinstitut für Berufsbildung, 2014, p. 83). These two facts signal an obvious disparity, and the question is why. In order to understand and clarify possible reservations and misunderstandings, a personal dialogue between employers, young people and counsellors would be useful. For example, there could be a regular format for this in the youth employment agencies: What concerns do employers have? Where can trainees get stuck? Are job offers, say, designed in such a way that they appeal to young people with a migrant background as well? For counsellors, a comprehensive knowledge of current application processes is also important. Since there are always new developments and trends in job applications, the team should include a counsellor who focuses on the topic and then passes on their knowledge:

- CVs are ranked by tracking systems (Applicant Tracking Systems). According to which criteria are they sorted?

- Many existing important skills are not recognised or explicitly called for.
- Special strengths of applicants with a migration background, such as multilingualism and intercultural competence, are not sufficiently communicated.
- Cultural differences in the application process between Germany and the country of origin are not clear to the applicants, with the result that behaviour and language do not contain the right codes.
- Social media plays an increasingly important role. On platforms such as LinkedIn or Xing, applicants can present themselves with content such as short videos and professional CVs. What are the current standards here?

Counsellors must adapt quickly to changes and be well informed. This requires close cooperation between counsellors, schools and employers. Overall, Germany has many good offers and support options for young people who cannot find a training position after school. The Youth Employment Agency's approach of supporting young people as early as possible and offering them a wide range of help likewise appears to work well. Nevertheless, the people who need support the most are often the hardest to reach, and we should therefore always be on the lookout for new solutions and opportunities.

5 Conclusion

The German career counselling service faces with new challenges in preparing for the "fourth industrial revolution", which will impact the labour force in the coming years in various ways.

5.1 Part 1: Gains and Losses

The first part of the chapter tries to predict the future labour market, the fourth industrial revolution and its consequences on counselling. There are forecast winners (e.g. IT) and possible losers (e.g. logistics), the expansion of digitalisation, the problematic demographics and predicted skills shortages in Germany. Education policies and job expectations in the past few decades have led to fewer and fewer young people taking up vocational training. There has been a clear shift towards academic qualifications. This may cause difficulties in the future job matching processes.

5.2 Part 2: The Graduate Dilemma

The second part of the chapter focuses on a perspective from the everyday practice of a career counsellor;it describes the specific situation of non-EU graduates in the

Stuttgart area who are taught courses entirely in English, speak very little German and therefore find it difficult to enter the German labour market after graduation. These graduates have generally been educated to master's degree level and are highly motivated and experts in their fields. More needs to be done to support these graduates in language learning at an early stage if they plan to stay in the German labour market. Some interventions and solutions are presented which support this client group in finding their way into a career in Germany.

5.3 *Part 3: Early Intervention*

The third part concentrated on the integration issues of some exemplary clients with a migration background in Berlin and how counselling can help these young people find their place in the labour market. Again we found a situation where the available training places and applicants show a mismatch which needs to be overcome. Job/training expectations often fail to match a person's individual skills or qualifications. Therefore, early information and counselling on realistic job/training prospects are needed. In addition, internships, special coaching, mentoring programmes, vocational language training and preparation courses are offered. Support is also given in the application process and in understanding cultural standards (i.e. punctuality, behaviour codes) potential employers expect in Germany. This support always aims to enable students to be accepted for an apprenticeship or a job.

Germany suffers from a double bind: on the one hand, there is a defined skills shortage in various sectors and at different levels; on the other hand, there are young people and graduates who have considerable difficulty finding their place in the German labour market. In this chapter, we have tried to look into the predicted future development of the labour market, the reasons for these discrepancies and also possible solutions. Young people with a migration background and graduates with a lack of German language skills have been identified as potential groups in the population which could help to alleviate future skills shortages. However, much more needs to be done to integrate these two groups into the training and the labour market.

References

Bachmann, R., & Stepanyan, G. (2020). It's a Woman's world? Occupational structure and the rise of female employment in Germany. In *Beiträge zur Jahrestagung des Vereins für Socialpolitik 2020: Gender Economics*. ZBW—Leibniz Information Centre for Economics.

Beicht, U. & Walden, G. (2019). *The influence of migration background, social origin and gender on the transition of school leavers who are not entitled to study into vocational training* (Discussion paper for the Federal Institute for Vocational Education and Training).

Bonin, H., Gregory, T., & Zierahn, U. (2015). Kurzexpertise Nr. 57: Übertragung der Studie von Frey/Osborne (2013) auf Deutschland [Brief expertise no. 57; Application of the Frey/Osborne (2013) study to Germany]. Link: https://www.bmas.de/SharedDocs/Downloads/DE/Publikationen/Forschungsberichte/fb-455.pdf?__blob=publicationFile&v=1

Bundesinstitut für Berufsbildung (BIBB). (2014). Data report on vocational education and training report 2014.

Bundesinstitut für Berufsbildung (BIBB). (2019). Data report on vocational education 2019.

Bundesministerium für Arbeit und Soziales (BMAS). (2022a). *Transformation of the world of work*. Link: https://www.bmas.de/EN/Labour/Transformation-of-the-world-of-work/transformation-of-the-world-of-work-art.html

Bundesministerium für Arbeit und Soziales (BMAS). (2022b). *Umsetzungsbericht nationale Weiterbildungsstrategie* [*Implementation report on the national continuing education strategy*]. Link: https://www.bmas.de/DE/Service/Publikationen/a805-umsetzungsbericht-nationale-weiterbildungsstrategie.html

Bundesministerium für Bildung und Forschung. (2020). *Berufsausbildungsbericht* [*Vocational training report*]. Link: https://www.bmbf.de/SharedDocs/Downloads/de/2021/berufsbildungsbericht-2021.pdf;jsessionid=F41AA694A21B7F52EDC0CD3D1193D520.live721?__blob=publicationFile&v=4

Enggruber, R. & Rützel, J. (2014). *Vocational training of young people with a migration background: A representative survey of companies commissioned by the Bertelsmann Stiftung*. Link: https://www.bertelsmann-stiftung.de/fileadmin/files/BSt/Publikationen/GrauePublikationen/LL_GB_Integration_UnternBefr_Links_2015.pdf

Euler, D., & Severing, E. (2014). *Durchlässigkeit zwischen beruflicher und akademischer Bildung [Permeability between vocational and academic education]*. Bertelsmann Stiftung.

Euroguidance. (2022). *Guidance system in Germany*. Link: https://www.euroguidance.eu/guidance-system-in-germany

Frey, C., & Osborne, M. A. (2013). *The future of employment: How susceptible are jobs to computerization?* University of Oxford.

Hochschulkompass. (2020). *Hochschulkompass* [*College compass*]. Link: www.hochschulkompass.de

Index für die digitale Wirtschaft und Gesellschaft (DESI). (2020). Fragen und Antworten: Ergebnisse des DESI 2020 [questions and answers: Results of the 2020 DESI]. Link: https://ec.europa.eu/commission/presscorner/api/files/document/print/de/qanda_20_1022/QANDA_20_1022_DE.pdf

Integrated Micro-Electronics Inc. (IMI). (2022). *Industry 4.0: Skills for the future of work*. Link: https://www.global-imi.com/blog/industry-4-0-skills-for-the-future-of-work

Nationales Forum Beratung in Bildung, Beruf und Beschäftigung (NFB). (2022a). *German national guidance forum in education, career and employment*. Link: https://web.archive.org/web/20200511211403/https://www.forum-beratung.de/english/index.html

Nationales Forum Beratung in Bildung, Beruf und Beschäftigung (NFB). (2022b). Career *Guidance in the life course*. Link: https://www.forum-beratung.de/cms/upload/English/nfb_2014_Career_Guidance_in_the_Life_Course.pdf

Organisation for Economic Co-operation and Development (OECD). (2019). *OECD employment outlook 2019: The future of work*. OECD Publishing.

Pahl, J.-P. (2018). *Fachhochschule: Von der Fachschule zur Hochschule für angewandte Wissenschaften [Fachhochschule: From technical school to university for applied sciences]*. wbv.

Schütte, F. (2013). Konkurrenz von akademischer und nicht akademischer Bildung [competition between academic and non-academic education]. In E. Severing & U. Teichler (Eds.), *Akademisierungder Berufswelt? [academisation of the professional world?]* (pp. 43–62). wbv.

Wissenschaftsladen Bonn e. V. (WILA). (2022). *Perspektiven für Agrarwissenschaftler*. Link: https://wila-arbeitsmarkt.de/blog/2019/10/21/berufseinstieg-mit-agrarwissenschaften/

Wolter, M. I., Mönnig, A., Schneemann, C., Weber, E., Zika, G., Helmrich, R., Maier, T., & Winnige, S. (2018). *Wirtschaft 4.0 und die Folgen für Arbeitsmarkt und Ökonomie* [*Economy 4.0 and the consequences for labour market and economy*]. https://www.bibb.de/dokumente/pdf/qube_welle5_W4.0_final.pdf

World Economic Forum. (2018). *The future of jobs report 2018: Insight report*. Link: https://www3.weforum.org/docs/WEF_Future_of_Jobs_2018.pdf

Zukunftsinstitut. (2022). *Dossier megatrends* [*Megatrends report*]. www.zukunftsinstitut.de/megatrends/

Greece: Challenges and Perspectives in Vocational Guidance in a post-crisis era

Kalliopi Marioli, Dimitrios Sannas, and Evangelia Tsilimigkra

1 Introduction

Since 2010, Greece has suffered an 11-year financial crisis. The Greek economy entered a long-term recession, resulting in a more than 25% decrease of the gross domestic product (GDP) (Hellenic Statistical Authority, 2020a). Although there were some signs of economic recovery between 2016 and 2018, there has been a further decline in the economy since 2019. In December 2014, the unemployment rate was over 26%, leaving 1.25 million people outside the job market. Unemployment rates have improved since then, but remain high, reaching 16% in 2020 (Hellenic Statistical Authority, 2021).

Since 2015, Europe has experienced its biggest refugee "crisis" of the past centuries. Millions of people who have been forcibly displaced from their countries are attempting to reach countries in the European Union. Many refugees land on the shores of Greece.[1] Since 2015, the country has received over a million individuals. Currently, approximately 160,000 asylum seekers and refugees are living in Greece (UNHCR, 2021b).

From a technological perspective, Greece has largely followed the bigger European countries and was lagging behind in the adoption of new technologies and technological developments. However, the COVID-19 pandemic since March 2020 accelerated the development in this area, including in the private and public sectors, providing a more positive outlook for the future of jobs in Greece.

This chapter focuses on refugees and asylum seekers in Greece, and Athens in particular, along with the growth of the older workforce and their integration in the

[1]The geographical location of Greece between the three continents of Europe, Asia and Africa makes it an entry point for people who want to enter Europe.

K. Marioli (✉) · D. Sannas · E. Tsilimigkra
Athens Solidarity Centre, Solidarity Now, Athens, Greece
e-mail: kmarioli@solidaritynow.org; marioka@ppp.uoa.gr; dsannas@solidaritynow.org

C. Enoch et al. (eds.), *Vocational Guidance in Europe*,
https://doi.org/10.1007/978-3-031-06592-7_5

labour market, and finally on the rapid advancement of technology and how it has affected everybody's working capacities and lives. These three areas in relation to vocational counselling and the resulting challenges and perspectives are derived from the writers' experience in providing career counselling services to more than 1300 individuals from vulnerable groups (including asylum seekers and refugees, the long-term unemployed, homeless people or people under the poverty line) from February 2018 to September 2021.

2 Counselling for Migrants and Refugees: Intercultural Awareness, Access to Education and Recognition of Qualifications

A critical aspect of integration for refugees is their educational qualifications. These, along with a sufficient knowledge of the country's language (Greek) or sufficient knowledge of the international lingua franca (English), are an essential requirement for communicating in daily life and furthermore for gaining access to the labour market.

According to Greek law, adult refugees have access to secondary education. Refugees receive the right to participate in educational programmes that are specifically for adults, relating to employment and vocational training, under the same terms and conditions that apply to Greeks. It is worth noting that there are no specific provisions facilitating the access of refugees to higher education in Greece. They may access universities under the same conditions as Greeks, following participation in entry examinations organised on specific dates by the Greek state. However, an important obstacle is the difficulty of having their secondary education recognised and therefore entering the exams.

Those who have not completed their mandatory education may enrol in the second chance schools, which are public schools for adults who have not completed their compulsory education, which is 9 years in Greece. They were established by the Law 2525/1997, and they offer afternoon courses in subjects such as linguistics, mathematics and physical sciences.[2]

Besides the second chance schools, reception classes for adult students with little or no knowledge of the Greek language have been established since 2010 in primary and secondary schools in areas that have been designated as Educational Priority Zones. These classes include a two-cycle programme within the mainstream class schedule. The first cycle is designed for students who speak little or no Greek.

[2]The Law 2525/1997 established the unified general high schools (Article 1). Before this law, the high schools were separated into general, technical, musical and vocational schools. The law also established the pupils' access to university (Art. 2), and the all-day nursery and junior schools and the second chance schools (schools for adults who have not finished their compulsory education) were formed (Art. 4, 5, 6).

Students of this cycle receive intensive Greek courses and may also join a few of the mainstream courses if they wish to. The second cycle is designed for students with an average command of the Greek language.

Attending a language course in school is especially important for those who are not fluent or have difficulties with speaking the national language. However, learning the language and attending school has been a challenge for both young and older refugees. Additional language courses (Greek, English and other languages) are provided by NGOs and are usually taught by volunteers and not necessarily by specialist teachers, and many refugees complain that they are of low or poor quality and lack continuity.

The courses taught by NGOs fall into the category of informal education, which is governed by the General Secretariat for Lifelong Learning of the Ministry of Education. Centres for Lifelong Learning (KDVM in Greek) and public or private Vocational Training Institutes (IEK in Greek), along with NGOs, civil society actors, refugee communities and other actors, supplement the adult education (Youth and Lifelong Learning Centre, 2021).

The problem with adult education is that it is largely fragmented, project-restricted, and not integrated into a general state policy. The adult education programmes lack continuity and sustainability, which hinders their effectiveness. Moreover, it must be noted that adult refugees who want to participate in technical and vocational education schemes have to face a complicated procedure due to the lack of an adequate system for the certification of the qualifications which they received in their countries of origin.

At present, the validation of skills remains a task that should be performed not by private authorities but by public actors. The public institutions for the recognition of foreign certificates are the Department of Studies, Programmes and Scholastic Issues of the Ministry of Education, the Interdisciplinary Organization for the Certification of Qualifications and Vocational Guidance (EOPPEP in Greek) and the Hellenic National Academic Recognition Information Centre (DOATAP in Greek) (Hellenic National Academic Recognition and Information Centre, 2021). EOPPEP is the National Organization for the Certification of Qualifications and Vocational Guidance, an all-encompassing statutory body that invests in better quality and more efficient and reliable lifelong services in Greece (National Organization for the Certification, 2021).

The process of recognising the qualifications of all Greek citizens, including third-country nationals, does not take into consideration the special circumstances of the refugees, who cannot always obtain/access/translate the relevant documents. This greatly hinders the validation of their skills and the recognition of their qualifications. In order to remove this obstacle, the Council of Europe collaborated with the Ministry of Education, Research and Religious Affairs to implement the European Qualification Passport for Refugees (EQPR) (Council of Europe, 2021). It is a capacity-building project that was launched in 2017, aspiring to validate the level of education, work experience and language proficiency of refugees who do not have their full educational documents. Refugees who have attended at least one year of higher education in their own country can apply for this passport and will receive it after an evaluation process. The document includes the refugee's qualifications and knowledge. However, the EQPR document is so far not recognised as an official document, like a school certificate, so its holders cannot use it either to access public universities or to attend higher education classes. They can only use it to verify their education and therefore to find a job (Council of Europe, 2021).

3 Counselling for Migrants and Refugees: Access to the Labour Market

The positive effect of employment on social inclusion and personal well-being is undoubtedly crucial. Working boosts self-reliance and enables refugees to meet members of the host society. It also provides them with a first-class opportunity to develop their language skills and contributes towards restoring their self-esteem. As such, access to the labour market is a key factor in ensuring an effective social inclusion. However, no public integration policy or strategic plan is in place to facilitate the access of refugees to the labour market.

In Greece, the law allows refugees to work six months after the registration of their asylum claim. According to the law, they have the same working rights and obligations as Greek citizens (UNHCR, 2021a). After registration, they are eligible to acquire a Tax Registration Number and to register with their local unemployment offices, thus receiving their unemployment card. The unemployment card allows them to access jobs posted by the unemployment offices, but does not allow them to apply for programmes run by the unemployment office in the same way as it allows Greeks to do this. In addition, those who work under a legal contract that gets terminated can apply for unemployment benefits.

Since 2019, asylum seekers have received a temporary social security number called PAAYPA when they apply for asylum and a permanent one when their request for asylum is granted (Hellenic Republic Ministry of Migration and Asylum, 2021a).

Although these procedures sound simple, they put refugees at a disadvantage. They must deal with severe obstacles that hinder their access to employment, starting with their lack of Greek language skills, along with their difficulties in obtaining the necessary documents for work and the multiple obstacles from the maze-like bureaucracy. In addition, they find it difficult to have their previously acquired knowledge and skills recognised, and their stay in isolated refugee camps makes it difficult for them to acquire new skills and knowledge. Also, they must face discrimination and a lack of connection to the Greek job market or relevant social networks. To top things off, they also lack familiarity with the local culture and the work environment. Furthermore, they must face high unemployment rates due to the economic recession, from which Greece has not yet fully recovered, plus the COVID-19 pandemic, which reduced the number of available positions even more.

According to our experience at the Athens Solidarity Centre, refugees are less likely to be engaged in paid work than Greeks and more likely to work on temporary jobs or in the informal market—especially those who do not speak a second language and/or have not completed secondary education—often working in packaging, tailoring and as domestic workers. Many also work in migrant-owned shops in big cities.

Those who work without a contract or in temporary jobs are in a more serious situation because they cannot apply for unemployment benefits once their work ends, which can happen at any time, and they can become victims of maltreatment by their employers. In this way, they are denied additional income until they find a new job and additional protection for their rights. Refugees who lack official papers in particular do not usually access counselling services and cannot benefit fully from the counselling sessions, as they cannot get a job with a contract and claim their employment rights. Therefore, they can benefit from training on employment rights.

On the other hand, refugees who are well-educated, are skilled in either Greek or English and have good fortune usually work as interpreters or cultural mediators for NGOs and international organisations on a contractual basis.

In addition, there is no integration policy or strategic plan in place to facilitate refugees' access to vocational training and thus the labour market. Aside from the significant initiative of the state-supported Helios project, which aims to promote the integration of refugees into Greek society, NGOs are the main, and often the only, providers of employability services and vocational training. NGOs have an emphasis on the private sector, and their interventions and activities are based on established patterns of employment services.

All the aforementioned issues mean that the professionals involved in counselling services need to adopt new roles. For example, the role of the navigator who is there to assist the clients through the several administrative issues to access work. Moreover, the counsellors need to help their clients to focus more on their transferable skills rather than their official education. They also need to help them to adapt their previous working experience to the needs of the Greek job market, in order to become more employable. In addition, the counsellors need to take on yet another role, that of the advocate to the authorities with regard to work and education rights.

Finally, the counsellors become mediators between the clients and the different services provided. Since the services are scarce (language courses, vocational courses, psychological support, etc.), the counsellors need to be aware of the opportunities and to connect clients to these as needed. The counsellors also need to become facilitators between the employer and the client, assisting their communication.

Within this framework, it seems that Greece is lacking a policy, or at best has a fragmented policy, regarding the vocational training initiatives for refugees. Since most of the programmes are on a project basis, they depend on external funding, lack sustainability and are by no means part of a general plan and strategy. If we consider the overall economic situation and the fact that the available funding is focused mainly on the humanitarian response rather than integration, it becomes apparent that the refugees' access to training, vocational counselling and consequently the labour market is seriously hindered.

Despite the previously mentioned efforts by NGOs to provide employability support to refugees, there is still a lot of work to be done. The rates of labour absorption, hindered for the last 2 years by the COVID-19 crisis, are still low. Despite the examples of high-skilled refugees employed in the humanitarian sector as interpreters or cultural mediators, their access to the labour market generally remains limited and highly problematic. The pre-existing overall socio-economic situation, which has escalated due to the recent COVID-19 pandemic, and the lack of relevant policies are the main factors that contribute towards the insecurity, precariousness and unemployment amongst refugees.

4 Counselling for Migrants and Refugees: Specific Supportive Measures

Greece, like many EU countries, has placed an emphasis on solving the refugee crisis, but it sets personal trauma, deteriorating physical and mental health and a lack of social support for refugees against a lack of understanding and an inability for many reasons—political, social and economic—to intervene effectively.

In Greece, this intervention is mainly carried out by private organisations and NGOs. By "stepping in", they fill the lack in government policies and in personnel by providing refugees with support for the basic challenges they face such as poverty, social exclusion and marginalisation due to stereotypes, racism and xenophobia within the country. Refugee integration is threatened by the dilemma between needs and the means for successful integration. These good practices are carried out by private organisations, which are generally in partnerships with organisations from either European or other countries, and are therefore usually short term and almost always funded by EU funds. Some examples are provided below:

4.1 Athens Solidarity Centre

The doors of the Athens Solidarity Centre were opened in December 2014 by the NGO SolidarityNow. Since then, it has been an example of cooperation between a public body (the Municipality of Athens), the local civil society, institutional supporters and holistic psychosocial services (SolidarityNow, 2021).

The centre welcomes all people in need indiscriminately—i.e. regardless of nationality, origin, sexual orientation and religious or political beliefs. The only criterion is their vulnerability, for example people with no or low income, refugees and asylum seekers, minorities, NEETs, etc. Over the past 7 years, it has tried to provide an answer to the complex needs that have emerged as a result of the economic crisis and been exacerbated by the refugee crisis. The centre serves hundreds of people in need every day. They receive high-quality free social, psychological and legal support services, employment support services and accountancy services. Since December 2014, it has served 73,000 people from vulnerable groups.

The employability service has operated since 2016 and provides vocational guidance and counselling, support with job searches and networking with potential employers and training programmes, and thus has an important impact on its beneficiaries' livelihood.[3]

4.2 Odyssea Academy

Odyssea is a Greek non-profit organisation that was founded in early 2016 by a group of social entrepreneurs, architects, engineers, financiers and communication experts working together to develop innovative models and solutions to systemic social issues (Odyssea Academy, 2021).

Its goal is to help people to develop new skills and to find work. The academy process includes free vocational training courses for adults in a variety of subjects, education in soft and digital skills and employability services. Courses are intensive and hands-on, taking place at a large training centre equipped with the latest technology and training tools.

4.3 Equality Works

Equal Work and Education for All—Equality Works is an employment and education integration project that was implemented by the NGO Generation 2.0 between March 2020 and August 2021. The project aims to reinforce equal access to work and education for all and provides support and empowerment to unemployed immigrants, refugees, asylum seekers or people outside formal education or vocational education who reside in the prefecture of Attica. In detail, the activities that will be implemented within the framework of the project keep at their core the one-on-one career counselling sessions, while the vocational guidance sessions are reinforced for the people seeking an educational path. At the same time, the participation of individuals in Job Readiness Groups, as well as in the Soft Skills Development Seminars, is encouraged. The Informative Seminars on Labour Rights are supplemented by the Advocacy Training sessions, vital training for equal access. Finally, the Peer Learning, an innovative activity, offers the opportunity of skills

[3] Disclaimer: the writers are currently working/have worked at the Athens Solidarity Centre.

development, with the beneficiaries of the service being the instructors, every time that somebody wants to share their know-how and knowledge in a field (Generation 2.0, 2021).

With regard to self-employment, the project focuses on Women's Social Entrepreneurship to meet the needs for education and guidance towards this end, as well as to help to develop the necessary skills in groups.

4.4 Helios Project

Helios Project (Hellenic Integration Support for Beneficiaries of International Protection) is implemented by the International Organization of Migration (IOM) and receives funding directly from the European Commission's Directorate-General of Migration and Home Affairs (IOM, 2021). It is a fully developed project that is aimed at all adults who are beneficiaries of international protection as well as their families. It caters to the needs of beneficiaries of international protection who have been recognised as such. The purpose of the project is to promote the integration of beneficiaries of international protection and increase their prospects of self-reliance by providing services or activities such as accommodation support, integration-related courses (e.g. Greek language courses, courses for the development of professional skills) and job counselling to enhance job readiness, raise awareness in host communities and promote social cohesion (Hellenic Republic Ministry of Migration and Asylum (2021b).

5 Demographic Change: Introduction

Greece has shown a constant decrease in births since 1932, with the most significant drop between 1980 and 1990. In addition, there has been a further drop in the number of births since the beginning of the financial crisis in Greece in 2010. For the first time this decade, the number of deaths has exceeded the number of births (Hellenic Statistical Authority, 2020b) (cf. Fig. 1). It is worth mentioning that Greece never experienced the post-World War II baby boom of other countries. At the same time, the life expectancy at birth increased from 68 years in 1960 to 82 years in 2019 (World Bank, 2019). The population aged 65+ is now 22% of the total population in Greece, compared to 7% in 60s, following the trend of most Eurozone countries (World Bank, 2020).

The brain drain has also contributed to the ageing workforce, as the net result of immigration in Greece between 2008 and 2018 is 200,000, with most of them being in the critical age range of 25–44 (Hellenic Federation of Enterprises, 2018).

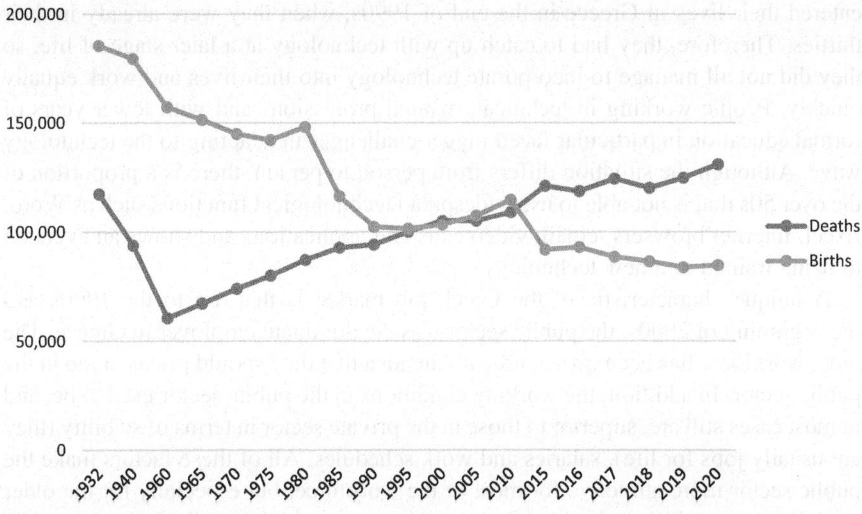

Fig. 1 Births and deaths for the period 1932–2020 in Greece (Hellenic Statistical Authority, 2020b)

6 Demographic Change: The Challenges of an Older Workforce

At the Athens Solidarity Centre, we provide employability services and job-search support for several vulnerable groups. Amongst them, the one that faces several difficulties in finding and retaining decent employment is the older workforce, especially low-skilled workers who are 50+ years old. As Greece is suffering from a financial crisis that has lasted 11 years, many of them are currently long-term unemployed and face severe challenges in re-entering the job market. The main challenges are discrimination by the employers, their lack of modern digital skills, their preference for the public sector and a lack of motivation for re-skilling.

Employers in Greece exhibit a strong preference towards younger personnel, especially those under 40 years old, with a stronger preference for people aged between 20 and 30. As the basic salary in Greece is very low (550 euros/month net), they face difficulties in motivating older employees with this salary level. In addition, they believe that younger personnel are more open to working overtime, in shifts or late in the evening. They also question the reliability of older employees for more manual or labour-intensive jobs that require greater physical strength and stamina (e.g. warehouse workers, drivers or technical professions such as electricians and plumbers). In the case of white-collar office jobs, employers are afraid that older personnel will be more conservative, will find it harder to adapt and will lack digital knowledge and skills. Although it is prohibited as discriminatory practice, many job advertisements are posted with an age limit, usually 35–40 years old.

For the over 50s, computer and network technologies such as Internet, MS Office applications such as Word and Excel and email communication are something that entered their lives in Greece in the end of 1990s, when they were already in their thirties. Therefore, they had to catch up with technology at a later stage of life, so they did not all manage to incorporate technology into their lives and work equally quickly. People working in technical, manual professions and with fewer years of formal education in particular faced bigger challenges in adapting to the technology wave. Although the situation differs from person to person, there is a proportion of the over 50s that is not able to use widespread technological functions such as Word, Excel, Internet browsers, email, video calls and applications and shows an aversion to being trained in a new technology.

A unique characteristic of the Greek job market is that, up to the 1990s and the beginning of 2000s, the public sector was the dominant employer in Greece. The older workforce has been grown up with the idea that they should pursue a job in the public sector. In addition, the working conditions in the public sector used to be, and in most cases still are, superior to those in the private sector in terms of stability (they are usually jobs for life), salaries and work schedules. All of these factors make the public sector more attractive for most of the workforce, but especially for the older workforce that still has the idea that there are a lot of jobs available in the public sector. Since 2010, however, this has not been the case, as public sector positions have suffered heavy cuts, and openings are more and more scarce and highly competitive. Furthermore, the older workforce relies on short-term positions that are announced by the Labour Force Organization for 8-month or 12-month contracts and subsidised by the public budget. The above expectations make them less willing to pursue opportunities in the private sector.

Finally, a section of the older workforce is less willing to undergo re-skilling and to be retrained in their own or alternative professions. They consider training and vocational counselling to be something that should have been done by their 30s and that it is now too late. In the era of COVID-19 and the transfer of most training to an online mode, re-skilling has become less accessible and attractive to this group in connection with the digital skills' gap, as relevant training programmes require some basic or more extensive digital skills, a reliable connection and equipment.

It is worth mentioning that immigrants of the older generation in particular have difficulties in securing even the baseline pension when they approach 67 years of age due to many years of unregistered work in the past and long-term unemployment during the past decade.

The above factors influence the work of the job counsellor. Firstly, the older workforce is more reluctant to ask for help from a career counsellor, as they consider it to be a process that they should have gone through earlier in life. Secondly, they attach more importance to their circumstances and to luck, doubting how much they can do themselves to manage their career. This is a challenge from the counsellor's perspective, as he or she is striving to improve the clients' career management skills. In addition, they are often very disappointed, with a low level of confidence, and sometimes show reluctance to actively engage to the counselling process. Dismissal by employers because of their age further exacerbates the feelings of disappointment.

7 Demographic Change: Opportunities and Sources of Support for Older Workforce

One area in which age does not play such an important role is the area of care, either care of the elderly, childcare or nursing. Meanwhile, care is an increasing job market for the exact same reason—the demographic change—and could be an opportunity for the ageing workforce. Up to now, however, it is low paid and usually unofficial. Furthermore, women are usually preferred to men due to traditional gender roles. Another work opportunity for the older workforce is the different state programmes. The more successful programmes are those in which the older workforce, the over 50s, are employed by municipalities or state-owned organisations with 8- to 12-month contracts. On the other hand, other programmes that subsidise a percentage of the salary of the older employees have not been so successful in motivating employers to hire older personnel. This kind of programme usually requires the employer not to have engaged in dismissals in the previous period, which is rare in financially drained Greece.

Another initiative that is worth mentioning is the ACT 45+ programme, which is implemented by ActionAid Hellas and INE GSEE. It is a part of a European project to support the employment of the under-skilled workforce over 45. Finally, the Athens Solidarity Centre employability service actively supports the older workforce, both Greeks and migrants, with re-entering the job market or accessing training (re-skilling and up-skilling) through career counselling sessions. The centre also provides a computer room and free Wi-Fi for open use. However, more initiatives for this demographic group are necessary.

8 Demographic Change: Suggestions for Vocational Guidance

Access to computer facilities and Wi-Fi can be a substantial measure, especially for individuals with limited resources. The supervision and assistance of personnel is also critical during the use of digital resources, in order to bridge the gap in skills and knowledge and make it less intimidating. A dedicated open-access space with simple equipment that can be used for online training, job interviews and job searches, amongst other things, can be useful. In terms of training in digital or other skills, the older workforce could benefit from a slow exposure to technology and new areas of work and step-by-step training.

The older workforce is often suffering from disappointment and a lack of motivation due to the long-term recession and sometimes long-term unemployment. Efforts to overcome long-term feelings of disappointment and despair should be a goal of the career counsellor. At the same time, they need to support their clients in developing a greater sense of agency for their own lives and help them to create a short-term and medium-term action plan. Finally, they can support them by discussing their perceptions about public sector opportunities with honesty and objectivity, in order to help them to identify real opportunities and manage their expectations.

9 Jobs of the Future: The Future of the Labour Market in Greece: Technology and New Needs

The labour market in Greece has changed during the past decade. The rapid evolution of technology and the new needs that it brought with it have created a new reality. The rapidly advancing technological change made the traditional professions more machine-oriented, which means that traditional functions and operations have changed and/or been replaced by new ones. The new, more machine-oriented operations require a minimum knowledge of digital skills for their successful completion. For example, a traditional warehouse officer or storekeeper is now expected to know (or at least to be able to gain the skill quickly and accurately) how to use a scanner machine or to be able to transmit data in a digital file. This means he or she needs to have at least a basic IT literacy and familiarity with technology.

Starting from 2000, the gradual digitalisation of the manual professions has taken place in Greece, including of course all types of bureaucratic work. More and more companies have started to use computers and to save all their data in digital, electronic files, rather than on paper. After this, the Internet quickly gained a large share of all the economic activities and created new needs such as the need for a website for any commercial activity provided by companies in the private sector. At the same time, manufacturing industries gradually replaced their old-fashioned tools and techniques with modern ones that are adapted to the new era.

During the last three years (starting from 2019), the COVID-19 pandemic has led to a completely different perspective of the modern Greek job market. In a really very short period of time, a rapid digitalisation of many professions took place (except for those that require a human presence in the workplace). Almost every profession in the services sector, also including the public sector, turned to remote work. Professions in the IT sector, teaching, sales, counselling/consultancy and customer services, for example, transferred to a remote basis, using technology and rapidly growing platforms such as Zoom and MS Teams. Following the end of the lockdown periods, many of the companies providing the above services continued to operate—either completely or partially—on a remote basis.

Also, a large part of the sales activities switched to e-commerce, and many physical stores quickly created electronic shops so as not to lose their activity and customers. A significant point to consider is that many physical stores (mostly smaller units) that have not adapted to the new circumstances were unable to survive after the end of the lockdown period.

10 Changes in Human Capital: Technical, Soft Skills and New Flaws of Human Capital

The above-mentioned changes to the job market have led to significant changes in the workforce. New needs appeared in terms of the technical qualifications and the soft skills of the employees. With regard to the technical qualifications, a minimum level of IT literacy is now required for almost any type of work. This means that basic computer literacy skills such as the ability to use email and the Internet, the knowledge of communication platforms such as Skype and at least a basic knowledge of electronic filing and archiving tools such as Microsoft Word and Microsoft Excel. For example, the current minimum requirements for a typical secretarial position in Greece are a knowledge of Microsoft Office, a knowledge of the English language and most likely a university degree.

With regard to the linguistics qualifications for jobseekers/employees in Greece, it is noticeable that more and more companies and jobs have set a minimum requirement of a good English knowledge over the past decade. This phenomenon is a result of the gradual globalisation of the Greek economy and the opening of its activities to foreign markets.

Apart from the need for the English language, (excellent) knowledge of a second or even third language is a strong asset for a jobseeker or a professional in Greece, as it gives a competitive advantage for many job opportunities. As many multinational companies and global call centres have their headquarters or subsidiaries in Greece, the need for multilingual professionals has significantly increased—especially with regard to the French, German, Italian or Arabic languages. Aside from this, strong linguistic skills are mandatory for work in companies in the Greek private sector that are expanding their activities in Europe or overseas, as well as Greek or international NGOs that are getting involved in the field of humanitarian aid/refugees. Qualified bilingual employees with a refugee or migrant background usually fill new positions arising in the field of interpreting or customer services.

Other technical skills required after the "tech revolution" and the digitalisation due to the pandemic include coding skills, a knowledge of databases, web development and web design, advanced office skills, electronic medical prescriptions, e-commerce and social media marketing. For this reason, training in the above skills was offered free of charge to employees as well as unemployed people by various private educational institutions in Greece that are funded by European funds. Other skills currently in demand are logistics skills, project management, HR skills and accounting skills. Familiarity with high-tech devices such as smartphones and tablets is also required by many employers. Also, it is noticeable that a degree from a university, college or technical institution is a minimum requirement to get a skilled job nowadays, as many jobseekers/employees in Greece have at least a master's degree.

Last but not least, more and more attention is being paid to the soft skills of the professionals, something that was not given too much emphasis some years ago. The reason for this is that, as the job market becomes more competitive, employers are looking for those characteristics that match the company's culture and better meet the demands of the role. The soft skills that are in demand in the modern Greek job market are communication, teamwork, critical thought, decision-making, problem-solving, the ability to multitask and emotional intelligence.

Changes in the demographics of Greece due to the large flows of migrants and refugees during the last decade are estimated to lead to changes at the workforce as well. Many refugees with qualifications (language and IT skills, experience in their country of origin, technical skills or academic qualifications) are entering the competition of the Greek job market, looking for opportunities. On the other hand, unskilled migrants and refugees work in areas such as agricultural production, tourism and manufacturing.

11 Conclusions

This chapter has examined the challenges and perspectives of vocational guidance in Greece in relation to the refugee humanitarian crisis, the demographic change and the future of jobs. The ageing workforce in Greece, in combination with their lack of digital skills, results in long-term unemployment for this group and a difficulty in meeting the demands of the available positions. On the other hand, the flow of asylum seekers and refugees can create an opportunity for Greece, as it brings a new flow of skills, experience and knowledge, balancing the effects of the ageing population and the brain drain.

The rapid digitalisation of the public and private sector because of the COVID-19 pandemic can cover Greece's digital gap and modernise the world of work. Counsellors will have to focus more on the development of soft and transferable skills and help clients to embrace the digitalisation of the job market.

The role of vocational counsellors is critical in helping the above groups to recognise their strengths, interests and values, identify opportunities in the environment, build a medium- and long-term plan and goals and re-construct their career, and in connecting them to the most relevant educational and job opportunities. Counsellors need to further expand their role and become advocators, facilitators, mediators and trainers in the future.

References

Council of Europe. (2021). *European qualifications passport for refugees*. https://www.coe.int/en/web/education/recognition-of-refugees-qualifications

Generation 2.0 NGO. (2021). https://g2red.org/equality-works/

Hellenic Federation of Enterprises. (2018). *Study on brain drain executive summary*. https://www.sev.org.gr/Uploads/Documents/Brain_Drain_executive_summary.pdf

Hellenic National Academic Recognition and Information Centre. (2021). http://www.doatap.gr/en/

Hellenic Republic Ministry of Migration & Asylum. (2021a). https://www.gov.gr/upourgeia/upourgeio-metanasteuses-kai-asulou/metanasteuses-kai-asulou/eurese-prosorinou-arithmou-asphalises-kai-ugeionomikes-perithalpses-allodapou-paaupa

Hellenic Republic Ministry of Migration & Asylum. (2021b). *Helios project*. https://migration.gov.gr/en/migration-policy/integration/draseis-koinonikis-entaxis-se-ethniko-epipedo/programma-helios/

Hellenic Statistical Authority. (2020a). *Gross domestic product timeseries*. https://www.statistics.gr/el/statistics/-/publication/SEL15/-

Hellenic Statistical Authority. (2020b). *Natural movement of population 2020*. https://www.statistics.gr/documents/20181/20f115d5-b960-da2b-715f-8c72fc6edf16

Hellenic Statistical Authority (2021). *Workforce timeseries*. https://www.statistics.gr/el/statistics/-/publication/SJO02/-

IOM Office in Greece. (2021). https://greece.iom.int/en

National Organization for the Certification of Qualifications and Vocational Training. (2021). https://www.eoppep.gr/index.php/el/

Odyssea Academy. (2021). https://odyssea.com/about-odyssea/

SolidarityNow NGO. (2021). https://www.solidaritynow.org/en/kentro-allileggiis-athinas/

UNHCR. (2021a). https://help.unhcr.org/greece/living-in-greece/access-to-employment/

UNHCR. (2021b). *Greek fact sheet 2021*. https://data2.unhcr.org/en/documents/details/88966

World Bank. (2019). *Life expectancy at birth*. https://data.worldbank.org/indicator/SP.DYN.LE00.IN

World Bank. (2020). *Population ages 65 and above % of total population*. https://data.worldbank.org/indicator/SP.POP.65UP.TO.ZS

Youth and Lifelong Learning Foundation. (2021). https://www.inedivim.gr/en & https://www.inedivim.gr/en/node/8272

Ireland: Access to Guidance Provision for Migrant Groups within Youth Information and the Further Education Sector

Susan Scott

1 Introduction, Acknowledgement and Recognition of Additional Supports for Disadvantaged Groups

This chapter begins by recognising the ongoing and vital interagency support of national organisations which have specialist remits including information guidance and supports. Services such as: Money Advice & Budgeting Service (MABS), Free Legal Aid Centre (FLAC), Citizens Information Services (CIS), Mediation Services and special interest groups like the Migrants & Refugee Rights groups, although this list is in no way exhaustive.

1.1 Guidance and Counselling Provision at Second-Level Education and in the FET Sector

In line with the requirements of the Irish Education Act 1998 that schools provide students with "access to appropriate guidance to assist them in their educational and career choices" (section 9c), and the implications of the Department of Education's White Paper "Learning for Life" in 2000, guidance provision and adult guidance services in Ireland are embedded in and delivered through education provision and under the remit of the Department of Education. This is very different to the model of career guidance delivery across most of the EU where career guidance is more often a function of the Public Employment Services (PES).

S. Scott (✉)
Crosscare Clondalkin Youth Service (A Dublin Social Care and Youth Work Agency), Dublin, Ireland
e-mail: cysinfo@crosscare.ie

C. Enoch et al. (eds.), *Vocational Guidance in Europe*,
https://doi.org/10.1007/978-3-031-06592-7_6

Nonetheless, guidance-related activities and services also exist outside of the education sectors, but with some significant and noteworthy differences. For example, in Ireland, engagement with public employment services is typically compulsory and can have financial implications for jobseekers, whereby the jobseeker is at risk of penalty if they do not engage. In contrast, the education-embedded career guidance services have no such conditions and engagement is entirely voluntary.

While career guidance services and activities are also provided across other education and labour market sectors, this chapter focuses on voluntary points of contact with career guidance services within second-level, community, FET and the Adult Guidance sector. A framework to explore themes of social inclusion, equality of access and opportunities presented itself more readily within these specific career guidance settings. As a guidance counsellor working within the informal educational setting of Youth Information (which supports disadvantaged and at-risk young people and young adults), barriers and issues identified from our area of expertise are highlighted in this chapter.

In compiling this chapter, the policy work completed by National Centre for Guidance in Education (NCGE, 2016, 2017) to date on behalf of all the stakeholders in career guidance provision is acknowledged. Examples of cooperation, collaboration and opportunities to share good practice are used, and a number of reports and recommendations have already been made about career guidance provision in Ireland which inform our discussion.[1]

2 The Role of the National Centre for Guidance in Education (NCGE)

The National Centre for Guidance in Education is the agency of the Irish Department of Education with responsibility for leading and shaping guidance policy and practice to enable learners to make informed and appropriate life choices. NCGE's mission is to develop, support and influence guidance policy and quality guidance provision in the education and training sector as part of lifelong learning in accordance with national and international best practice.

Amongst the tasks undertaken by NCGE since 2011 is the twice-yearly hosting of the National Forum on Guidance (NFG) on behalf of the Department of Education. This provides stakeholders with an opportunity to discuss issues of interest and development in guidance across all sectors. NCGE (2016, 2017) convenes working groups and committees to focus on specific issues pertaining to guidance on behalf

[1]For more general information about the VET and the counselling system in Ireland, you can find more information on these Websites: https://www.asti.ie/document-library/presentation-from-ine-hyland-emeritus-professor-of-education/https://careersportal.ie/courses/calculator/pointsCalculator.html

of the Department of Education and the Department of Further and Higher Education, research Innovation and Science.

Significant to this chapter, the "Adult Education Guidance Initiative" (AEGI) was established on a "pilot" basis in 2000 in response to Learning for Life: White Paper on Adult Education (2000) which describes "guidance" as referring to *"a range of activities designed to assist people to make choices about their lives and to make transitions consequent upon those choices*".

The AEGI offered free and confidential Career Guidance and Information Services to adults (over 18 years of age) including impartial adult educational information, one-to-one and group career guidance to help people make informed educational, career and life choices. From 2000 to 2007 the AEGI evolved through 4 "Pilot Phases" from 11 local services based in the Vocational Education Committee (main providers of Adult and Literacy Education, VECs) to 39 local VEC-based AEGIs.

The AEGI had National Coordination support from NCGE through the "pilot phases", developing an adaptive, professional and accountable model of Adult Guidance and Information delivery. Following significant developments and the incorporation of "Adult Education" into "Further Education and Training" along with the establishment of SOLAS and the amalgamation of the 37 VECs to 16 Education and Training Boards, the AEGI became more usually referred to as the *Adult Education Guidance Services* and are housed in the local ETB. As the ETB AEGS operate within the ETB Further Education and Training (FET) sector, the 2012 DES AEGI Operational Guidelines remain in place pending the development of a nationally agreed Guidance Strategy in FET (DES, 2021).

Information and Guidance Services in the Further Education and Training (FET) sector provide impartial careers and education information and one-to-one and group guidance, which help people make informed educational, career and life choices. FET Information and Guidance Services are provided to adults aged 18 years and over, and those over 16 who have left school early who are interested in or participating in programmes on the National Framework of Qualifications Levels 1–6.

NCGE has the responsibility to advise DoE and DFHERIS regarding policy and practice in Guidance as provided in the FET sector through various services, including

- FET / Adult Education Guidance Services.
- Colleges of Further Education (CFEs) and PLC Programmes.
- Youthreach / CTCs.
- Training Centres.
- Adult and Community Education.
- Prison Services.

The delivery of Further Education and Training is the responsibility of the 16 Education and Training Boards (ETBs), funded by SOLAS (the further education and training authority). Guidance in Further Education and Training is informed by the DES (2014) Further Education and Training Strategy.

July 2020 saw the launch of the SOLAS FET Strategy *"Future FET: Transforming Learning"* which as stated by DFHERIS Minister Harris is "an ambitious new strategy based around the three core pillars of building skills, fostering inclusion, and facilitating pathways". While impartial, professional and integrated Guidance Counselling facilitates all three "core pillars" of the SOLAS Strategy, notable is SOLAS' statement on page 54 of the Strategy:

> 7.4 Facilitating Lifelong Pathways: Critical to facilitating lifelong learning pathways is the pivotal role of ETBs in providing guidance on education, training, employment and careers to all within their regions. The approach to guidance is inconsistent across FET settings and provision, and this must be rectified with an integrated approach to guidance across ETBs. This should ensure that impartial guidance is available to all who seek it within the ETB region, and that the ETB positions itself to ensure that it works effectively for all FET provision and all FET learners. Despite many different information resources, FET also lacks a good centralised single 'go to' IT portal which can offer more accessible information and advice without the need for face-to-face contact, and FET must support the development of such a resource as recommended by the recent Government Review of Career Guidance. This must include accessible labour market intelligence that can inform potential learners of the likely available future job and career opportunities from particular course choices.

3 An Introduction to Integration in Ireland

Ireland has a history of weathering economic recessions and has more experience of outward migration and emigration, so after two and a half decades of incoming migration it is all still relatively new to us to manage and plan for. A figure of just over 11.5% of the population in the 2016 census is mentioned as being of migrant origin. The foreword of the recent Department of Justice and Equality's Migration Integration Strategy 2017 (MIS) speaks of Ireland having an opportunity to "get it right, to build on what has been done before and to plan for the future". It anticipates that "inward migration will continue over the next decades and that Ireland will remain culturally diverse into the future" (Dept., of Justice & Equality, 2017, p 6).

It also envisages greater participation of second- and third-generation migrants at all levels of society in the decades ahead. The Strategy is the first step towards realising the long-term vision of Ireland as a society in which migrants and those of migrant origin play active roles in communities, workplaces and politics. It sees the guiding principles for Ireland of the future as those of solidarity and opportunity for all, underpinned by respect for diversity (as above p 6).

MIS (Dept of Justice & Equality 2017, p 6) recognises that "migrants have differing needs and opportunities depending on their circumstances". Under specific actions (as above p 5) it lists

- Monitoring of current school enrolment policies over time to assess their impact on the enrolment of migrant students.
- The inclusion of a language component in education and training programmes for unemployed migrants with poor English proficiency.

- Initiatives to ensure that migrant needs in relation to skills acquisition and labour market activation are addressed.

Themes of social inclusion, educational disadvantage, economic marginalisation and "breaking the cycle" of poverty are well known in Ireland. Various policies and practical measures to tackle issues for different sections of the population have been developed and implemented over the years (Dept. of Social Protection Social Inclusion Policies, 20th Sept 2019).

Ireland has experienced a high level of social, economic and educational change in a relatively short time frame. It was once common practice for people to leave school at 14 years to enter the workforce. The introduction of measures now seen as pivotal such as "free second-level schooling" in 1967 created an opportunity for many people to extend their educational experience and widen their career options. Reflections on this measure 50 years on can be found in ASTI (2018). Development of alternative educational routes to formal second-level schooling namely "Youthreach" in 1989 was another such measure where young people who had disengaged from the mainstream provision could be re-engaged and catered for in more appropriate way (ESRI, 2019).

The opening up of diverse employment opportunities widened career horizons. Expansion of "vocational training" introduced the concept of Post Leaving Courses (PLCs) in 1985 with the support of the European Social Fund. Such changes increased accessibility to further and third-level options and in turn enhanced social mobility and inclusion policies and practices. ERSI (2019, Vol 50, No. 3 Autumn 2019, pp 557–585)

Subsequent reforms like the addition of two extra formats to accompany the Established Leaving Certificate Exam in 1994/5 have also helped more young people to remain in school and complete second-level education. The Community Development Sector simultaneously grew in strength and was a key player in lobbying and advocating for greater social and structural supports for people. Particularly for those who found themselves in new "green field" communities without adequate resources. This social alienation created problems including anti-social behaviour and increased marginalisation and at times lack of employment options. Community development here is understood as

> a process whereby those who are marginalised and excluded are enabled to gain in self-confidence to join with others and participate in actions to change their situation and to tackle problems that face their community (Lee, 2003).

4 Growth of Guidance Provision

All these factors had an impact on improving social and economic mobility and creating more diverse learning and training pathways for people to consider. Coupled with the policy, financial and infrastructural supports, a range of localised and national services were also put in place which could offer people a more personalised approach to help them maximise their options in life. This included

Guidance provision in a variety of settings including secondary school, youth information and within the community, FET and Adult Education sectors.

An article on the *"History of Counselling in Ireland for the Journal of Counseling & Development. July 2012. Volume 90 371"* offers a comprehensive contextual background to how the interaction of State, Church, development of marriage counselling and economic conditions all played their part in the rise and recognition of the practice of counselling in Ireland. It goes on to say that in the last 30 years (to when the article was written) "Ireland experienced rapid growth and public attitudes towards counselling become more positive, especially with the increased secularisation of a once strongly religious Catholic society."

The article describes a "second phase of counselling in Ireland as beginning in the 1960s, when career guidance counselling was initially introduced to vocational training schools in Dublin (Chamberlain, 1983)". These schools prepared students for occupations and "operated outside of the Church jurisdiction". The Church did however "largely control primary and secondary education". Secondary level or post-primary in Ireland as it is commonly known tends to refer to a more academic school system. The article continues by saying that

> The idea of providing career guidance counseling to second level schools spread to them in the 1960s as well (Chamberlain, 1983). The psychological service of the Irish Department of Education and Skills supported this development. As part of this movement, University College Dublin introduced a course for career guidance teachers in the 1960s, emphasizing counseling as well as career choice. More recently, the term guidance counselors has been adopted, which is the equivalent of school counselors in the United States (O'Morain, 2012).

The foundation of the Institute of Guidance Counsellors (IGC) in 1968 further promoted "professionalism among counsellors within second-level schools" and "third-level colleges and universities), adult guidance services, private practice, and in other settings in Ireland" (IGC, 2021). The author suggests that "despite these beginnings, the concept of counselling in Ireland did not take hold in the general population until the 1970s".

A role description for secondary school Guidance Counsellors as outlined in Grad Ireland (2021) specifies that they "advise students and young people so they can make more informed choices about their future in relation to employment education and training". It details that amongst the responsibilities are "assessing ability and potential in students, providing one to one counselling and liaising with other professionals in the area". Reminding us that "Guidance counselling in Ireland is made up of 3 separate but interlinked areas: personal and social guidance counselling; educational guidance and vocational guidance and counselling."

NCGE by Consultation re Guidance Counselling Qualifications developed the "Programme Recognition Framework" (PRF). In March 2016, the Department of Education and Skills published this Framework. The PRF sets out criteria and guidelines for providers of initial education programmes in guidance counselling who intend that their programme graduates will work in guidance services under the remit of the Department. The Department of Education and Skills recognises graduates from initial education programmes in guidance counselling from working in educational institutions under the remit of the Department. This includes School and Further Education (FE) settings (such as Colleges of Further Education, PLCs and the Adult Education Guidance Services—AEGS).

The pressures on second-level school guidance counselling services have been documented along with the request for the restoration of the ex-quota guidance allocation. For further information on School Guidance Counsellors, please see the Houses of the Oireachtas Dail Eireann Debate (2019).

Due to the high demands of the second-level guidance counselling role, a decision is often made to concentrate more time on students in exam years. The increasing complexity in young people's personal lives for example anxiety, school refusal and poor mental health all play a part in stretching the resources of school guidance provision.

In 2017, NCGE launched their "NCGE Whole School Guidance Framework (WSGF)", followed in 2019 by professional development training for Guidance Counsellors and the managers/principals of post-primary schools. This Framework has now been adopted by over half of the post-primary schools in Ireland, and this has radically changed delivery of guidance counselling in that context.

Challenges to resources, staffing and priorities of pandemic responses have tempered further WSGF training; however, online webinars and CPD provision has been welcomed by post-primary guidance counsellors across Ireland. The WSGF model was developed collaboratively following National Consultations in 2016. It supports schools in planning and delivering a comprehensive whole school guidance programme that meets the needs of all students. The Framework presents a continuum of support model for the school guidance programme and sets out three areas of learning to facilitate post-primary students' development in 8 areas of competence.

The areas of learning include "understanding oneself" (personal/social development), "educational opportunities" (educational development) and "career decision-making" (career development). A social constructivist approach to guidance-related learning and development with the term "career learning and development is used". Careers are viewed as being socially constructed through a range of learning experiences and interactions with others (peers, parents, teachers, guidance counsellors, employers and so on). This approach helps the guidance conversation to be supported across the whole school community and beyond (NCGE WSGF, 2017).

5 Guidance Counselling Supporting "Key Transitions" in School

A number of key decisions and transition are made during second-level school, and knowledge of these, along with their options and choices (or lack thereof), is important if students and parents are to make the best of the system on offer. During this process Guidance Counsellors have a range of educational systems and structures to explain to students and their parents. But for various reasons—some of this information gets lost in the process.

For many migrant students and parents this might be the first point of contact with the world of guidance. It is important for school guidance therefore to identify potential barriers to understanding and to ensure young people and families from disadvantaged backgrounds get the support they need to explore these options in a timely way. Subject choice for Leaving Certificate has a bearing on the types of third-level (University) college course that can be applied for. Similarly understanding the "Points System" is equally important as courses are allocated on a points basis. See Careers Portal (2021), for calculating your points. Choosing from one of the 3 Leaving Cert Exam options has major implications as one of them does not equip you with the immediate option of applying to the Central Application Office (CAO, 2016, 2021) for a third-level course. Effectively applying for courses and navigating the CAO (who for a fee process the college applications and distribute the offers) can be a daunting experience for some students and their parents. Making mistakes and missing deadlines can lose a person an offer of a desired course. The IGC (2021) have a resource for parents and sixth year students called "6th Year the results are out—what now?" This explains how the points and course allocations work.

Awareness of other training and education options such as apprenticeships, traineeships and the direct application process for PLCs available in the FET sector is invaluable if people are to make full use of all the options. Understanding the progression options and specific routes to move seamlessly between the different educational levels is necessary. Securing funding for college including the Government Maintenance Grant known as SUSI (2021) and being aware of the specific "access" pathways such as HEAR and DARE are all crucial knowledge bases to acquire (IUA, 2021). A written submission, to the Joint Oireachtas Committee on Education and Skills: *Barriers to Education facing vulnerable groups* by Kathleen Lynch (2018, p 3), discussed how education is both an intrinsic and positional good—intrinsic in enabling a person to exercise capabilities, choices and freedoms generally in life, helping them realise other rights and enabling them to overcome other social disadvantages.

In its role as a *positional good* "it enables the person to gain social advantages vis-à-vis others, particularly in relation to employment".

> The more and better a person's educational credentials one has the more likely one is to gain good and profitable employment and be able to exercise political power and influence (Lynch, 2018, p 3)

Education is also described as *a public good* enriching cultural, social, environmental, political and economic life for all of society, where "the collective value of education is greater than the sum of its personal value to individuals" (Lynch, 2018, p 3) . Her research suggests that vulnerable groups face several ongoing challenges in relation to benefiting from education. She acknowledges that some children from these groups have highly specific barriers such as travellers, those in State (social) care, or in direct provision, but that

> all children and families share one common factor that impacts on their ability to benefit from formal education, namely their access to economic resources that enable them to compete equally with others. (Lynch, 2018, p 6)

She says this fact applies to all groups including those from ethnic minority backgrounds, but

> how these resources are translated into competitive advantage for different groups varies considerably, but the sociological fact remains that any vulnerability is exacerbated by lack of money (Lynch, 2018, p 6)

It is interesting to note the use of the phrase *"cultural capital such as insider knowledge of how systems work"*. From a Youth Information perspective, understanding these very systems and pathways often presents barriers and challenges to students and parents alike. Part of the NCGE WSGF mentioned earlier is a move towards facilitation and enhancing communication with parents, guardians, other agencies and appropriate supports. The WSGF recognises and embraces inputs and expertise from other services with direct experience of engaging with this cohort. The feedback received from information practitioners stated that migrant groups experience difficulties and barriers in understanding and accessing some of these systems including "education". It could be suggested that part of a Youth Information role is to help people cultivate some of this "insider knowledge".

6 The Intersection of Formal School Guidance and Youth Information Work

In many instances, this is where the intersection of formal school guidance and Youth Information work often takes place. A typical query might be about any or all of the above key educational themes/systems/transitions presented earlier. At other times a parent might simply say that their child/student is not doing well in school and ask about other options. Part of that Youth Information conversation is to initially re-direct the parents back towards school supports like guidance and the student support team. This can be particularly important especially if the parent does not know that those supports exist within the school.

A second task might be to assist the parents in framing their questions, concerns or needs, so that they are fully heard by the school. This can involve an informal talk through "any anticipated issues", guiding the conversation so that essential points are covered and strengthening the person's voice and personal confidence in dealing with school personnel. This is particularly important for some parents who may have a fear of dealing with the authorities or the education system or who have had a negative school experience themselves. Similarly, people from non-traditional backgrounds may need more time to absorb and discuss the information and be assisted to "know what to ask for". Another option is for the Youth Information Officer (YIO) to contact the school guidance colleagues on behalf of the family. An open arrangement currently exists where the YIO also takes calls from colleagues in the school on behalf of students and parents to see what additional supports the Youth Service or the community setting can offer them. The Department of Education guidelines state that guidance should be a key aspect of Adult Literacy and Community Education programmes and should be available at all stages, including pre-entry and pre-exit, on an integrated basis.

The Adult Educational Guidance Service (AEGS) provides personal, educational and vocational guidance, which supports learners to make informed decisions about course choice and certification (if required), progression plans, recognition of prior learning (RPL), etc. Guidance in Back to Education Initiatives (BTEI) including progression plans, RPL, etc. may be formal and non-formal. Delivery of Outreach "Educational Pathways" guidance information sessions can be given to groups of adult learners in or integrated with local employment service provision. This is quite like the work undertaken by the YIO who would also be invited to "take an information stand" or "make a presentation" at a Parent's Night or Open Event in a local school. These are invaluable opportunities to take guidance work out of the office or centre and into the community. It also provides Youth Information services with an additional opportunity to publicise our services which are available out of school hours and when schools are closed during the summer holidays.

These outreach, network and training events also give parents with more complex or personal needs an additional route to get assistance and information independently of the school setting. Both the Youth Information and Youth Service have strong links with our local second-level schools in the area, with particular supports given to the Tusla Education Support Service (2021) School Completion Programme (SCP) and "iScoil" (2021) re-engagement initiative for early school leavers.

The YIO role can be viewed as part of a community chain of guidance supports. In some local circumstances, this has evolved very organically. The location of Clondalkin Youth Information and Youth Service in West Dublin is within an Adult Education complex which also houses Adult Guidance services and a "Youthreach" Centre. On a practical level, this facilitates a more personalised response with quick and effective cross-referral to each of our respective services.[2]

7 Challenges to Equity of Service Delivery

There are significant challenges in the equity of service delivery nationally, and development of a "Whole of Government" approach underpinning the "community chain" of supports is needed to ensure fair treatment for all into the future. One of the weaknesses identified to more comprehensive guidance delivery service is historical allocation which applies equally for Youth Information provision resulting in no coverage for young people in certain counties. A similar finding in the evaluation of

[2]For more detailed information about guidance for young people, please visit: https://www.tusla.ie/services/educational-welfare-services/scp/For students: https://www.iua.ie/ourwork/access/

the National Youthreach Programme under Policy implications ERSI (2019, p 20) mentions that "the location of Youthreach and Community Training Centres is geographically variable and largely reflects legacy issues rather than current need".

The emergence of the Further Education and Training (FET) sector in Ireland since 2014 highlighted the need for a strategic approach to guidance and information delivery.

8 Expanding the Reach of Youth Information through Collaboration

An interagency approach to "raise the profile and improve the reach" of Youth Information Services was undertaken in 2020 in conjunction with the online Youth Information provider Spunout (2021). The Youth Information Network comprises a small collection of Youth Information Officers/workers from the key Youth Work Agencies located throughout the country (many of them on part-time hours or with their time divided between Youth Work and YI). The Youth Information Live Chat partners are Youth Work Ireland (YWI), Young Men's Catholic Association (YMCA) and our Youth and Social Care Agency (Crosscare) and Spunout.

This Youth Information Live Chat initiative involves the YI workers providing cover for evening shifts from 4 to 8 pm during the week where young people, young adults, parents and youth workers can access a "person-to-person" Live Chat. During the "Chat" they get the information and guided supports they require and/or referral to other specialists for their issues. A 24/7 free Crisis text service is available too for young people if they would like someone to talk to beyond the Live Chat operational hours. There is a ticket service for "out of hours queries received" and these are answered each evening by the staff providing the Chat service. To date this has proved a successful and valuable service. A high number and a wide variety of queries have been received and answered from the general public, as well as from migrant and other under-represented groups. Please find a few samples below from our Live Chat data collection system relating to migrant type queries.

Migrant—can I stay in Ireland if I study or get a job

Migrant—How do I move to Ireland to work and study? What do I need to do to move from Africa?

Direct Provision—Can I get SUSI if I live in Direct Provision?

Asylum seeker—Can I access SUSI if I am an asylum seeker?

Asylum seeker—How to register a child for stamp 4 visa (they had previously been on their parent's visa but are now 16)

Asylum seeker—I had legal status to live in Ireland when my parents make the application but my parent made a mistake and then they took back our

(continued)

visas. So I don't have any documents but want to apply for grants for college. Can I still do that/

Citizenship—I have a PPS number, does that mean I am a citizen in Ireland?

Citizenship—Can I access the healthcare system if I am not a citizen?

Citizenship—My parents want to apply for citizenship through naturalization but we don't understand how to do it?

Another advantage of this service is the opportunity for an "in-centre" or "face-to-face referral" to take place. For example, if a query is received from a person in a county where there is a nearby Youth Information Service, a personalised referral to that service can be made with the person's permission. This is usually offered when the person has high needs or presents with a complex query that would benefit from the personal face contact, supports and follow-up.

9 Youth Information and Youth Services: Allies in the Inclusion and Integration Process

A Youth Information Services offer a suite of programmes to young people (15–25 years) and "those acting on their behalf". Provision of Youth Information is located within the Youth Work Sector in Ireland. It combines the Principles of Youth Work where applicable, but has its own specialised skills set. It is recognised that styles of Youth Information provision vary across the different European countries.

A recently completed *Youth Information Competency Framework* developed at a European wide level is due to be launched. This was done to assist providers explain and promote Youth Information work and to ensure more effective recruitment of staff who embrace the competencies, ethos and ideals and practices of YI work. It is envisaged that this Competency Framework will guide future discussion about professional recognition and protection for Youth Information providers working in this sector (EURODESK & ERYICA, 2021).

The European Youth Information Charter—Adopted in Cascais (Portugal) on 27 April 2018—by the General Assembly on the European Youth Information and Counselling Agency (ERYICA, 2018) states that:

> Access to information and the ability to analyse and use information is increasingly important for young people in Europe and beyond. Youth Information helps them achieve their aspirations and promotes their participation as active members of society. Information should be provided in ways that enlarge the choices available to young people, and that promote their autonomy and empowerment (EURODESK & ERYICA, 2021).

Youth Information providers subscribe to the belief that Youth Information is a right for young people which supports the democratic process. The ERYICA Charter (2018) says that

> Generalist Youth Information work covers all topics of interest to young people and can include a spectrum of activities such as: informing, counselling, supporting, coaching, training, networking, and referral to specialist services in-order to empower young people (EURODESK & ERYICA, 2021).

This Charter outlines the principles of Youth Information work as being independent, accessible, inclusive, needs based, empowering, participative, ethical, professional and proactive.

> A right to information has also been recognised in the Universal Declaration of Human Rights, in the Convention on the rights of the Child, and in the European Convention for the Protection of Human Rights and Fundamental Freedoms in the Council of Europe concerning information and counselling for young and young people's access to rights (EURODESK & ERYICA, 2021).

Youth Information is a complementary arm of Youth Work where young people and those acting on their behalf can get access to free, confidential, impartial information within a supported environment. This can be done independently or through their connections with Youth Services. It is there to support the Youth Workers as a resource to their own roles and may also be seen as a type of "public good" in the community. Youth Work activities can be free for some and are generally low cost for all. They introduce young people and those at risk and/or with fewer opportunities to different group activities. These include drama, arts, outdoor learning, sports, media and special interest topics. "Peer-to-peer learning" is a key concept within Youth Work. It is a developmental process and cultivates leadership skills while promoting the concept of volunteering and giving something back to the community/society. Exposure to new horizons through social and informal learning opportunities takes place through EU-funded activities like Youth Exchanges. As well as the "fun element", developing positive peer and significant adult relationships is a very important outcome in Youthwork. A clear social inclusion remit underpins Youth Work where activities are flexible and respond to the growing needs of young people and families especially those alienated from mainstream provision. The vision of Youth Work is:

> for all of our young people to have ambition for themselves, to be confident individuals, effective contributors, successful learners and responsible citizens; and to be nurtured, safe, active, healthy, achieving, included, respected and responsible. We believe that youth work has a significant role to play in realising this vision for young people (NYCI, 2020)

NYCI represents the interests of the Youth Sector, develops policies, promotes good practice and conducts research on behalf of young people and young adults engaging with Youth Work Services. Their report ***"Make Minority a Priority"*** NYCI (2020) shares insights from minority ethnic young people growing up in Ireland. It makes recommendations to Youth Sector Organisations on how they might improve approaches to inclusion of youth from migrant backgrounds. 50 young people aged 15–24 years from 20 different ethnic backgrounds took part in the research. The themes covered were on "identity and belonging"; "parental and community relationships"; "racism and exclusion"; "leadership skills"; and "integration". There is a body of learning from the Youth Sector that could also be utilised within more formal educational settings. Lack of awareness of the current resources available from this sector is a missed opportunity for promoting inclusion and integration activities.

In the *Evaluation of the National Youthreach Programme* ESRI (2018, p 21) under *"Governance"* the findings suggest greater scope for ETBs to play a role in encouraging the sharing of good practice across the two settings of Youthreach and the Community Training Centres. This could be taken further to include other settings like that of the Youth Work sector who are also under the jurisdiction of local ETBs.

The "development of" and "value placed on" personal skills with young people from all backgrounds is a major aim within the Youth Work sector. But the lack of recognition of the value placed on these soft skills for vulnerable young people has also been flagged in the Youthreach evaluation. ESRI (2018, p xii).

> Current metrics for reporting on the programme are seen as progressing the aim of progression in education, training and employment but coordinators/managers and learners expressed frustration at not being able to capture the value of the programme in enhancing the personal and social skills (such as communication and organisational skills) of young people using the programme.

These are essential skills sets for young people to develop if they are to re-engage fully with formal structures and embed themselves more firmly in the life of the community and society. A second resource developed for the Youth Sector by NYCI called *Skills Summary* was designed with youth in mind and is helpful for those who want to develop their skills with a view towards employment. It can be individually accessed for those with strong IT and motivational skills or can be used in a supported environment such as a Youth Work or training setting.

10 How Are Alternative Training and Education Options Accessed?

If "alternative training and education" options are sought by a parent or young people from the YIO, then the range of available options are presented, and clients are encouraged or facilitated to make direct contact with those services.

Listed below are for some alternative learning settings from one community alone in West Dublin. Examples include Clondalkin Youthreach, YESS, ALP, Rosse Court Training Centre, Carline and Sportivate. A local version of these kinds of options are often replicated throughout the country, but there may be a higher concentration of services in the bigger towns and cities.

One disadvantage as an information provider is that it is difficult to know exactly what services are there, without a central point of reference. This gap of a centralised "go-to" resource was also acknowledged in the 2018/2019 DoE *Review of Career Guidance* and is a significant challenge to guidance provision in the FET sector. There is wide recognition of the need for a more coordinated response including developing appropriate cross-sector channels of communication and continuity of support.

The Youthreach Programme referred to earlier was developed in 1989 by the government in response to high numbers of Early School Leavers (ESLs) in Ireland. It remains the main national programme providing young people with access to second chance education and training. Educational and social supports are delivered through Youthreach Centres and Community Training Centres (CTCs). This evaluation was commissioned by the State Agency SOLAS under the Department of Education and Skills (DES) led strategy 2014–2019. Key findings in this evaluation note that while numbers of ESLs have dropped over the years, the young people who are presenting as participants are "more marginalised and with greater levels of need" (ESRI, 2019, p xii).

Coupled with this is "a prevalence of mental health difficulties amongst this group". With many experiencing "trauma (adverse childhood experiences)" and exposure to substance misuse. It is suggested that the staff need additional resources to increase their capacity to respond to these "complex needs", if they meet the DES requirements to

> provide early school leavers (16–20years) with the knowledge, skills and confidence required to participate fully in society and progress to further education, training and employment (ERSI, 2019, p xi).

Lynch (2018, p17) speaks about how children's education cannot be prioritised when family tension is created through poverty:

> Two major national studies by Annette Lareau (2006) in the US and Richard Layte in the UK (2017) both show how family resources impact on how parents interact with each other and relatedly with their children. Lack of money and resources increases stress in families, which in turn, impacts negatively on children emotionally and even cognitively; this has a downward spiralling impact on their educational performance. Very poor families in particular experience considerable anxiety over lack of resources, which, in turn, lead to personal conflicts; this means that time is invested in managing poverty and its attendant tensions so children's education cannot be prioritised

Geographical access was noted as one potential barrier to young people accessing a Youthreach or CTC and an interesting point was made about how

> informal networks are commonly used to access information about Youthreach prior to entry. This means that for some groups of learners, particularly those with a migrant background, may not have access to these networks and are therefore unaware of the programme. Furthermore, the interviews with learners highlight the part played in negative school experience, negative relationships with teachers, learning and mental health difficulties (ESRI, 2019, p xii).

Additional points of learning which can be taken away from this evaluation include inequity of provision of service in terms of facilities and resources. It also mentions contractual difference and difficulties in retention of staff. It implies that stress and the impact of unequal resourcing lowers staff moral and affects relationships with students which are key to positive re-engagement in this context.

> The learners interviewed contrasted the level of support and care they received in Youthreach with the negative relations they had with their teachers in mainstream education (ESRI, 2019, p xiv).

Contributors report that supporting high mental health needs requires adequate counselling supports, but there is a difficulty in securing referral to external psychological services. Centres which are part of the Special Education Needs Initiative (SENI) "receive additional funding" and were more likely to be able to contact and connect in with external agencies and supports. Access to Guidance for Youthreach learners although viewed as an "important support mechanism" is "variable across centres", ESRI (2019, p 21), which suggests

> the need to consider more focused progression planning for learners, increased one to one contact with staff to discuss future plans and the introduction of 'bridging courses' to facilitate transitions to further education, training or employment. They also advocate for 'ensuring a continuity of supports for learners over the transition, especially in terms of mental health.

The current SOLAS FET Strategy 2020–2024 (p 52) envisages a restructuring and simplification of the current provision to aid more successful transitions especially for this cohort. It says there is a need to link their training to "pathways within FET and beyond", to ensure it evolves to meet the changing and more complex need of learners.

11 Adult Guidance and Youth Information: Potential to Collaborate and Better Meet the Need of Groups

The model of Adult Guidance delivered through the (ETB) AEGS is hugely influential in assisting marginalised people to avail of return to education, retraining, social participating and exploring career progression options. Although only one element of FET guidance provision, the (ETB) AEGS model includes provision of impartial and professional guidance to the general public and to target groups (including migrants, international protection applicant, literacy, numeracy, digital skills and language learners and community education). This Adult Guidance model is integrated into the wide arena of FET provision. This implies extensive access to wide client groups including the most marginalised and specific migrant communities.

As noted, there is crossover in terms of the age groups that Youth Information and Adult Guidance work with. The Youth Information age remit is 15–25 years and Adult Guidance services assist young people 16+ from an ESL or "not in education or training" (NEETS) background.

Both Adult Guidance and Youth Information are highly "relational" specialities. They take information and guidance out of centre to "where people are", they develop and modify resources to make them more applicable to respective client groups and they put people first in the guidance conversation. They also cross-refer people and actively act or advocate on their behalf in certain situations to ensure the best outcome for them.

For a comprehensive view of Guidance provision across all sectors in Ireland and with specific reference to guidance provision for immigrants, please refer to the following document from CEDEFOP (2020) *inventory of lifelong guidance and practices—Ireland.*

AEGS work with asylum seekers, migrants and international applicants and NCGE has also supported the IRC Irish Refugee Council with the development of an information booklet. NCGE delivered an information sharing and good practice training session on *Social Inclusion Challenges and Opportunities* in 2019. This brought cross-sector services providers together to share information on specific training and employment programmes for migrant groups. It also presented research on racism and discrimination in the Irish workplace.

In 2020, NCGE published overarching research from their Adult Guidance Management system. This refers to their work with Adult Guidance clients and outlines the ethos and methodologies employed, including qualitative feedback from recipients of the service. A section on "Barriers to participation and progression for clients accessing FET services" NCGE AGMS (2020, p 54) says that the current AGMS categories of barriers are largely "situational" whereby these barriers stem from "a person's personal circumstances". The reports cites previous research on barriers in the FET sector where a different conceptual view of barriers is taken under the headings of: "motivational/ dispositional, economic/social-welfare, organisations and informational/guidance".

A visual snapshot of the barriers faced by FET participants can be found in NCGE AGMS (2020, Chart 49, p 55). The research says that "typical clients face numerous barriers, but the recording system only allows for the recording of 1 barrier per client or an option to choose 'combination'". Breaking down those barriers and promoting social inclusion remains a key priority for the (ETB) AEGS, linked to the SOLAS aim to expand "FET access for socially, economically or educationally disadvantaged groups" DES (2014, p.5). What is significant throughout the "pilot" phase and the emergence of the (ETB) AEGS model is that an expectation of local "networks" to facilitate the delivery of appropriate supports for all was envisaged. This expectation faces the challenge of the massive change in the delivery of FET in Ireland, again presenting "pockets" of excellent supports without the consistency that would make the "networking" of supports an expectation everywhere.

In Sect. 6 *"Fostering Inclusion"* of the current SOLAS Future FET: Transforming learning—The National Further Education & Training (FET) Strategy 2020–2024 (p 43) the commitment to Social Inclusion is reaffirmed

> fostering Active Inclusion and community development have always been a central tenet of the work of ETB's and FET providers, with extensive reach into and across local communities. FET ensures that supports are available to allow any individual, regardless of background or formal education level, an opportunity to learn and develop.

The implementation of the SOLAS FET Strategy—*Future FET: Transforming Learning 2020–2024* (p 54) states that

> Despite many different information resources, FET also lacks a good centralised single 'go to' IT portal which can offer more accessible information and advice without the need for face-to-face contact, and FET must support the development of such a resource as recommended by the recent Government Review of Career Guidance.

This must include accessible labour market intelligence that can inform potential learners of the likely available future job and career opportunities from particular course choices.

12 Discrimination and Inequalities for Migrants in the Irish Workforce

Current research on the migrant experience in the Irish workforce clearly points to inequalities and discrimination existing in different employment sectors. It details specific employment sectors where this is happening and in what ways it is experienced by different migrant groups. The additional support roles that guidance, information and advocacy can play for migrant groups when accessing employment and combating discrimination have also been flagged.

Lynch (2018, p 21) referred to earlier in this chapter adds additional insights into the belief that "equal opportunity for all based on merit within the Irish education system" is possible to achieve. She says that research does not support this, especially where economic inequalities exist as disadvantaged groups experience these effects more disproportionally. Highlighting that

> access to socially privileged' peers matters and this cannot occur in a segregated schooling system. Yet, in Ireland barriers to immigrants in particular are being generated in segregated housing policies that results in particular schools serving highly vulnerable/privileged groups to the exclusion of other.

Lynch (2018, p 7) says that "children in Irish schools are well aware of the economic and social pecking order, and their relative chances of educational success' compared to others in more privileged schools".

> Their aspirations and hopes are adjusted accordingly, as are those of their parents, and their teachers with a down-spiralling effect for those who are most disadvantaged'. The lowered expectations, and the tensions and anxieties impact directly on learning, and are also exacerbated by macro-level policies outside of education, such as housing.

This research suggests that if the government is to "promote substantive equality in education" there is a need to "seriously reduce the economic inequalities in Ireland on an ongoing basis between the wealthiest and poorest in particular". This includes significantly more equal distribution of wealth and income to have substantive equality of opportunity in education. And, because all forms of inequality are intersectionally related, we need to address inequalities and barriers at macro, meso and micro levels simultaneously". Lynch (2018, p 33)

Recommendations include the development of public policies which "promote equality of condition, economically and socially, outside of school and colleges so that there can be more equality of outcome within schools". A point is also made about entry to higher education being

> highly class stratified, and while the proportion of students attending higher education has increased for all classes since free education was introduced, those from working class and lower income backgrounds are significantly over represented in lower points courses in the 9 Institutes of Technology (now Technical Universities) where they have fewer career options: at the other extreme, 50 per cent of students from Irelands most affluent areas study at one of the three elite universities in Ireland (UCD, TCD or UCC), four times the rate of those from disadvantaged areas (Lynch, 2018, p 9).

Additional recommendations suggest that the government has a role in "ensuring that all forms of employment are as secure as possible, so that any given job guarantees a sustainable livelihood (and opportunities for further education and progression)", and that this "is key to creating a more sustainable and less exam-focused education system" (Lynch, 2018, pp. 5–6).

These findings connect "fear regarding employment and long-term economic security" as driving "fear and anxiety in education" and say that "because precarious work is so pervasive, there is less and less incentive to stay in education for those in low-skilled areas especially" (Lynch, 2018, p v). This is especially important for vulnerable groups as many of them enter the less-skilled sectors of the economy where there is often limited security.

Lynch (2018, p16) mentions how the current pattern of clustering of immigrant children in secondary schools in urban centres located in more generally disadvantaged areas is detrimental and that this shows a high level of "ethnic segregations in schools and related to housing which must be urgently addressed". If this pattern persists into a second or third generation (as it has in other European countries), this has serious implications for prolonging the barriers immigrants experience in advancing in education and society. This kind of cross-sectoral research is important for informing guidance practice especially around understanding career expectations and future employment options and the role that poverty and other inequalities play particularly in the lives of low-income families and some migrant groups.

13 Current Reports on Migrant Experience of the Irish Workplace and Employment Sector

Research is available from projects and reports undertaken to date, which explore migrant experiences of the Irish workplace and employment sector. *Covid 19 and non-Irish nationals in Ireland*—EMN/ ERSI (2019) complements the MIS Monitoring Report on Integration & Equality 2020.

This publication was prepared in line with the Migrant Integration Strategy and was funded by the Department of Children, Equality, Disability, Integration and Youth. It describes itself as an early snapshot of the pandemic in Ireland and how it varies by nationality. This report compares the early impact of COVID on non-Irish and Irish nationals. It alerts us to the "potentially unequal impact" of the pandemic/

economic crisis, and stresses that this needs to be continually monitored so that policy responses can prevent the emergence of greater divisions in society. The impact of the COVID pandemic is discussed in terms of the health and socio-economic issues of some vulnerable people in the population. The research notes that "migrants, foreign citizens and asylum seekers have been identified as particularly vulnerable to the direct and indirect effects of Covid 19". Economic issues, risk of infection and exposure to derogatory or xenophobic language are some of the factors cited. The researchers raised an interesting point about what they called "remotability", meaning the option for people to be able to work from home during the crisis. The ability to do this was often connected to certain occupations and professions, whereas others needed to be more physically present for their jobs. Some service, sales and craft and plant occupations could not avail of this option, which increased risks for people working in these areas and had some economic or labour force implications. It goes into great detail in terms of what specific groupings of people were most impacted under the different research headings and in what ways. The findings suggest that migrant workers may represent "a particularly vulnerable workforce during the pandemic due to the nature of work in which they are typically employed". It recommends continual monitoring needs to be done "to prevent vulnerable groups being adversely affected due to the impact of the pandemic" (EMN/ ESRI, 2019, p 51).

Ethnicity and Nationality in the Irish Labour market is the fifth report conducted by the Economic and Social Institute (ERSI, 2018) as part of the Commissions Research Programme on Human Rights and Equality. It explains the principle of equality and stresses that "the right to a life free from racial discrimination is articulated most comprehensively in the International Convention on the Elimination of All form of Racial Discrimination". (Foreword) The Commission protects and promotes human rights and equality in Ireland, "building a culture of respect for human rights, equality and intercultural understanding". This report emphasises that employment is important for integration and inclusion in the community and society. It says that "quite simply, in a just society, everyone should have equal access to employment opportunities, experience equal treatment in the workplace and enjoy labour market outcomes regardless of their ethnicity". These central tenets to the Commission's work have contributed to the successful appeal to the Supreme Court, which found an outright ban on access to employment for applicants for International Protection to be unconstitutional.

Once again, it is a very comprehensive and detailed report which looks at different migrant groups' experiences of discrimination in terms of accessing work opportunities as well as within the workplace. It reminds us that "experiences of different ethnicities in Ireland cannot be reduced to simple generalisations", and that some ethnic groups for various reasons are at an advantage in the Irish labour market, both in terms of access to employment and progression (ESRI, 2018 Foreword).

In the summary, this report mentions that "employment leads to financial independence and reduces the risk of social poverty and social exclusion; it also facilitates immigrants into society as a whole".

Those taking part in the research were also asked if they "experienced discrimination according to a definition that reflects Irish Law". The definition of discrimination in this context was where people believed that they were "treated less favourably due to membership of a specific group" (ERSI, 2018, p 69).

An interesting finding here which the authors say is consistent with previous research, is that "those with higher education tend to report more discrimination in the workplace, perhaps because of heightened awareness and higher expectations of equal treatment" (ERSI, 2018, p 78).

Overall, the findings reflect a diversity of experience amongst national and ethnic groups in the Irish labour market. It identified that non-Irish individuals, especially individuals of non-white ethnicity, experience higher rates of discrimination in the labour market.

> Many minority ethnic/national groups and particularly those of Black ethnicity experience more negative outcomes in employment and occupational attainment and are at greater risk of discrimination in recruitment and in the workplace than White Irish individuals (ERSI, 2018, p 86).

This report acknowledges that legislative measures are in place to respond to employment discrimination. But it pushes for "other measures to prevent discrimination...and...promote equality of opportunity". It clearly sees a role for awareness-raising efforts amongst some minority, ethnic and immigrant groups, but stresses that these need to be "coupled with provision of information to immigrant communities about equality legislation and the supports available to them".

There is recognition here that "ethnicity is a key locus of disadvantage", but this report feels this is "rarely measured in repeated survey data in Ireland" and that "regular collection of ethnicity in the labour market is a key priority at this time" (ERSI, 2018, p 90). This absence of base-line data was also raised as a deficit in the MIS strategy and report. The Migrant Integration Strategy (2017) predicted a greater contribution to Irish society and increased benefits from the labour market for second-and third-generation migrants. This report suggests for that to happen successfully, it is important to measure and monitor challenges in order to capture the experience of immigrants in Ireland.

One other finding of interest to guidance providers related to the need for better information on qualifications recognition supports and for greater awareness amongst migrants about services that may facilitate their access to employment, or access to progression routes. While this is a typical element of the (ETB) adult guidance and information delivery, those services are not nationwide.

During the "pilot phases" of the (ETB) AEGS, considerable expertise was developed by the staff of the Adult Education Guidance Initiative. These pilot projects generated publications and guides that could be distributed across adult and community education and made available through the "network" of community supports. Current (ETB) AEG service delivery includes information and career guidance workshops, delivered in a variety of settings, including the "Direct Provision" or international protection centres. There is a challenge to ensuring appropriate access to "online" and/or "self-directed" information services. An example is the government-funded Quality Qualifications Ireland (QQI). QQI provide NARIC Services: NARIC Ireland provides advice on the academic recognition of a foreign qualification by comparing it, where possible, to a major award type and level on the Irish National Framework of Qualification (NFQ). This report recommends that "this system should be promoted among both immigrants and employers to prevent skills being 'underutilised and facilitate occupational mobility'" (ERSI, 2018, p 88).

An equally important opportunity exists for a wide variety of supporting organisations including information, guidance and advocacy services to raise "awareness of equality legislation amongst the general public". The research found that "invoking employment equality legislation and accessing redress for discrimination relies on the individual's knowledge of their rights under equality legislation and their capacity to make a complaint" (ERSI, 2018, p 87).

14 Barriers and Issues from Practitioners Working with Migrant Groups

A small informal qualitative sample was requested from practitioners working on behalf of migrant groups. They were asked to contribute their top 5 issues or barriers and contextual observations. A range of replies were received, and despite the differences in services, there appeared to be common themes in terms of the personal or structural barriers presented.

Employment—difficulties finding employment—needs deeper help understanding employers' needs—I think employment is difficult for them for making CVs and trying to get employed, etc.—*For Refugees:* Discrimination that black migrants face accessing the labour market—Changing CVs and making them more "Irish"—isn't just an asylum seeker/refugee thing—can be a lot around cultural norms—Cultural things generally like "eye contact, etc.", can be tricky. Most stuff we don't even know about as providers—Not being allowed to work while waiting for a decision is a huge challenge as it often forces people to work on the black economy.

Housing/accommodation—Housing/accommodation is a huge challenge for this cohort—Direct provision clients trying to register for a GP/applying for a medical card/notifying the Health Service Executive (HSE)—a) There are a lot of hoops that you have to jump through and b) you have to know that you need to jump through them—Help navigating accommodation—where to get HAP (Housing Assistance Payment) if living outside of Dublin but working in Dublin until late at night. Which county council to apply to for that payment. There's a lot to navigate for anyone—never mind someone new to the country—*For Refugees:* Difficulties in sourcing accommodation—Housing is a major issue—The other major issue highlighted is the lack of housing.

Irish educational system, training and language issues—Issues connecting with and understanding the Irish Education System—I think the education system can be difficult for migrants and refugees especially with the language barrier and getting used to the culture of the Irish Education System—Recognition of existing qualifications—Re-skilling/up-skilling—Language supports—Funding education—Digital Competency training—Language is also a difficulty. The English we speak is not necessarily the English they heard on TV or whatever. It has a big impact on how kids get on in school, or as adults applying for work—assuming they are allowed to.

Migration status—as a worker knowing the various migration statuses and knowing how to move from one to the other and what they mean can be difficult too. Makes it hard when someone wants help

- *Non-EU migrant group* (important to distinguish from the EU—as there are immigration barriers that have a massive impact for this group—Security of Residency—nearly all immigration is "temporary" and needs at a minimum to be renewed. All changes in circumstances can impact on this, so it is a constant stressor. For undocumented migrants it is probably the major issue behind all their concerns.
- *Family reunification*—many migrants are separated from family, and not all are able to sponsor them to come to Ireland, e.g. Afghan citizens are hugely worried about family over there.
- *Citizenship (linked to security of residency)* is a topic of concern. Often in a good way as in "something to work towards", but long processing times and uncertainty around success can make it difficult.
- *Education/employment*—either lack of recognition of qualifications, or lack of suitable opportunities to get into jobs that match their skills and qualifications—this feeds into the point below on "finances", and relates to "wellbeing and successful integration being dependent on a person feeling valued by and valuable to the society".
- *Finances*—income, housing, social protection, etc. no different to anyone else, but the limitations of income have a big impact on migrants; importantly they have fewer safety nets (either savings, or family supports, or access to social welfare). Housing is a massive issue with the majority of migrants renting, and higher numbers in homeless services.

Dealing with INIS—migrant worker with high level of English and friends in similar situation– biggest challenge and ongoing is dealing with the Irish Naturalisation and Immigration Service (INIS) when trying to get Visas, renew them or get Citizenship. Difficulties include waiting for months/years to get a response and not even getting an acknowledgement when documents, letters or email are sent to them. Someone else suggested that one person would book an appointment with an "official" and then sell that slot to someone else who needed it?

- *Social Isolation*—Social Isolation and lack of support—low finances, low savings and lack of social safety nets.
- *Mental health and trauma*—The effect of trauma that many migrants and asylum seekers will have faced. Many will still be experiencing PTST—migrant issues: the potential for counselling or life coaching to assist has come up with the United

Nations Migration (IOM) Agency—we have partnered with them to make referrals to a counsellor, for undocumented migrants in particular.
- *Rights and entitlements—For refugees:* Family member joining sponsor—registering with local authority, INIS, PPS, social welfare, etc.,—For refugees: digital divide—more services have to be accessed online, e.g. revenue and welfare—For refugees: not having sufficient understanding of English to access services.
- *Access to information*—A university graduate migrant with strong English language skills said that they found the general, public information service "Citizens Information" accessible but said that many friends did not know where to get accurate information when they arrived in Ireland.

The challenge is that without specialist, qualified and impartial guidance provision, the choices that are "available" are not mediated with the client/service user: this lack of context in decision-making is noted amongst adult guidance and information providers who often can only support the individual to "unpick" poorly informed choices.

15 Conclusions

In looking at the range of queries received, and the issues and barriers presented above, there is a clear role for guidance services working with migrant clients in a voluntary setting. There is also a mandate to support this group within Youth Information and Adult Guidance underpinned by a clear social inclusion remit. But these services are only of value to migrants and other vulnerable groups if they are available, accessible to them and they know that they exist. As per other recommendation for FET and Guidance Sector, clarity around what is available in terms of information and guidance support is required. Many of themes identified in the practitioner's feedback are currently being supported. These include understanding education systems and training pathways, qualifications recognition and funding sources for college. Assistance with forms and applications is available along with CV, employment and career management skills. Specific language supports exist within FET provision including English for speakers of other languages (ESOL) classes. Guidance in general connects people to social and other personal support outlets. But there is probably scope for stronger connections with translation services and other "language-related supports" on behalf of clients, which could help guidance practitioners especially with resource development or interpretive functions. Similarly certain supports around housing and understanding your rights and entitlements and accessing services are also available in a guidance setting. But there are limitations to the role, and recognising the limits and boundaries is important. Maintaining high expectations from other service providers (for quality provision) who take over the tasks is needed for greater accountability and improved client outcomes. This is important too if we are to keep the client at the centre of our services in a respectful and meaningful way. Respondents were keen to reiterate that immigrants is a broad term and covers a multitude and that refugees and asylum seekers as a subset of the first group have different needs and higher levels of challenges and complexity. They also remind us of the individual diversity within groups in terms of personal supports, social capital and previous educational attainment or employment experience, which they bring to the conversation, along with their queries and needs.

Information, guidance and advocacy providers also need to know of existing services and available supports for effective cross-referral and to maximise service reach and outcomes for clients. This again could be addressed as per the Guidance in FET strategy recommendations already referred to. But it also involves collaboration with key statutory agencies with migrant support functions. Some work may need to be done on finding a common ethos and practice for this collaboration to be most effective. It is clear from the needs represented above that there is a specialist role in migrant supports that falls outside the generalist supports that broad-based guidance services can offer. Recognition of existing services and supports structures with acknowledgement of their specialist "expertise" is crucial by funders to enhance social integration plans. It is interesting to note that some of these expert services are encountering structural barriers with state services on behalf of their respective client groups. The complexity of migration and residency status, long turnaround times for decisions and lack of clear communication channels for people is clearly creating anxiety and tension for migrant groups and for those working on their behalf and those barriers need to be addressed at national level. Clearer cooperation pathways between state and voluntary services with an emphasis on removing structural and informational barriers are required. The National Housing Crisis is a well-documented phenomenon and is currently affecting wide sections of Irish society, but it is impacting more significantly on the mental health and broader integration potential for migrant and vulnerable groups.

The National Child Care Subsidy has also been cited by respondents as "not going far enough to help low-income earners" and has impacts for meaningful employment and child safeguarding. A complementary role can be seen between second-level, community/Youth Information, FET and Adult Guidance services. These offer a range of entry points for migrant and other groups to access guidance, information and career supports across the lifespan. Adequate resourcing and parity of recognition across guidance roles is necessary for staff recruitment and retention and maintaining morale. This is also important to ensure continuity of organisational knowledge bases. The disparity in resourcing creates stress and a tension and a competitive edge between scarce services. Additional CPD opportunities especially around working with people with higher needs such as migrant groups and cross-sectoral sharing of learning to inform practice were also suggested. Effective data collection to measure individual and nuanced impacts on different population groups was recommended as a requirement for future research, reports and key learning around supporting migrants.

References

ASTI. (2018). *Free second level education: The context for change and lessons for today. Talk by Áine Hyland at an ASTI conference 50 years on: Reflecting on the legacy of free second level education Gresham Hotel – 28th April 2018.* Link: https://www.asti.ie/document-library/presentation-from-ine-hyland-emeritus-professor-of-education/

CAO. (2016). *Press statement census 2016 - Non-Irish nationalities living in Ireland 2016.* Link: https://www.cso.ie/en/csolatestnews/pressreleases/2018pressreleases/pressstatementcensus2016non-irishnationalitieslivinginireland2016/

CAO. (2021). *Central Applications Office – for applying for college using the CAO process.* Link: www.cao.ie

Careers Portal. (2021). *Calculating your points.* Accessed November 1, 2021, from https://careersportal.ie/courses/calculator/pointsCalculator.html

Cedefop. (2020). *Inventory of lifelong guidance systems and practices – Ireland.* CareersNet national records. Link: http://www.cedefop.europa.eu/en/publications-and-resources/county-reports/inventory-lifelong-guidance-systems-and-practices-ireland

Dept. Justice and Equality with a special responsibility for equality, migration & integration. Migrant integration strategy a blueprint for the future 2017–2020. Link: https://www.justice.ie/en/JELR/Migrant_Integration_Strategy_English.pdf/Files/Migrant_Integration_Strategy_English.pdf

Dept. of Social Protection. (2019). *Social inclusion policies 20th Sept 2019.* Link: https://www.gov.ie/en/collection/f96bb9-social-inclusion-policy/

DES. (2014). *Further education and training strategy 2014–2019 (Section 10).* Link: https://www.solas.ie/f/70398/x/920e2fa0b6/fetstrategy2014-2019.pdf

DES. (2021). *Adult education guidance initiative guidelines 2012.* Link: https://www.ncge.ie/sites/default/files/AEGI_Operational_Guidelines_2012__FINAL.pdf

ERSI. (2018). *Leaving cert applied programme discussion paper for NCCA.* Link: https://ncca.ie/media/3759/scr-lca-discussion-paper.pdf.

ERSI Research Series no 82, Dublin. (June 17th, 2019). *Evaluation of the national youth reach programme 2019.* Link: https://www.esri.ie/publications/evaluation-of-the-national-youthreach-programme

ERYICA. (2018). *Youth information charter.* Link: https://www.eryica.org/charter

ESRI. (2019). *Evaluating post leaving certificate provision in Ireland. The Economic and Social Review*, Vol. 50, No. 3, Autumn 2019, pp. 557–585. Policy Paper. Link: https://www.esri.ie/publications/evaluating-post-leaving-certificate-provision-in-ireland

Eurodesk and ERYICA. (2021). *First European competence framework for youth information workers.* Link: https://eurodesk.eu/projects/youthinfocomp/

Grad Ireland. (2021). *Job description for Secondary School Guidance Counsellor.* Link: https://gradireland.com/careers-advice/job-descriptions/guidance-counsellor-second-level

Houses of the Oireachtas (Friday 6th September 2019). Dail Eireann Debates – *School guidance counsellors, questions 249, 293 & 294.* Link: https://www.oireachtas.ie/en/debates/question/2019-09-06/294/

IGC. (2021). *Resources 6th year the results are out – what now?* Link: https://igc.ie/wp-content/uploads/2021/09/6th-YEAR-THE-RESULTS-ARE-OUT-WHAT-NOW-1-2.pdf

iScoil. (2021). *Empowering young people to re-engage in learning and succeed in their educational goals.* Link: https://iscoil.ie/

Lee, A. (2003). Community development in Ireland. *Community Development Journal, 38*(1), 48–58. Link: https://www.jstor.org/stable/44257727

Lynch, K. (2018). *A written submission, to the Joint Oireachtas Committee on Education and Skills.* Link: https://researchrepository.ucd.ie/handle/10197/9559

NCGE. (2016). *Programme recognition framework: Guidance counselling criteria and guidelines for programme providers.* Link: https://www.ncge.ie/policy/PRF

NCGE. (Tuesday, September 5, 2017). *A whole school guidance framework.* Link: https://www.ncge.ie/resource/ncge-whole-school-guidance-framework

NCGE AGMS. (2020). https://www.ncge/sites/default/files/NCGE-FET-AGMS-Overarching-Report-EN.pdf

NYCI. (2020). *Skills summary a free tool that will help you assess your careers skills, including communication skills, interpersonal skills and much more.* Link: http://www.skillssummary.ie

O'Morain, P., (2012) Journal of Counseling & Development. July 2012. Volume 90 371, *History of Counselling in Ireland.* Link: https://www.padraigomorain.com/history-of-counselling-in-ireland/

SOLAS. (2020). Strategy *"Future FET: Transforming learning" 2020–2025.* Link: https://www.solas.ie/f/70398/x/64d0718c9e/solas_fet_strategy_web.pdf

Spunout Ireland's Online Youth Information Website. (2021). Link: www.spunout.ie

Students Universal Support Ireland (SUSI). (2021). *Organisation for distribution of government means tested grants for college*. Link: www.susi.ie

Tusla Education Support Service. (2021). *SCP – School Completion Services.* Link: https://www.tusla.ie/services/educational-welfare-services/scp/

Lithuania: Are We Ready for Tomorrow Challenges? A Thematic Analysis of Career Development and Prospects within Lithuania

Liepa Mikulevičiūtė

1 Introduction

The main purpose of this chapter is to understand existing issues and challenges that the Lithuania's careers industry faces. Discussion will revolve around most prominent challenges such as lack of qualified professionals within the industry, lack of guidelines to shape industry itself, inefficient careers education and absence of individualised guidance in state schools and vocational centres.

To eradicate the challenges mentioned, a governing body such as a careers guidance association could be formed as a solution. Association would collect best practice data and create tailored guidelines for the Lithuanian educational system covering all different areas of careers guidance. Their main purpose would be to inform and educate schools and other industry professionals to ensure that pupils are provided with quality careers guidance. This guidance would help school professionals to use the resources and frameworks when delivering career education within schools. The governmental guidelines should also provide clear careers education delivery plans that the institutions should follow throughout the year. Assessments to establish the effectiveness of these programmes should be done annually. Numerous young people need to have access to personal career guidance advice to discover their potential and match that with a career path. It is considered that providing high-quality career guidance could help students to choose preferred career paths which could then lead to easier integration within the Lithuanian economy labour market. Moreover, Lithuania's working force is experiencing demographic change where the ageing population is not being replaced by younger professionals; which led to an increasing shortage within the labour force, for example, in industries such as education (Vilkoitytė & Skučienė, 2020). Suggestions for increasing engagement

L. Mikulevičiūtė (✉)
St. Brendan's Sixth Form College, Bristol, UK
e-mail: Lmi@stbrn.ac.uk

C. Enoch et al. (eds.), *Vocational Guidance in Europe*,
https://doi.org/10.1007/978-3-031-06592-7_7

within roles in demand focus on the need to integrate careers education that would help young adults to identify their strengths and match them with the right career path. In order to encourage young people to choose studies to become an educator it is important to implement motivational incentives that would focus on the specific areas that are in urgent need of professionals. To tackle unemployment within older generations it is recommended that the government considers implementing flexible working hours and accessible training structures that would increase the older generation's motivation to remain employed.

Because 39% of Lithuanians aged 25–64 have low skills in areas such as problem-solving and technology focused environments, they may need more attention in helping them to integrate within the local labour market (Cedefop, 2020a, 2020b). Others may need help to re-skill to meet the demand of future jobs that will appear due to automation. The aim of the chapter is to investigate the challenges that the career guidance face and suggest solutions that would result in it being more accessible to people across various socio-economic backgrounds, therefore, would help to avoid skills mismatch and to provide equal opportunities to all.

This chapter will investigate the key challenges that Lithuania's career sector face. First section will look into the overview of key challenges in Lithuania's careers education, its structure and delivery. More depth will be provided in the areas of career guidance in schools as well as the urgent need of different subject teachers and how blended learning in school can help with improving digital skills. The further structure of the chapter will identify the future job demand in Lithuania, how it may change the labour market and what does that mean for career guidance practitioners. The section about demographic change will explore the challenges that the older generations face when accessing career education and for those wanting to re-skill. Finally, recommendations will be provided as headings where each subsection will provide more details on why those recommendations should take place.

2 The Overview of the Key Challenges in Lithuania's Careers Education

Careers education in Lithuania has been established in 1999 with an aim to provide a process that is focused on providing structured and systematised learning that helps students to choose a profession and acquire career competencies. It was initiated by the Open Society Foundation of Lithuania where education programmes have been delivered in primary and secondary schools. Teachers had examples of lessons provided to them that focused on helping educators to develop student competencies. Throughout the years careers education has been recognised and integrated within the documents of the national strategy. The importance of careers education has been identified as one of the educational components (Gudžinskienė & Railienė, 2012). While the environment for life skills and career competencies development is in place there are many different programmes delivered by specialists who are trained at different levels. Even when there are trained specialists and educational programmes taking place few challenges exist that the career development system has not addressed. First, the career programmes in schools lack structure and are not related to one educational subject in both formal and non-formal education. Furthermore, the lack of structure impacts students and leads them to struggle when choosing the career path and causes the lack of motivation to invest their attention towards it (Gudžinskienė & Railienė, 2012).

The priority that the Ministry of Education, Science and Sport currently has is to establish a career development and professional guidance system that would help to recognise the individual as a person with unique experiences and a set of skills. It is important that schools provide an opportunity to explore different career paths and would provide the required support to identify different and accurate opportunities for young adults. At the moment Lithuania does not have efficient career-oriented education and it is one of the key challenges that need to be addressed (Židžiūnienė, 2021).

Career guidance is one of the key elements in shaping the professional competencies in the Lithuanian market. It determines the success of an individual's integration within the economic and social context. Currently, the main career guidance is delivered in state schools within the general education set-up, where the responsibility of career guidance relies on the student himself, teachers and administrational staff (Augienė, 2018). It is the responsibility of an educator to deepen their competencies within the career education practices and delivery by participating in various events and courses. The practitioners can choose which events to attend based on the value they will get (Vaitulionienė & Augienė, 2018). Other institutions delivering career services include career guidance information centres such as universities or youth creativity houses and the Lithuanian Labour Exchange, and organisations in the private sector such as Kalba.lt, Kastu or Digiklasė. The careers guidance can be delivered in secondary schools, high schools, universities or in organisations that provide help for those who are seeking employment opportunities (Digiklasė, 2021; Kalba.lt, 2021; Kastu, 2021; Luobikienė, 2015). School staff, teachers, pupils and parents can also access a database Mukis.lt which is a non-formal education career-focused website that provides useful links and relevant resources (Mukis.lt, 2021). Another platform LMNŠC (The non-formal education centre for the students of Lithuania) has been established in the seventh of April 2021 as a result of requirements that were made by The Minister of Education, Science and Sport. The aim of this centre is to merge different institutions such as Lithuanian Pupil's Information and Technical Creation Center, Lithuanian Young Naturalists Center, Lithuanian Pupils' and Students' Sports Center and Lithuania Youth Tourism Center. The main function of this organisation is to initiate and participate in the preparation of legal acts, submit proposals for development, create and implement innovations on the issues of non-formal education, help prepare and improve the in-service training programmes for teachers and to offer methodological assistance (LMNŠC, 2021). It is important to recognise this progression towards more efficient careers education however, due to a large load of material career education in schools should focus on providing guidelines to students as well as staff about using such resources to find the most accurate and relevant information for each individual.

Higher education institutions mostly use Karjera.lt system that focuses on providing career services to young adults that study in their educational facilities, for graduates, employers, career professionals, students and their parents (Karjera.lt, 2021). The services are accessible for university students during their studies or for 5 years after graduation. Currently, there are 6 universities and 14 colleges that use this platform to provide career guidance services (Karjera.lt, 2021a). Idialogue is another platform where mentors and career consultants can register to provide consultations or mentoring to those who need it. People can also access individual expert consultations; however, the qualifications of these professionals vary based on their experience and field of expertise. While some have background and qualifications in coaching, others have experience in developing organisational success, organising career-focused courses, have experience in recruitment or qualifications in psychology (Idialogue, 2020). This raises concern if those with different professional backgrounds and no recognised career guidance qualifications can provide informed and quality-focused career guidance.

Because career development requires a knowledge of certain theories, practices and guidance it is important to note that the different level of careers and other qualifications that the practitioners have can influence their ability to deliver effective career education within schools. Furthermore, if a practitioner is not a qualified career service provider, they may not recognise which areas they lack understanding in and as a result provide mediocre career guidance (Augienė, 2018). Therefore, it is important to ensure that the Ministry of Education provides resources, guidelines and policies for schools and career guidance practitioners to deliver a high-quality career service.

2.1 Career Education Delivery in Schools

Vocational centres are less efficient in delivering career services compared to schools. This is because schools have better access to career guidance delivered by trained career specialists. Meanwhile compared to general education institutions in vocational centres it is more often that the career advice will be delivered by the vice-principal or module leader (Antanaitienė & Sajienė, 2012). Therefore, it is important to acknowledge that all institutions need equal access to trained staff and professionals who have informed knowledge about the career education processes. The purpose that the career's advisor has within the school set-up is to help pupils to discover their career paths, recognise personal skill sets, teach how to research different opportunities, develop soft skills set and introduce current labour market trends. Career advisor aims to prevent wrong choices based on personal interests. Thus, career education has a primary meaning within the school operations (Augienė, 2018). Career advice can be delivered by any member of the school staff. The school staff that can provide career services include teachers, support staff, social workers, librarians, psychologists. Social workers and psychologists are the least involved in providing career service even though they are the closest to those who would have competencies in helping an individual to discover their true value, skills and qualities (Antanaitienė & Sajienė, 2012). Therefore, career guidance is delivered by staff that do not have accredited qualifications in career guidance; furthermore, only some universities cover career guidance theory within pedagogy degrees or offer careers guidance focused postgraduate degrees (KTU, 2021; MRU, 2021; VDU, 2021a, 2021b; Vilniaus Universitetas, 2021). This suggests that the support given by different school staff might not be fully informed by the best practices or may have various levels of career guidance-based knowledge. There are no requirements for such a role; therefore, the preparation for such professionals is not present. Because there are no industry standards the services provided are not at the same level where everyone prepares the programme based on their own experiences, learning and competencies (Vaitulionienė & Augienė, 2018). While large city schools may have a career advisor who has related qualifications, the smaller city schools may not have such professionals; therefore, it is usually an additional responsibility for the school's teachers to integrate career guidance in between their teaching practices and gain all required knowledge on their own (Totorienė & Augienė, 2018). Since there are no particular people in charge of delivering career services this may result in a threat where students are not aware of the services in their schools and do not know they can have access to such support (Antanaitienė & Sajienė, 2012).

While parents do play a significant role in delivering career support to their children it creates a structure where children from lower working-class families may not have equal opportunities in discovering their path and developing the right set of skills to succeed (Li & Qiu, 2018; Totorienė & Augienė, 2018). Schools should take responsibility for taking the primary role for career guidance and use parent influence as a mechanism to help pupils discover themselves and their potential. It is important to notice that while the parents may want the best for their children they may be subjected to their own experiences and opinions, this is where career consultant plays a key role in providing a partial opinion and informed guidance in helping the pupil to discover their true wishes impartially and without bias.

Some schools have career information points such as career offices or help desks where students can get resources about different career paths. People working in career information points are usually those who provide lessons and workshops that discuss how to choose a career, as well as organises employer visits and career-focused events within schools. However, not all schools have such information points and there is still a lack of individual consultations where students would receive individualised career guidance. Therefore, these career information points mostly manage professional events with a purpose to spread a message about the different career paths, but the attention towards individualised advice is exceptionally low. The events usually are weekly class meetings, gatherings discussing career information that may be led by career consultants or trips to the workplaces. Additional resources for gaining information about prospects are through external organisations that visit schools to provide extra information (Antanaitienė & Sajienė, 2012).

The guidance for career development practitioners suggests that the schools should implement a careers programme delivery action plan for everyone to follow. It would help schools to implement the delivery programme that runs smoothly across all school departments. However, if such a plan is not present, it can suggest that the schools will deliver substandard, or no career guidance services. The career development programme can be successful only when all school staff contribute towards the goal of developing pupils' understanding about the future possibilities and their skill set integration within the labour market (Augienė, 2018). It is thought that to achieve the best outcomes in careers development there is a need for effective communication within the different school departments where careers advisers would be able to share information among social workers, schools' psychologists and class leaders. However, some smaller regional schools may not have a career education programme or a person responsible for it; therefore, the amount of work becomes too much of the responsibility for the remaining school staff. Non-existing career education department within the school could be identified as a challenge that needs to be urgently addressed (Totorienė & Augienė, 2018).

3 The Current Education Challenges for State Schools

3.1 The Need for Personal Career Guidance in Schools

The key challenge related to the careers sector is that there is no effective careers education delivery within the schools and vocational centres. Young people make inaccurate career choices due to a lack of understanding of how to identify the right path, the external pressure from family or when they cannot get into the universities they initially aimed to (Antanaitienė & Sajienė, 2012). There is a need to help young people to learn how to identify the right set of skills and how to apply them in the right context within the world of work. When a young person is not able to recognise their attributes and is not self-aware it can lead to a skills mismatch and can result in missed opportunities. Employers highlight that the lack of qualified employees creates limited opportunities for innovation. The lack of skilful employees can prevent businesses from growing. Thus, 26.5% of small companies in Lithuania express their concern in facing such challenge. It is thought that skills mismatch is having an impact on youth unemployment (Hogeforster & Wildt, 2020). This is important to note because employers see young people as individuals lacking life and social skills which suggest that there is a demand for a career education that would help them to quickly integrate into the workplace and deliver satisfactory results. Career education must integrate the learning of these life and soft skills within the curriculum to prepare young adults to face real-life problems.

It is thought that the schools do not provide individualised career service, or it is delivered in a way that does not bring any positive results. The programmes that are delivered are done in a more generalised way and lack consideration of individual needs and experiences. It suggests that career education should be integrated in a way that is not just part of the extra curriculum but is part of the whole pupil's progression (Totoriene and Augienė, 2018). It may hardly be possible to achieve success in career guidance when one approach is implemented upon a large scale of students. However, if career education is only possible through group sessions due to limited resources that the institutions have, then group learning training should be established for professionals that the sessions delivered are as effective as possible (Meldrum, 2017).

The usual proportion of time dedicated to career development is not accurate to the actual need required to deliver the programme. The research conducted in 2018 by Totorienė and Augienė shows that staff of some schools get one additional hour per week while one representative stated there are no additional hours to deliver career guidance. Furthermore, it is overlooked as one of the responsibilities that is already integrated within teachers' contracts and should be delivered among other duties. Usually, there is no space allocated where careers services would be delivered so professionals need to look for different classrooms and available spaces where they could run the programme. Depending on the school and its resources, the challenges may present where some professionals can only offer group and not individual sessions (Vaitulionienė & Augienė, 2018). Furthermore, when career education is delivered in a generalised manner the diverse needs of each pupil cannot be addressed. The school staff faces challenges of not having enough information about delivering career service. There are limited resources or databases that could be used to provide individual service. Those providing the service lack training and seminars that would help them to implement career education within their everyday roles (Merfeldaite et al., 2020). Back in 2018, it was stated that there was not enough funding that the schools could establish fully competent career departments which remains a challenge to this day (Vaitulionienė & Augienė, 2018). There is a need to improve the career resources that career specialists could access free of charge and use within their daily practice. Further attention is required for the career guidance qualification and its professional development. There is a need for experience-based training and events where career professionals could meet to share and discuss current and best practices and further development actions. Especially because there are no industry standards those who do not have any knowledge of career guidance industry would benefit from such events of learning where to start and how to integrate career education within their teaching or counselling practices (Merfeldaite et al., 2020).

3.2 *The Urgent Need for Different Subject Teachers*

The finances for the education industry have been increasing in the last few years; however, that does not help to rectify the increasing challenges. According to the Department of Statistics, the funding reached 2, 3 billion euros in 2020 which was

238 million more than in 2019 the 81% (1.9 billion euros) came from government funding. The funding is around 3180 euros per student which were 330 euros more than a year before. Therefore, the increased funding does not help to rectify the current education challenges. The 2020–2021 data shows that there are around 459,000 school and university students (LRT, 2021). The increasing numbers of students, high demand and not enough funding bring various challenges by putting more pressure on schools' staff which impacts on them choosing to leave their job roles.

The current data shows that there is an urgent need for schoolteachers. Education is experiencing a crisis where the near future forecast provided by the Department of Statistics shows the lack of about 2000 teachers for state schools. However, the number of teachers is increasing in private schools. According to data provided the number of states schoolteachers dropped by 4000 in the last four years. Meantime the numbers in private schools increased up to 1425 teachers in the last 4 years. This increase may be related to the increased number of private schools that has expanded up to 14.6% in 2020 which is double compared to 7.3% back in 2010 (Orion, 2021). The Minister of Education, Science and Sport Jurgita Šiugždinienė highlights the urgent need to solve this problem, saying that the education industry is falling behind around 10 years and the results of the current solutions will be seen only in five years from now. The areas that are proposed to have the biggest lack of school staff are STEM, primary teaching and the support staff (LRT, 2021). Due to low wages attracting teachers to the high demand areas becomes even more challenging for all institutions providing secondary education including state schools and vocational centres who provide education curriculum and vocational training (SKVC, 2021).

Moreover, some schools already implemented plans to deliver 30% of online learning; however, teachers see this as a big challenge. Therefore, some teachers decide to resign due to the stress caused by blended learning. Teachers are not satisfied that they will have to not only teach in class but also do the same for kids who are isolated at home while not receiving any additional pay increase (Dranseikaitė, 2021). The current salary of teachers is 1400 euros per month before tax with an aim to increase the pay up to 10% within the next year (LRT, 2021). Vocational education centres also experience staff shortages due to salaries that are equivalent to general education teachers (Švietimo, mokslo ir sporto ministerija, 2020). The expectations of vocational education teachers to have LTQF (Lithuanian Qualifications Framework) or EFQ (European Qualifications Framework) level 6 qualifications as well as have vocational qualification while getting low salaries create more barriers for people to enter the profession (Hogeforster & Wildt, 2020).

The education industry is experiencing another challenge of not having enough young educators that would replace senior professionals. The 50% of teachers are the age of 50 years old; thus, there is a lack of teachers that are younger than 30 years old and who are recent graduates from university and could implement up-to-date knowledge and more innovative ways of teaching (LRT, 2021).

Back in 2000–2010, around 37,000 young people have graduated with a pedagogy degree where every year the 570 of those students have chosen to work as teachers (Civitta, 2021). In comparison during last year, there have been a total of

576 students who applied for a teaching degree. Furthermore, only 24 students have been accepted to study within the area of demand including IT (Information Technology), Maths, Chemistry, Biology and Physics. The governmental analysis centre of strategy prognosis shows that in the next 4 years, there will be a demand of 716–739 Mathematics teachers as well as 642–694 teachers of the Lithuanian language. There will also be a lack of IT, Sciences, English language teachers. In the upcoming 4 years, it is expected that around 34 graduates will be Maths teachers, 43 Lithuanian language and 16 Physics. Thus, not everyone who graduates as a qualified teacher will choose to work in a school setting.

Meantime, it is suggested that around 365 graduates of Sports educators will be in lower demand within schools where the available roles should be around 264–298 teachers (Murauskaitė, 2021a). Lithuania is experiencing a crisis of not having enough specialists to not only deliver career education but also to deliver the general education to future generations.

Furthermore, those choosing the higher qualification of an educator often do not meet the entry requirements and choose to study for a degree where their overall school grades are accepted. Therefore, Sports educators or Dance teacher studies seem to be more popular than those that are in demand while there is an insufficient number of students choosing to study STEM related teaching degrees. Ideally, it is thought that universities should take upon the responsibility of easing the entry requirements when accepting future educators to those subject areas that are in the biggest demand. Those choosing Sport or similar educator studies usually see this as a universal degree where competencies and skills can be transferable (Murauskaitė, 2021a).

The government considers what further actions would encourage young people to choose educator studies in university and propose providing them with a motivational incentive of 300 euros scholarship on entry (LRT, 2021). This would cost a total investment of eight million euros in 4 years. However, that raises the question of whether it is enough to attract those with an interest in the subject areas that are in the highest demand? Especially if the scholarship will be given out not depending on what subject area was chosen. Furthermore, it is questionable if the employability rates of school's teachers will increase because of these scholarships (Murauskaitė, 2021a). There are some promising prognoses that show an increased number of people choosing educational studies after already gaining higher qualifications. Some teachers choose to re-qualify and gain additional qualifications to become multiple subject teachers. This suggests some promises for the future (LRT, 2021).

The proposal could be to offer more specified scholarships with a focus on specific subjects in demand. Government suggest that those students could receive scholarships for their studies with conditional offer to dedicate the first few years after their studies to work in a school for a certain time after their graduation (Murauskaitė, 2021a). To extend on this further suggestion for the government would be to encourage universities to offer placements in schools and nurseries as part of the educator degrees, or to consider apprenticeship schemes for those who do not want to invest in university and would prefer practical learning on the job.

3.3 Blended Learning and Its Integration within Education

It is expected that Covid will carry on disrupting the current education system. The current challenge is addressing the need to implement such measures that do not affect the future of the current generation. The aim for the 2021/2022 academic year is to ensure that the schools can deliver face-to-face learning instead of remote one. The associate of the municipality M. Sinkevičius highlights that remote working has its benefits but is not as effective as learning in schools (Murauskaitė, 2021).

The research conducted by the Ministry of Education has reached out to 94% of general education schools. The data showed that around 40% of those schools chose the "Microsoft Office 365 for Education" package. The most used platforms for meetings and video calls were "Microsoft Teams" (45%) and "Zoom" (34%) (Nacionalinė švietimo agentūra, 2021). Integrating these packages within teaching and learning practices should play a key role within education because it can help to develop digital literacy that is often required within the world of work.

"Norsat" conducted research showed that year 9 and 12 school students struggled the most when studying online. Thus, 28% of students have stated that they felt a tremendous change in their energy levels when moving to online learning, 25% felt slightly tired. Around 10% of students have experienced sleep disturbances. The findings suggest that students get more exhausted when spending time on the screen (LRT, 2020).

"Kurk Lietuvai" has started an EdTech programme to establish an innovative education ecosystem that would attract small businesses and start-up companies to create innovative technological solutions that would help to enhance the education sector. This would help to improve the quality of education delivery and tackle the challenges that the education sector faces. While 86% of schools have used an electronic journal as their main resource, they had limited virtual resources to engage students in education (Filatovaitė & Stakėla, 2021). Google representatives have presented a "Google for Education" resources package that would help students to reach learning remotely, flexibly and from any location. Google had a significant impact on helping Lithuanian schools to cope with the COVID-19 challenges. They have provided more than 300,000 free electronic study platforms and 10,000 hours of courses that helped to develop teacher competencies in working online. Furthermore, Google can offer an accessible teaching method that could be more accessible and efficient (Nacionalinė Švietimo agentūra, 2021). Implementing more accessible learning could also help in delivering careers education and guidance online, because students could access it on demand.

Moreover, while students are facing difficulties in learning online it is important to recognise that integrating technology within learning is essential to increase student's digital skills and knowledge. Obtaining digital skills can allow students to gain competitiveness as well as enhance creativity and innovation. However, while digitalisation has its benefits not everyone has equal access to online learning. Online teaching also presents various challenges to teachers where they try to create a value in delivering their content online. Thus, delivering career service becomes a secondary priority for school staff who already face challenges of coping with blended learning demands. Because pandemic had influenced people's mental and psychological health individualised career service should play a key role in helping people to gain motivation and other required skills like problem-solving that are essential for their progression towards chosen career path and constantly changing world of work (Petkevičiūtė & Balčiūnaitienė, 2021).

4 Future Jobs

According to OECD skills studies Lithuania's work society is influenced by globalisation, digitalisation, demographic change and climate change. Therefore, change within these key factors is required to develop a certain set of skills that would help to thrive in work and life. The current changes that COVID brought to education and world of work called attention to the need for up-skilling as well as re-skilling (OECD, 2021). Around 50% of businesses have experienced an insufficient demand in 2020 because of the pandemic. The decline has been seen across various sectors like manufacturing, construction and trade where the construction sector has experienced the biggest shortage of employees (Versli Lietuva, 2021). It is expected that the negative consequences of COVID will not last for long term and can be resolved in a near future by targeting most affected sectors. According to IFM (International Monetary Fund) organisation, the economic recovery requires attention towards reforming structures in sectors such as education to increase productivity and efficiency. This is essential to create an environment for economic growth and competitiveness (Lietuvos Bankas, 2021). Lithuania has one of the highest rates for qualification mismatch compared to other EU countries because many employees work in a lower qualification job while holding higher qualification degrees. Additionally, other people who look for employment do not have qualifications that are required in most of the job advertisements (Jankaitė & Budrytė, 2021). Thus, this becomes a challenge for those looking for a job and highlights a need of up-skilling, getting work-based training or accurate career guidance that would help to establish effective progression route towards obtaining skills and knowledge required.

The European Centre for the Development of Vocational Training forecast of future employment shows that by 2025, the growth will be mostly seen in business and public sector services. It is predicted that around 27% of job opportunities will be within high-level occupations in STEM, business and teaching sectors. Another 20% growth forecasts the need of those occupations that will apply scientific and artistic concepts, strategies and policies in sectors like engineering, healthcare, business and public sector. Around 12% increase will be seen for craft and related trades workers. This growth of skilled workers in Lithuania is expected to be higher than the predicted 5% which is combined all together across other EU countries (Cedefop, 2015).

So far, Lithuania's use of the technology in labour market is the lowest in the EU where there are only 5 robots per 10,000 workers. While there is a threat that robots may change many industries, its implementation would depend on countries investment and funding. The education system needs to prepare for further technological advancement thus, more job vacancies will be available in this sector. Therefore, young adults need to start developing technical skills to keep up with the change (Vilikanskytė, 2020). Development of such skills is one of the key challenges that Lithuania's society face. Moreover, young people lack cognitive and socio-economic skills. Meantime, only few adults aim to develop their technical, soft or cognitive skills further (OECD, 2021). The unemployment rate among young people of age between 16- and 29-year-old has reached 71,400 in 2021 and has increased by 44,600 compared to 2020. The unemployment rate for those up to 29-year-old has increased by 10.1%. Young people shape around 25.8% of all unemployed population of Lithuania. The biggest number of unemployed and unqualified young people has been between 16- and 19 years old. Around 58,900 people that are younger than 30 have been employed in the last year. Around 58,875 youths have found employment, 7024 have joined the ADRP (Active Labour Market Policies) that aim to help working-age population to integrate within labour market to prevent the dependence on benefits (Martin, 2015), and 10,854 have started their own business. The skill development programme showed the best results where more than 88% of young population managed to secure employment (Užimtumo tarnyba, 2020). To avoid unemployment numbers growing it is important to provide young people with opportunities to learn essential skills that will be applicable to future jobs; furthermore, young people should learn to re-skill throughout their career. This could be done through strengthening Lithuania's education system and implementing a well-developed career guidance service within all schools. Attention for the government is needed for implementing a successful curriculum (OECD, 2021).

While most of the jobs in demand will be of higher-level qualifications some medium-level qualifications jobs may face increased demand due to high replacement demand (Cedefop, 2015). For example, thinking about the fact that many teachers are at the pension age and are planning to leave education and retire (see Sect. 3.2).

The Vice Minister of Education, Science and Sport stated that one of the main aims of the government is to establish vocational learning that would demonstrate clear value to the economy. Looking into the fast pace of technological development, it is considered that the educational system should reflect this development and prepare the professionals who would succeed in this entrepreneurial world. The Vice Minister argues that the education system is not capable of changing as fast as businesses do. Thus, it is considered that the careers curriculum in Lithuania do not prepare competent specialists who could apply the required skills in the labour market (Židžiūnienė, 2021).

Moreover, this may present challenges for career guidance practitioners when the job roles arise from labour market development and automation trends which may suggest areas of employment demand. Meanwhile, the purpose of careers guidance appointments is for the practitioners to deliver impartial services when providing personal guidance to their clients and addressing their individual needs while exploring various opportunities. Career practitioners may also be presented with a need to help their customers identify existent skills and gaps within their client's knowledge and create strategies helping them to enter those roles that are in demand or may require a higher level of competencies and qualifications. When implementing careers education within schools practitioners may face challenges of developing the careers services delivery strategy and integrating it into teaching practices within whole institution.

5 The Identification of the Future Job Demand in Lithuania

According to future projections of 2030, the digital technologies used across services and businesses will continue to grow. There will be a need to develop several types of skills where technological, creative, cognitive and interpersonal skills will be essential within the labour market. The development of those skills will require education that helps to train for jobs that will appear in the future (McKinsey & Company, 2017). Around 20% of jobs in Lithuania are at substantial risk to be automated. Another 40% of jobs experience change in their tasks due to automation (OECD, 2021). The biggest attention should be focused on the following industries: life sciences, engineering, information and communication technologies. While attention is also required in developing the education system that would provide knowledge, skills and qualifications for the areas in demand (Jankaitė & Budrytė, 2021).

The ISM University of Management and Economics conducted research that showed increased automated work force in some of Lithuania's sectors. Researchers have identified which areas in Lithuania could be the most and least automated.

Resilient to automation: Neringa, Alytus, Šiauliai, Vilnius district.

Most likely to be automatised regions: Palanga and Birštonas.

According to the Association of Lithuanian Municipalities, the different likelihoods of automation are dependent on how foreign investments are distributed. Unskilled jobs are at the highest risk of being automated in those municipalities that have the least investment. However, automation is also being seen as a great way to create more higher-skilled positions such as robot maintenance specialists. Thus, this way new jobs can be created, while low-paid jobs are changed to better paid roles (Vilikanskytė, 2020). The most secure jobs will be those that include creativity, problem-solving and humanitarian soft skills (Vilikanskytė, 2020). Focusing on these attributes would help to boost job satisfaction and productivity of an individual which would then lead to strengthening the economy and developing the highly skilled workforce.

According to HR agencies the biggest demand is being seen in IT, e-commerce, engineering and sales industries. While automation can create new well-paid jobs the current situation in some sectors like IT, business and finance experiences the challenge of finding qualified workers. Based on the lower qualifications the biggest demand for workers is seen across industrial and construction sectors. One of the reasons why it is hard to find senior-level specialists is due to expectations that employers have regarding employee experience. Usually, requirements are as high as 6–8 years even in those roles where the biggest demand exists (Jankaitė & Budrytė, 2021).

6 Demographic Change

Lithuania is experiencing ageing population and the percentage of those at retiring age is increasing. The EU demographic trend shows that Lithuania's population is getting older. Back in 2012, the forecast predicted that by 2025, Lithuania's working-age population will fall by more than 19%. By the 2050s, the average age of Lithuanians is predicted to be around 46 years old (Cedefop, 2015; Wysocka, 2021). Meanwhile, the average European dependency ratio of those who will be working is projected to reach 50.2 years by the 2060s (Creighton, 2014). The current ageing of population is expected to have implications on economic growth, productivity and social aspects such as working hours and retirement (Cedefop, 2015; Wysocka, 2021). It may also impact increased unemployment numbers and pensioner poverty (Creighton, 2014). This suggests that career practitioners and government need to focus on developing sustainable strategies that would help to shape the future labour market.

Another factor that affects the demographic change of working force is migration because 71% of Lithuania's emigrants are at the working age between 15 and 44 years old. This has an impact on the shortage of labour power in certain areas, especially those that require higher qualifications because young people tend to leave for countries where they will earn more for their qualifications (Europos migracijos tinklas, 2021). Back in 2017, one of the key issues employers faced was attracting talent for roles in demand, retaining skilled workers from immigrating to other countries and attracting qualified workers who are in shortage of required skills due to poor preparation before leaving education (Versli Lietuva, 2017). The migration flows have shown some positive turnaround in 2019 for the first time in the last 20 years (OECD, 2021). Professor Vilmantė Kumpikaitė-Valiūnienė (KTU School of Economics and Business) highlights a few periods that the emigration took place. First, it started after Lithuania got back its independence, then after Lithuania joined the EU, finally it was influenced by the economic crisis when people experienced financial instability. The fourth wave of emigration was affected by the low wages. Other reasons for emigration include professional development opportunities, an open-minded society and life-changing experiences (KTU, 2017). While people are migrating to other countries it becomes harder to fill in high demand positions in Lithuania. It is important to ensure that those with developed skills choose to stay and work in Lithuania, but this depends on the career choice and progression opportunities (Jankaitė & Budrytė, 2021). The solution could be offering employment opportunities with realistic requirements that match individual skills, experience and competencies, effective career guidance that would help young people to match their skills to desired jobs and promotion of economic stability as well as easier access to professional development.

7 Career Education Challenges for Older Generations

Around 20% of Lithuanians are at the age of 65 years. (Europos migracijos tinklas, 2021). Age can influence a person's abilities to reach success and ability to adapt to changing economy (Martinaitis et al., 2021). Lithuania faces challenges within providing a lifelong learning and effective adult learning system in the country (EAEA, 2020). Around 39% of adults aged 25–64 have a low skill within areas of problem-solving and technology focused environments. The 9% of those between the age of 35 and 54 are more likely to experience low levels of education which may result in increased threat of being unemployed. Moreover, 9% adults of this age group have low numeracy skills (Cedefop, 2020a, 2020b). Adults lack essential skills including digital literacy, numeracy and problem-solving. Additionally, there is a low use of skills such as teamwork, autonomy, professional development and progression within career as well as lack of appraisal processes that would encourage an increase in performance. One of the challenges is that those of older working age tend to have lower motivation and may not be inclined towards learning new skills. Low motivation can be impacted by factors such as adult courses being too expensive for most people or not providing a clear value for money; which may discourage individuals from training. People that are later in their career may avoid training due to time constrains and inability to manage full-time employment and personal life demands (OECD, 2021). Consequently, establishing a flexible working policy could be an effective way to schedule work and earn income for those who might have commitments or wish to maintain work and study balance.

The challenge is presented when people are employed in roles with skills miss-match and excess or shortage of required attributes provided in the job description. Working in not suitable jobs can affect people's motivation to perform or commit to the job. Not everyone who is looking for work wishes to be employed as a full-time worker because people do not want to commit to long hours for low pay. Therefore, to encourage older people to join the labour market it is essential to consider shorter working hours, ability to train and gain a vocational qualification that would be applicable to the workplace right away, as well as consider better health care, tax incentives and a package of employee benefits (Wysocka, 2021).

It is important to tackle the efficiency of an ageing population and their involvement within the market to tackle the shrinking workforce. Especially because Lithuania is among one of the most ageing populations among other EU countries. One of the factors why an ageing population may struggle is because those with lower qualifications tend to work physically and emotionally harder jobs. This could be solved by offering older generations fewer demanding jobs; however, they should still be willing to re-skill and learn new things to be employable. Those of older age often lack motivation to remain within their employment after reaching pension age due to low financial reward compared to the difficult working conditions (Vilkoitytė & Skučienė, 2020).

7.1 *The Current Education Challenges for Adults Wanting to Re-skill*

To provide a solution to the issues of an ageing population Lithuania has been focusing providing lifelong learning. Adults are encouraged to continue their learning through adult education with the aim of supporting people's integration within the labour market. The Lithuania's strategy of 2030 is to enable each individual to pursue their potential (Pata et al., 2021). The aim is to form a society that is independent, confident, creative and proactive. Through lifelong learning, society can develop required skills and knowledge towards information communication technologies. National programmes can help people to understand their potential and talents (State Progress Council, 2012).

Adult learners can access a wide range of vocational courses through vocational education. However, the problem with vocational centres in Lithuania is that it has stigma around being a choice of those with low grades and mediocre performance in schools (Hogeforster & Wildt, 2020). The vocational education can be accessed through "Užimtumo tarnyba" who can provide the funding for the courses. According to their data there are around 195,180 unemployed people and around 197,708 of those who registered have been employed during 2021 (Užimtumo tarnyba, 2021). The total number of those who have registered to get help from "Užimtumo tarnyba" have reached 277,199 in 2021 where 37.8% are age of 30–49-year-old; 36.4% are those of age 50+; 26% those who have been unemployed for a long time; 38.3% those that do not have any vocational training and 34.5% who live in small cities or countryside. Around 5400 job seekers have used initiative to join the vocational training scheme where 72.6% of people who have attended the training have been employed within the 6 months of completing the qualification. The most popular areas for training have been transport, business administration and educational sectors. (Užimtumo tarnyba, 2020).

Those with better education tend to be more likely employed and earn more. In the case of job role being dismissed due to automation people with lower qualifications will be able to find only low-skilled and may find it hard to progress further in their career due to narrow skill set. Older workers do not explore potential opportunities as they do not see much potential in the labour market. By accepting low-skilled jobs older people do not need to worry about putting effort in up-skilling and can focus on waiting for their retirement, especially when there is a lot of uncertainty about the possible career improvement (Martinaitis et al., 2021). While the level of skills does not depend on the accessibility of education, the training for unemployed people is considered not effective. There is a need to make the training programmes in accordance with the needs of employers. There is a need to create an environment where training can be done not only in theory but also in a practical setting too. This would help to apply the content of training programmes (EEPO, 2015).

Trainees should go under traineeships that would give them practical skills and would prepare them to face real employment upon completion of the programme. Graduates of such learning would have bigger chances to be employed by the company where they completed the practice (Hogeforster & Wildt, 2020).

If employers would get involved in adults training, it would boost post-training employment rates (EEPO, 2015). However, even if the interaction with the employers within different industries is seen to be beneficial, it is usually limited to local opportunities and for economically less developed areas it may be harder to create work-based training due to lack of local opportunities (Totorienė & Augienė, 2018).

Vilnius Coding School is currently one of the organisations providing career change services for adults. The focus is on the personal qualities required to enter the IT industry and provides personal career guidance that helps to choose the coding language, prepare for an interview and enter employment. The career guidance is delivered by professionals who have qualifications related to recruitment, IT consulting, certified coaching specialists and psychologists (Coding School, 2021). However, while the first career consultation is free the following process requires some investment to identify the existent IT knowledge. The services are free for school students and alumni members. The 8 weeks course offers to gain basic skills of programming and costs around 900 EUR; therefore, the prices of re-skilling may influence the lack of motivation (Coding School, 2021a). The biggest age range for those attending the coding schools is those of age 26–35 years old and around 56.3% of students find work placement within 3 months' time. 76.4% of students identified careers consultation to be beneficial when looking for an IT job (Coding School, 2021). Therefore, governmental funding incentives should be considered for those who wish to gain IT related skills. Also, in a partnership between coding school and government a new initiative could be considered to establish a specific programme focusing on ageing population that wish to up-skill and learn digital literacy and gain IT qualification that would help them to be more employable in the future.

8 Recommendations

The following section will propose recommendations as headlines for challenges discussed throughout this chapter. Each subsection will investigate recommendation within more detail and description in terms of why it should take place.

> There is a need for access to resources and training for professionals who aim to do career guidance.

Many young people struggle when choosing their career path; therefore, there is a need to develop careers education in schools and vocational centres. Career education should provide not only group sessions but also individualised guidance that would allow young person to identify their strengths and interests while teaching them how to integrate their skills and strengths when choosing the right path. The career choice becomes a continuous process within a life where an individual no longer stays with one choice rather than exploring different opportunities that arise from the competencies, behaviours and skills that change during various experiences they have throughout life (Antanaitienė & Sajienė, 2012). The priority of career education should be focused on individual skill sets and competencies recognition-based discovery workshops. But the challenges may occur where the career advisors do not have all relevant resources in delivering fully effective careers education programmes within the school (Augienė, 2018). Therefore, it is important to develop relevant databases where professionals can access resources to use within their practices. Looking for information can be time-consuming and overwhelming due to a load of information especially for those who just entered the careers guidance sector; therefore, these resources would help professionals to self-plan the careers curriculum in an easier way while accessing high-quality content. Schools should also implement effective careers departments that would work with teachers in order to provide training and guidelines on how to deliver a career curriculum within their subjects. Especially because the career development programme is successful when all school staff contribute towards the goal of developing pupil understanding about the future possibilities and their skill set integration within the labour market (Augienė, 2018). Career education should focus on not only providing personal guidance, but the group sessions that should aim to prepare young adults with essential skills that would help them to integrate within life after graduation and apply it to the workplace. Thus, clear training should be provided for professionals which would focus on establishing frameworks of delivering both personal and group career guidance.

Those who obtain qualifications in career guidance should have access to a database that would allow professionals to share different insights and knowledge about the best practices. There is a need for career industry events where professionals could network and engage with career education trends. Events focused on career professionals could be a great tool to develop practical skills like using technology in delivering effective and interactive guidance. The current databases such as Mukis.lt and LMNŠC (see Sect. 2) need further development to ensure that information is accessible to everyone. Ideally, teachers and students should have separate databases that it is easier to locate relevant resources. Thus, these databases should be widely promoted that everyone, including professionals, students and parents, are aware of them.

Career education should be integrated within the curricula and provide access for encounters with employers.

Life skills are essential when adjusting to society while being ethical and respectful when making decisions in everyday life. These skills give a young person confidence in dealing with difficulties and problems when reaching their goals, especially in the current quickly changing work environment. By using social skills such as communication and different behaviours, for example, being reliable, an individual shapes their professional competencies (Gudžinskienė & Railienė, 2012). Developing these set of skills is crucial for young people as it determines their success in the later outcomes of life while ensuring their well-being and professional growth. The development of these skills is essential for economic growth (OECD, 2021).

It is important to recognise what careers curricula should entail and how general competencies could be developed outside the educational set-up. For example, recognising the importance of employer encounters at an early age that could provide work experience to students (OECD, 2021). Hence, employers need support or clear policies and guidelines that would encourage them to offer support and work-based learning. This work-based learning should be offered to school students and adults who aim to explore different career paths and re-skill in different areas (OECD, 2021). By interacting with employers' students could familiarise themselves with interdisciplinary content applicable to multiple industries and career paths. Thus, the experience would allow students to link their experiences and learning to the subjects they are studying in schools. As a result of effective careers education students would develop essential skills and would be ready to integrate within the world of work after their graduation. Integrating career guidance within curriculum could also help to rectify the problem where many young adults do not choose higher qualification studies in STEM field because they do not see relevance between the subject they study in school and their future career prospects (Jankaitė & Budrytė, 2021).

There is a need to establish government guidelines, policies and professional bodies.

If any person can deliver career advice and guidance service with basic training, it suggests that the professionals may lack competencies and required skills that would help to increase student motivation for getting involved in careers education. Furthermore, there are no clear measure tools of success to understand if what schools are delivering meets Career Education Standards and establish what should be done to improve them within each school. Currently schools are not measuring their success of career education. This raises the question of how much of career education that is discussed in theory works in practice and if these standards should be improved. Therefore, there is a need for career guidance training standards that would ensure that all schools provide an equal level of service to all individuals. It is recommended to establish a professional body that would focus on the career industry and best practices by providing clear guidelines and training to those who want to pursue career guidance within the public and private sector. Furthermore, there is a need to establish an organisation that would focus on helping professionals to develop their skills and knowledge at conferences and professional events that would focus on sharing experiences and developing career practice. The training guidance standards should be established by a professional governmental body that would allocate career education funding to schools while monitoring the quality of career education delivery within the public sector. The same professional body should monitor the private sector to ensure that only qualified professionals provide personal career guidance as this would help to ensure the quality of advice given. There should be consistency in providing a career education to increase the value of the services delivered. The governmental guidelines should not only provide effective training to those aiming to deliver careers education but also have a set of standards and awarding bodies for schools to follow. The schools and other institutions should be assessed annually according to the quality guidelines and standards provided. This would help to establish an equal level of careers education across all schools and other institutions while ensuring no bias or favouritism in the process.

New incentives that would encourage young adults to pursue careers as teachers.

The career services in schools are mostly delivered by teachers. To tackle the lack of different subject teachers the funding and funded places in Higher Education (HE) should be linked to the demand of labour market attracting more students to those areas (OECD, 2021). Government should focus on the incentive of funding the studies with the condition for graduates to work back the time in the education set-up. Also, HE degrees focused on education should implement a module that would focus on delivering personal and group career guidance and services in schools with an understanding of how to integrate it into the curricula. This would help to prepare specialists that are qualified in understanding the importance of career education and would already know how to implement it within the learning. Additionally, the courses should cover the importance of keeping up to date with the labour market trends. Effective careers guidance requires to constantly update knowledge due to continuous changes of the world of work; therefore, professionals should have access to continuous professional development and training that would allow them to do so every few years.

Establishing support for those who are at the start and at the end of their working life's by helping them to integrate within the labour market.

Encouraging young adults to join the labour market in Lithuania.

Since there is a shortage of qualified specialists for jobs in demand more detailed research needs to be conducted to identify what could be done to prevent young people from leaving or to encourage them to return. The possible suggestions could be focusing on offering employment opportunities that match young people's skills, career guidance within the school set-up that would help pupils to relate subject areas to future jobs in demand while promoting economic stability that would result from choosing well-paid employment.

Supporting older generations aiming to join the labour market.

There is a necessity to provide flexible conditions for adult learning (OECD, 2021). While there are organisations offering vocational qualifications there is a need for creating new type of contract that would focus on flexible working providing adults with opportunities to schedule in their preferred hours that would come in line with their commitments, personal life and aspirations towards learning. It would be useful to offer tax incentives and employee benefit packages to increase older generations engagement within continuous learning and labour market opportunities. Based on individual circumstances older people should also have priority access to less demanding jobs. Moreover, the government could consider providing access to free courses or training on the job for adults wishing to up-skill towards entering sectors that experience labour shortage.

A need for further research with a focus on identifying areas of future jobs within Lithuania and ways to up-skill to meet the demand.

While automation will have an influence on shaping the future job market in Lithuania there is a need for more detailed research around this area. The research should focus on particular industries and roles that will be in demand in the future and should suggest relevant steps in preparing future generations for those changes. Thus, future job analysis should be shared across the resources provided to career specialist with links to the curriculum and future skills in demand. It is also important to establish a structure that would help older generations to up-skill to prevent unemployment.

9 Conclusion

This chapter has highlighted a lack of effective careers education and personalised guidance delivery within Lithuanian institutions. This may be influenced by the structure where careers service can be delivered by anyone across schools and other organisations including teachers, vice-principal support staff and anyone with the similar background. Those delivering a career education most often do not have the required competencies and qualifications as each institution has its own responsibility in training those who aim to deliver this service. It is suggested that while schools should take the primary role in delivering the career service it should only be done by those who have qualification within this area which would ensure that the guidance given meets the highest industry standards and is impartial and un-bias. This requires the governing bodies to be established that would not only set the standards but would also do annual reviews establishing the effectiveness of the programme. Having set guidelines would ensure that all schools, vocational centres, higher education institutions as well as private organisations deliver career education services at the same level and provide equal access and opportunities for all. Having set standards and qualification guidelines would create a better environment for delivering personal guidance which is currently not accessible for many young adults across the country.

Another challenge is that Lithuania face is a lack of teachers within those subjects that are in demand in line with prospects of future jobs, for example, STEM sector. While the government is developing incentives that would help to attach students to those subject areas there is a need for motivational incentives that would primarily focus on those areas that are experiencing a shortage. Moreover, if the government decides to fund higher degree studies for those who want to become teachers within subjects in demand the conditional offers should be made where students work at school for a certain period. This would allow them to get the experience after graduation while helping to change those professionals who are at retirement age and do not wish to continue their employment.

While students do struggle with blended learning more attention should be given to developing their digital literacy. Especially because many employers identify with a shortage of digital skills. Career education could help students to identify the relevance of these skills and world of work; for example, being more employable and having access to wider opportunities. Implementing technology within delivering learning could also help career practitioners to deliver guidance for those students who need it on demand as well as create online resources that students could access at any time.

More attention is needed for identifying what areas of future jobs will be in demand in Lithuania. While there are prognoses about the increase of digital skills and development of technological advancement it is important to identity which skills will be needed to meet the demand of those jobs and establish relevant educational programmes. These programmes could help to raise awareness of jobs in demand and assist people in matching their career interests with available roles. The development of these skills should start at the school level; however, in order to do so a well-developed career education and its integration within curriculum needs to be considered.

In addition, Lithuania is experiencing a demographic change where ageing population cause shortage of employees within some sectors. It is also predicted that an ageing population will have implications for economic growth and productivity. Due to skills mismatch and hard-working conditions, such factors may prevent people from investing their time in professional development. Due to low wages and an unfavourable working environment people chose to migrate to other countries, aspiring for a higher quality of life. A potential solution to this can be a consideration of flexible working hours, tax incentives and employee benefit schemes for an ageing population while establishing training with an access for all age groups who wish to gain desired skills to enter their preferred jobs. Overall Lithuania has to recognise the importance of career's sector and integrate that centrally within the whole strategy of education and economic growth. While the positive progress has started there are still many challenges that need to be overcome before the career education can start showing practical results; therefore, the continuous studies and analysis reports should be conducted to see the progression within this area.

References

Antanaitienė, A., & Sajienė, L. (2012). Bendrojo ugdymo mokyklų ir profesinio mokymo įstaigų vaidmuo mokinių profesiniam apsisprendimui: situacija ir pagrindinės problemos. *Acta Paedagogica Vilnensia, 29*, 133–143. [online] Available at: https://www.researchgate.net/publication/291256571_Bendrojo_ugdymo_mokyklu_ir_profesinio_mokymo_istaigu_vaidmuo_mokiniu_profesiniam_apsisprendimui_situacija_ir_pagrindines_problemos

Augienė, D. (2018). Bendrojo ugdymo mokyklos karjeros specialisto vaidmuo mokinių karjeros kompetencijas. *Švietimas: politika, vadyba, kokybė/Education Policy, Management and Quality, 10*(3), 102–104. [online]. Available at: http://oaji.net/articles/2019/513-1552893927.pdf

Cedefop. (2015). Skills forecasts country report – Lithuania. [online] *Cedefop.europa.eu*. Available at: https://www.cedefop.europa.eu/printpdf/publications-and-resources/country-reports/lithuania-skills-forecasts-2025

Cedefop. (2020a). *Empowering adults through upskilling and reskilling pathways. Volume 1: Adult population with potential for upskilling and reskilling* [online]. Luxembourg: Publications Office of the European Union., p. Cedefop reference series; No 112. Available at: http://data.europa.eu/doi/10.2801/475393

Cedefop. (2020b). Empowering adults through upskilling and reskilling pathways. Volume 1, Adult population with potential for upskilling and reskilling [online]. *Data.europa.eu*. Available at: http://data.europa.eu/doi/10.2801/475393

Civitta. (2021). Lietuvos Respublikos švietimo ir mokslo ministerija. Švitimo raidos scenarijų konkursas [online]. *Vilnius*, p. 430. Available at: http://file:///C:/Users/Liepa%20Mikule/Downloads/Civitta_Scenarijus.pdf

Coding School. (2021). IT Karjeros Centras visų kalbų programuotojams [online]. *Vilnius Coding School*. Available at: https://www.vilniuscoding.lt/karjeros-centras/

Coding School. (2021a). Programavimo pagrindai per 6 savaites Kaune [online]. *Vilnius Coding School*. Available at: https://www.vilniuscoding.lt/mokymai/6-savaiciu-programavimo-mokymai-kaune/

Creighton, H. (2014). *Europe's ageing demography* [online]. ilcuk.org.uk. Available at: https://ilcuk.org.uk/wp-content/uploads/2019/11/Europes-Ageing-Demography.pdf

Digiklasė. (2021). Mokiniams – Digiklasė [online]. *Digiklase.lt*. Available at: https://digiklase.lt/

Dranseikaitė, L. (2021). Rekordiškai daug mokytojų palieka mokyklas: visus gąsdina nauji mokslo metai [online]. *DELFI*. Available at: https://www.delfi.lt/news/daily/lithuania/rekordiskai-daug-mokytoju-palieka-mokyklas-visus-gasdina-nauji-mokslo-metai.d?id=87475003

EAEA. (2020). *Developments: No significant adult education policy developments in Lithuania*. EAEA Country Reports [online]. Countryreport.eaea.org. Available at: https://countryreport.eaea.org/lithuania/lithuania-2020/No%20significant%20adult%20education%20policy%20developments%20in%20Lithuania

EEPO. (2015). Upskilling unemployed adults (aged 25 to 64): The organisation, profiling and targeting of training provision. *EEPO Review* [online]. Luxembourg: Publications Office of the European Union, pp. 3–68. Available at: https://doi.org/10.2767/409552.

Europos migracijos tinklas. (2021). Migracija skaičiais - EMN [online]. *123.emn.lt*. Available at: https://123.emn.lt/

Filatovaitė, L. & Stakėla, L. (2021). Švietimo sektoriaus inovatyvumo skatinimas: EdTech ekosistemos plėtraI [online]. *Kurklt.lt*. Available at: http://kurklt.lt/projektai/edtech/

Gudžinskienė, V., & Railienė, A. (2012). Gyvenimo įgūdžių ugdymo ir ugdymo karjerai sąsaja: bendrojo lavinimo kontekstas. *Acta Paedagogica Vilnensia, 29*, 61–72. [online]. https://doi.org/10.15388/ActPaed.2012.29.1177

Hogeforster, M. & Wildt, C. (2020). Recent developments and challenges of the introduction of dual training for SMEs in countries around the Baltic Sea Region with a special emphasis on Lithuania. *11th International Scientific Conference "Business and Management 2020"* [online]. pp. 256–261. Available at: https://doi.org/10.3846/bm.2020.652.

Idialogue. (2020). Idialogue mokymai [online]. *Idialogue.lt*. Available at: https://www.idialogue.lt/e-parduotuve/2

Jankaitė, J. & Budrytė, M. (2021). Lietuvos Darbo Rinkos Apžvalga ir tendencijos [online]. *Kurklt.lt*. Available at: http://kurklt.lt/wp-content/uploads/2021/06/Darbo-rinkos-analiz%C4%97.pdf

Kalba.lt. (2021). Pirminė karjeros konsultacija – NEMOKAMAI! — Kalba.Lt [online]. *Kalba.lt*. Available at: https://kalba.lt/pirmine-karjeros-konsultacija-nemokamai/

Karjera.lt. (2021). Karjeros centraiIKarjeros konsultantai ir konsultacijos [online]. *Karjera.lt*. Available at: https://karjera.lt/web/guest/karjeros-centrai

Karjera.lt. (2021a). Karjeros centraiIKarjeros konsultantai ir konsultacijos [online]. *Karjera.lt*. Available at: https://karjera.lt/web/guest/karjeros-centrai

Kastu. (2021). Karjeros centras - Kastu.lt [online]. *Kastu.lt*. Available at: https://kastu.lt/karjeros_centras

KTU. (2017). Most Lithuanians still emigrate for economic reasons [online]. *EurekAlert*. Available at: https://www.eurekalert.org/news-releases/729969

KTU. (2021). Edukologija. Magistrantūros studijos, humanitarinių mokslų ir menų fakultetas [online]. *Stojantiesiems*. Available at: https://stojantiesiems.ktu.edu/programme/m-edukologija/#semester-1.

Li, Z., & Qiu, Z. (2018). How does family background affect children's educational achievement? Evidence from contemporary China. *The Journal of Chinese Sociology, 5*(1), 1–21.

Lietuvos Bankas. 2021. IMF positively evaluates resilience of Lithuania's economy, but urges to focus on productivity increase [online]. *Lb.lt*. Available at: https://www.lb.lt/en/news/imf-positively-evaluates-resilience-of-lithuania-s-economy-but-urges-to-focus-on-productivity-increase

LMNŠC. (2021). Apie centrą [online]. *Lmnsc.lt*. Accessed October 12, 2021, from https://www.lmnsc.lt/informacija/

LRT. (2020). Nuotolinis mokymasis kelia iššūkių visai šeimai: ekspertai pataria, ką daryti, kad vaikai nepervargtų [online]. *lrt.lt*. Available at: https://www.lrt.lt/naujienos/lietuvoje/2/1294456/nuotolinis-mokymasis-kelia-issukiu-visai-seimai-ekspertai-pataria-ka-daryti-kad-vaikai-nepervargtu

LRT. (2021). Artimiausiais metais šalyje gali trūkti per 2 tūkst. mokytojų, tačiau privačiose mokyklose jų daugėja [online]. *lrt.lt*. Available at: https://www.lrt.lt/naujienos/lietuvoje/2/1454697/artimiausiais-metais-salyje-gali-trukti-per-2-tukst-mokytoju-taciau-privaciose-mokyklose-ju-daugeja

Luobikienė, I. (2015). Career guidance in Lithuania: Tradition or fear of change? *Rural Environment, Education, Personality*, 1–8. [online]. Available at: https://llufb.llu.lv/conference/REEP/2015/Latvia-Univ-Agricult-REEP-2015proceedings-309-316.pdf

Martin, J. (2015). Activation and active labour market policies in OECD countries: Stylised facts and evidence on their effectiveness. *IZA Journal of Labor Policy, 4*(1) [online]. Available at: https://izajolp.springeropen.com/articles/10.1186/s40173-015-0032-y

Martinaitis, Z., Sadauskaitė, A., & Barzotto, M. (2021). *Adaptation trajectories of dismissed workers: A critical case study of the Lithuanian radio-electronics sector.* Work, Employment and Society.

McKinsey & Company. (2017). Digitally-enabled automation and artificial intelligence: Shaping the future of work in Europe's digital front-runners [online]. mckinsey.com/. Available at: https://www.mckinsey.com/~/media/mckinsey/featured insights/europe/shaping the future of work in europes nine digital front runner countries/shaping-the-future-of-work-in-europes-digital-front-runners.ashx

Meldrum, S. (2017). Group guidance – Is it time to flock together?. *Journal of the National Institute for Career Education and Counselling* 38(1), pp. 36–43. Available at: https://www.napier.ac.uk/media/worktribe/output-869984/group-guidance%2D%2Dis-it-time-to-flock-together.pdf

Merfeldaite, O., Railiene, A., Indrasiene, V. & Jegeleviciene, V., (2020). *Challenges for education career in the Lithuanian schools of general education: experience of career specialists* [online]. Available at: https://doi.org/10.17770/sie2020vol4.4836

MRU. (2021). Karjeros Valdymas [online]. *MRU*. Available at: https://www.mruni.eu/study_program/karjeros-valdymas/

Mukis.lt. (2021). Mukis - Mokytojams » Renginiai [online]. *Mukis.lt*. Available at: http://www.mukis.lt/lt/renginiai.html

Murauskaitė, A. (2021). 16 organizacijų sukirto rankomis dėl naujų mokslo metų: nesame naivūs, bus COVID-19 židinių, bet atsakingi esame visi [online]. *lrt.lt*. Available at: https://www.lrt.lt/naujienos/lietuvoje/2/1481924/16-organizaciju-sukirto-rankomis-del-nauju-mokslo-metu-nesame-naivus-bus-covid-19-zidiniu-bet-atsakingi-esame-visi?fbclid=IwAR0Z3Oh3A76SyvopZAqa8gjfZHR8nAeA7Jmv9EgU9fIPux-Tnusdo1QvuHQ

Murauskaitė, A. (2021a). Mokytojų rengimas plazda raudonomis vėliavomis: nebus kam mokyti matematikos, o fizinis ugdymas it medus traukia [online]. *lrt.lt*. Available at: https://www.lrt.lt/naujienos/lietuvoje/2/1403083/mokytoju-rengimas-plazda-raudonomis-veliavomis-nebus-kam-mokyti-matematikos-o-fizinis-ugdymas-it-medus-traukia

Nacionalinė švietimo agentūra. (2021). Po „EdTech" starto – siūlymai mokyklas praturtinti „Google" švietimo įrankiais - Švietimo naujienos [online]. *Švietimo naujienos*. Available at: https://www.svietimonaujienos.lt/po-edtech-starto-siulymai-mokyklas-praturtinti-google-svietimo-irankiais/

OECD. (2021). *OECD skills strategy Lithuania: Assessment and recommendations. OECD skills studies* (pp. 6–43). OECD Publishing. [online]. Available at: https://www.oecd.org/skills/centre-for-skills/OECD-Skills-Strategy-Lithuania-Report-Summary.pdf

Orion. (2021). Švietimas – geriausia investicija į mūsų ateitį [online]. *Am.orion.lt*. Available at: https://am.orion.lt/wp-content/uploads/2020/09/Svietimas_geriausia_investicija.pdf.

Pata, K., Maslo, I., & Jõgi, L. (2021). Transforming adult education from neo-liberal to holistically inclusive adult education in Baltic States. *Young Adults and Active Citizenship, 26*, 139–165. [online]. https://doi.org/10.1007/978-3-030-65002-5_8

Petkevičiūtė, N. & Balčiūnaitienė, A. (2021). Learning Challenges During Pandemic Situation: Lithuanian University Case. *Rural Environment. Education. Personality. (REEP) Proceedings of the 14th International Scientific Conference* [online] pp. 1–8. Available at: https://web.archive.org/web/20210510022709id_/https://llufb.llu.lv/conference/REEP/2021/Latvia_REEP_2021_proceedings_No14_online-155-162.pdf

SKVC. (2021). General Education|Education in Lithuania|Studijų kokybės vertinimo centras [online]. *Skvc.lt*. Available at: https://www.skvc.lt/default/en/education-in-lithuania/general

State Progress Council. (2012). *Lithuania's progress strategy "Lithuania 2030"* [online]. *lrs.lt*. Available at: https://rb.gy/2xunzm
Švietimo, mokslo ir sporto ministerija. (2020). Dažniausiai užduodami klausimai ir atsakymai apie etatinį apmokėjimą [online]. *Smm.lt*. Available at: https://www.smm.lt/uploads/documents/naujienos/klausimai_atsakymai_0425.pdf
Totorienė, R., & Augienė, D. (2018). Career education of 7th - 8th grade students: Career professionals position. *Education: Policy, Management and Quality, 10*(3), 105–114. [online] Available at: http://oaji.net/articles/2019/513-1552894026.pdf
Užimtumo tarnyba. (2020). Veiklos ataskaita [online]. *Vilnius*, pp. 18–21. Available at: https://uzt.lt/wp-content/uploads/2021/04/2020-veiklos-ataskaita.pdf
Užimtumo tarnyba. (2021). Užimtumo tarnyba prie LR Socialinės apsaugos ir darbo ministerijos [online]. *Užimtumo tarnyba prie LR Socialinės apsaugos ir darbo ministerijos*. Available at: https://uzt.lt/
Vaitulionienė, R., & Augienė, D. (2018). Ugdymo karjerai įgyvendinimas gimnazijoje: lūkesčiai ir problemos. Švietimas: politika, vadyba, kokybė/Education Policy. *Management and Quality, 10*(3), 115–127. [online]. Available at: https://www.lituanistika.lt/content/81152
VDU. (2021a). Studijų programos. Mokomojo dalyko pedagogika (STEAM): matematika, informatika, biologija, chemija, fizika, technologijos (Kaune) [online]. *VDU*. Available at: https://www.vdu.lt/lt/study/program/subject/274/
VDU. (2021b). Studijų programos. Profesijos edukologija [online]. *VDU Švietimo akademija*. Available at: https://svietimas.vdu.lt/studiju-programos/?/lt/study/program/subject/326
Versli Lietuva. (2017). Kodėl IMD pasaulio talentų reitinge Lietuva krito žemyn - Versli Lietuva [online]. *Versli Lietuva*. Available at: https://www.verslilietuva.lt/naujienos/kodel-imd-pasaulio-talentu-reitinge-lietuva-krito-zemyn/
Versli Lietuva. (2021). Verslumo Tendencijos Lietuvoje 2020 [online]. *Verslilietuva.lt*. Available at: https://www.verslilietuva.lt/wp-content/uploads/2021/07/2021.06.30_verslumo_apzvalga.pdf
Vilikanskytė, M. (2020). Many jobs in Lithuania can be replaced by robots – study [online]. *lrt.lt*. Available at: https://www.lrt.lt/en/news-in-english/19/1237432/many-jobs-in-lithuania-can-be-replaced-by-robots-study
Vilkoitytė, V. & Skučienė, D. (2020). *Elderly attitudes on the continuity of working careers* [online]. Vilnius University Press. Available at: https://doi.org/10.15388/STEPP.2020.16.
Vilniaus Universitetas. (2021). *Edukologija* [online]. Vilniaus universitetas. Available at: https://www.vu.lt/studijos/stojantiesiems/magistro-studiju-sarasas/edukologija#studiju-programos-planas
Wysocka, M. (2021). Effect of demographic changes on the labour supply in Lithuania and Poland. *Engineering Economics, 32*(1), 35–47.
Židžiūnienė, A. (2021). Edukacijos forumas „Kokybiško švietimo visiems visą gyvenimą UNESCO vizija: artėjame prie ar tolstame nuo jos?" - Švietimo naujienos [online]. *Švietimo naujienos*. Available at: https://www.svietimonaujienos.lt/edukacijos-forumas-kokybisko-svietimo-visiems-visa-gyvenima-unesco-vizija-artejame-prie-ar-tolstame-nuo-jos-2/

Luxembourg: "Somewhere Over the Rainbow" or "Is There Really a Land Where the Dreams of Social Justice and Equity Do Come True?"

Jean-Jacques Ruppert

1 Introduction

Questions of social injustice have for many years now been in the limelight and it is hardly surprising that guidance and career counsellors have also increasingly been faced with issues related to social justice. Hence, it is important to look into whether guidance and career counselling might play a part in dealing with social injustice and if so, investigate the scope and limits of the impact guidance and career counselling can have in the real world.

In their 2013 Montpellier communiqué the IAEVG appealed "to providers, practitioners, academics and policy-makers to increase their efforts by embracing social justice as a core value that guides their practices".

2 What About Social Justice or Should We Say Social Injustice?

Quite a few people consider social injustice as the greatest flaw of Western societies which are characterised by all kinds of inequalities between women and men, young and old, capital and labour, rural and urban dwellers, natives and immigrants, property owners and tenants—in any case, the list of differences or distinctions that make it possible to point at unequal distributions within our societies is endless. The issue of social justice or injustice is however hardly a new one.

Already in 1897, the German sociologist Georg Simmel put forward a hypothesis on social inequality in a "fairy tale" entitled "Rosen". His story begins in a fictitious

J.-J. Ruppert (✉)
Applied Vocational Psychology and Policy Research Unit, Belvaux, Luxembourg
e-mail: jean-jacques.ruppert@education.lu

C. Enoch et al. (eds.), *Vocational Guidance in Europe*,
https://doi.org/10.1007/978-3-031-06592-7_8

agrarian society in which there is an equal distribution of land. Everyone makes a decent living as people do not need more than the land provides, that is as long as they adjust their consumption to their income, something we may by the way have become unaccustomed to.

Now some of the landowners additionally begin to grow roses. This does not fail to create a conspicuous inequality. The author attributes this very noticeable inequality to already existing differences: small differences in wealth, different leisure behaviours, soil qualities that are differently favourable to the cultivation of roses, varying skills and so on. In other words, it does not take much to make a difference, to create a distinction. As you would expect a couple of roses generate more roses through cuttings, and as the rose growers learn more about the growing of roses, they refine their products more and more. This makes them and their gardens increasingly stand out from the non-rose growers and their rather barren gardens, with the differences becoming ever more pronounced.

Based partly on a sense of injustice, partly on admiration for roses, partly on indignation at the randomness of privilege, there is envy and there is protest against this state of affairs. And therefore the motives underlying this protest are based not only in inequality, but also in the demand to eliminate it. It comes to a conflict between the rose owners and those who want the roses to be equally redistributed. The latter win this argument not only because they are the larger group but also because not even the rose growers can completely close their minds to the ideal of social justice. The fact that minor differences born out of a mix of diligence and chance had become substantial inequalities, even the privileged rose growers could not present as a historical necessity, God's will or a moral proof of individual efficiency.

The rose bushes are then redistributed so that everyone has some and social peace is restored. But—as one can easily imagine—it does not stay that way long and the peace achieved is short-lived as the most ardent supporters of equality do not fail to notice further inequalities: some roses thrive better and smell more seductively than others, sunlight also favours some more than others and now even these most minimal and dare we say "natural" differences seem no less unbearable than the previous greater ones. It follows that further adjustments are made—again and again, and even Simmel refused to speculate on how often and until when these arguments and reconciliations repeated themselves:

> Ob und wann die Bürger unseres Märchenlandes das einsahen, wie oft die Revolution—immer um den noch gebliebenen Rest der Ungleichheit—sich wiederholte, weiß ich nicht. In hundert Jahren wird man es vielleicht wissen. Aber in tröstlicher Gleichgültigkeit gegen all' diese Wandlungen lebten die Rosen ihre selbstgenügsame Schönheit weiter (p. 360–361).

roughly translated as:

> Whether and when the citizens of our fairy-tale country realised this, how often the revolution—always around the still remaining residue of inequality—repeated itself, I don't know. In a hundred years, perhaps, we will know. But in comforting indifference to all these changes, the roses lived on in their self-sufficient beauty.

This fable emphasises a defining element of social injustice: it is not necessarily the objective fact but the subjective perception of differences that drives people to seek what they see as social injustice, a truth Harry G. Frankfurt from Princeton University also points out at the beginning of his book "On Inequality" (p.1) when he writes:

"First man: 'How are your children?' "
"Second man: 'Compared to what?' "

We very reluctantly have to agree with the Romanian/French philosopher and essayist Emil Cioran (1911–1995) that "nous en voulons à tous ceux qui . . . courent à nos côtés, gênent nos pas ou nous laissent en arrière" (Guerrini, 2002).

Freely translated as: "We resent everyone . . . who run at our side, who hamper our stride or leave us behind".

3 Is Social Justice Achievable at All?

Obviously, there is no denying that objectively there are growing injustices and inequities in our societies and it is or it should be up to politicians and policy-makers to address these. But beyond these indisputable facts we have to acknowledge that even in the German philosopher Gottfried Leibnitz's (1646–1716) "le meilleur des mondes possible", i.e. "the best of all possible worlds" (Essais de Théodicée sur la Bonté de Dieu, la liberté de l'homme et l'origine du mal—Essays of Theodicy on the Goodness of God, the Freedom of Man and the Origin of Evil. in: Caro, Hernán D. (2020). The Best of All Possible Worlds? Leibniz's Philosophical Optimism and Its Critics 1710–1755. Brill's Studies in Intellectual History. p.322 Leiden; Brill Publishers).

As well as in Simmel's "Rosen", despite never-ending redistributions, subjective feelings of social injustice are persistent and hence there simply is no way to eliminate them for good. Furthermore, we do worry that our societies are becoming ever more sensitive to social inequalities while at the same time never being able to achieve social justice. There is an unpleasant side to promises of social justice and equality: Everyone is promised everything, but in reality, only a few have career and life success and this opens up space for toxic feelings of injustice as depicted in "Rosen".

Let us furthermore have a critical look at the society we live in.

More than 50 years after Pierre Bourdieu's works on social reproduction, the French sociologist Camille Peugny's, 2013 book "Le destin au berceau: Inégalités et reproduction sociale" which roughly translates as "Destiny in the cradle: Inequalities and social reproduction" observes that in France today, seven out of ten children of white collar workers have a position of white collar worker a few years after the end of their studies; however, seven out of ten children of blue collar workers remain confined to blue collar jobs. So, more than two centuries after the Revolution, birth conditions continue to determine the fate of individuals. He concludes that one does not become a blue collar worker but that one is born a blue collar worker.

It can therefore be argued that our society, with its class-based constraints, has some parallels to the nightmarish model depicted in Aldous Huxley's "Brave New World" (1932) where children are created, "decanted" and raised in hatcheries and conditioning centres. They are from birth genetically designed to fit into one of five castes, which are further split into "Plus" and "Minus" members and designed to fulfil predetermined positions within the social and economic strata of the World State.

To make matters even worse, it is doubtful that education alone can change this situation. Of course, there is more to education than its utilitarian value but when push comes to shove, the value of a qualification is only as high as the labour market is willing to pay for it. A young person with a Ph.D. in astrophysics who cannot find employment corresponding to his/her qualification and drives a taxi for a living, is at the end of the day unfortunately still ("only") a taxi-driver, earning a taxi-driver's wages.

4 What About Guidance and Career Counsellors and Social Justice?

Let us despite these hardly encouraging premises be brave, venture into the land of dreams and lose ourselves in "The Wondrous Story of the Guidance and career Counsellors and Their Quest for Social Justice".

"Once upon a time there was a planet far, far away where social injustices and divisions had created wide economic and social gaps between, and within, countries. A great number of the inhabitants of this planet were out of work—among them many and often highly qualified young people. Those lucky enough to be in jobs, were often paid less than those taken on with the same or even lower qualifications a couple of years earlier. At the same time, employers complained of a dramatic shortage of skills and competences in jobseekers—the future looked very bleak indeed. Furthermore, a number of policies to promote social inclusion and cohesion had actually worsened the situation, proving to be ineffective in the creation of a democratic, participative and inclusive society. But not all was lost, as there was a group of indomitable individuals who still held out against this terrible state of affairs: the Guidance and Career Counsellors!

Deeply committed to social justice, advocating for and with their clients at both individual and system levels, they began to address the structural and societal barriers that oppressed the people. They argued that promoting

(continued)

equality of opportunity regarding access to education, training and employment was no longer enough. Indeed, they believed that all concerned had to strive to achieve nothing less than equity and equality of outcomes. The Guidance and Career Counsellors believed that social justice meant recognising that people should not be subservient to the demands of the labour market, and that consequently, the careers agenda should not be driven by solely economic rationalist arguments, but rather encompass a holistic view through which the needs of all human development could be taken into account.

So, one day, the Guidance and Career Counsellors decided to go and see the Policy-Makers and asked them to reassess the contribution that careers education, guidance and counselling could make to promoting a just society, and how the Policy-Makers could provide the material and political support to make this a reality. As the Policy-Makers were wise men and women, though obviously not as wise as the Guidance and Career Counsellors, they promised to embrace social justice as a core value of their future policies. The Guidance and Career Counsellors were overjoyed at this good news as it would help to ensure that career practice once more became truly meaningful, and real career choice was made available to all the people" (author's own story).

This brings us to the end of our little fairy-tale and back to the rather different realities of our time. If the 2013 Montpellier IAEVG communiqué was evidence of a real desire to think beyond current confines, such "blue-sky thinking" however must nevertheless operate within the parameters of the possible, for what is at issue here is nothing less than how counsellors should engage with the "real" world in order to promote social justice.

5 What Constitutes Social Justice in Our Western Societies?

The introduction to the 2012 UK Government report on Social Justice (www.dwp.gov.uk/social-justice) states that *"Social Justice is about making society function better ..."* and *"...to increase social mobility"* (p. 4):

> This is indeed all very nice and noble and there is no way one could morally argue a case against it. But as we all know, the idea of social justice is never a neutral one, it is at best a multidimensional and at worst a controversial and divisive concept. And if most of us will not have any issues with the principle of equality of opportunities, equality of outcomes might easily be a very much thornier issue.

To illustrate our qualms, let us with the following lines look *"Over the Rainbow"*:

> *"First (the Dodo) marked out a race-course, in a sort of circle and then all the party were placed along the course, here and there. There was no 'One, two, three, and away,' but they began running when they liked, and left off when they liked, so that it was not easy to know when the race was over. However, when they had been running half an hour or so, (..) the Dodo suddenly called out 'The race is over!' and they all crowded round it, panting, and asking, 'But who has won?' This question the Dodo could not answer without a great deal of thought, and it sat for a long time with one finger pressed upon its forehead, while the rest waited in silence. At last the Dodo said, 'EVERYBODY has won, and all must have prizes'"*. (Carroll, 1961, p. 21)

Well, contrary to this race in *"Alice's Adventures in Wonderland"*, we suppose we can all agree on the basic premise that in a real race going over a fixed distance, all the runners start at the same time and from the same spot—this is put into simple words what basic equality of opportunities amounts to. The organisers of a race might even make sure that all the runners have the same running gear and so on, thus eliminating many arbitrary formal barriers to the participation in the race. What the organisers of the race however will have no influence over is the different levels of talent that the individual runners possess, i.e. the informal barriers that might determine their performance in the race. Nevertheless, so far so good.

6 What About the Outcome of the Race?

We firmly believe that the organisers should not have any power over who finishes first, second, third and so on. Equality of outcomes would indeed mean that all the runners finish at the same time, that everybody wins and gets the first prize. Here we happily endorse the thesis of Nobel Prize winner and Indian economist and philosopher Amartya Sen whose lecture at Stanford University in 1979 was to permanently shake our thinking about distributive justice: In his talk entitled *"Equality of What?"* Amartya Sen (1980), (p. 195–220) referred to the philosopher "John Rawls" "A Theory of Justice" (1971) and advanced that justice should not be about the distribution of goods or money—for example, in development aid or as in Simmel's fable about the redistribution of roses, but about the opportunities that each individual finds to realise his or her dreams in life.

7 What Can Guidance and Career Counsellors Actually Do If They Want to Promote Social Justice?

Counsellors actually have two different roles to play:

On the one hand, they are a kind of coach supporting the runners before, during and possibly even after any given race. In the role of a coach, they must focus on the individuals. If they base their practices on the philosophical guiding principle of social justice, they should be in a position to give unbiased counsel to individuals regarding their potential participation in any given *"race"*, accompany them in their preparation and ideally follow them up afterwards. This gives them considerable influence at an individual level ensuring that informal barriers are eliminated. When acting as coaches, counsellors obviously have little to no influence on the circumstances that individuals face, but they can have considerable influence on the choices and decisions the counselees will make.

On the other hand, counsellors can be a kind of judge/referee aiding the organisers of a race in selecting the best runners. In this role, they must focus on the system. If they also base their practices on the philosophical guiding principle of social justice, they should be in a position to ensure that the selection process for the *"race"* is fair and unbiased. In other words that everyone has an equal chance to acquire the relevant skills, competences and qualifications necessary. This gives counsellors considerable influence at a system level ensuring that formal barriers are eliminated. It follows that when they are acting as judges/referees, counsellors have no influence on the choices and decisions that individuals will make, but they do or should have a certain influence on the circumstances that the counselees face.

8 What About Luxembourg? Might It Be the Land Where These Dreams Really Do Come True?

As this is not the place for a detailed portrait of the education and guidance systems in Luxembourg, we invite you to consult the following sites that will provide you with in-depth information (EURYDICE, 2021). We will therefore limit ourselves to a couple of facts about Luxembourg and some thoughts on the education system and the guidance set-up. Finally, for a critical assessment of education and guidance in Luxembourg, we would like to direct you to "La place de l'école dans la société luxembourgeoise de demain" by Romain Martin et al. (2008).

According to "Luxembourg in Figures 2021", a publication by STATEC, the Statistics Portal of the Grand Duchy, on 1 January 2021 Luxembourg had 634,700 inhabitants (p. 11). The massive increase of the resident population by more than 300,000 in the last 30 years is mainly due to immigration. On 1 January 2021, the ratio of foreigners in the general population was 47.2%. Foreign citizens' countries of origin are mostly one of the 28 member States of the European Union. So it is hardly surprising that the share of non-nationals in Luxembourg's resident population is the highest of all European countries. Furthermore, over 200,000 commuters from France, Belgium and Germany travel on a daily basis for work to Luxembourg.

Luxembourg is a trilingual country: the national language being Luxembourgish, "Lëtzebuergesch", spoken above all by the country's Luxembourgish population.

The legislative language is French, with French, German and Luxembourgish being the official administrative and judicial languages.

In addition to the three official languages, the immigrants' languages—especially Portuguese, French and Italian as well as English, play an important role in Luxembourg's economic and cultural life. Code switching, i.e., the necessity to switch from one language to another, is part and parcel of the residents' daily life. This trilingualism has a long tradition in Luxembourg with varying habits according to social background, context and political situation.

Given Luxembourg's linguistic particularity, it follows that the education system is also multilingual. In education Luxembourgish constitutes the language of integration and socialisation and German, French and English are progressively added. Furthermore, depending on the educational streams in secondary education students are in or on the options they have chosen, additional languages can be learned.

Compared to other EU member states Luxembourg has the highest number of pupils and students using another language at home than the language(s) of instruction with the time dedicated to teaching foreign languages being the highest.

If the nationals of any country logically constitute the target population of that country's education system, this observation applies—despite more recent positive developments to consider the specific situation of pupils and students of foreign origin—also to Luxembourg. The education system still is very much a school for Luxembourgers and it is therefore hardly surprising that many nationals who have succeeded in this highly selective system, consider it to be good or even excellent. Besides the mainstream Luxembourgish education system, an international provision is available that is mainly targeted at anglophone and francophone pupils/students in both elementary and secondary education.

We would however like to point out that the provision of formal and non-formal education has been vastly diversified during the past years such as to adapt to the linguistic and socio-cultural diversity of the population.

Here a one year "early childhood education" ("éducation précoce") for 3-years-old children has been a real success story—its purpose being to give non-national children the opportunity to learn Luxembourgish. A good understanding of Luxembourgish is crucial as from the age of six when compulsory schooling begins, the vehicular language is German, a logical approach as "Lëtzebuergesch" is close to German.

Although in cycle 3 of elementary education, pupils start learning French, the dominant language remains German, at least in theory as in practice teachers rely largely on a mix of Luxembourgish and German. For some pupils however this means that they have to master four languages: German, French, Luxembourgish and their mother tongue, e.g., Portuguese. If pupils of "Latin" origin frequently struggle with the German language, many Luxembourgish pupils find French a big hurdle.

Luxembourg's education system is thus faced with a very heterogeneous school population, both culturally, socio-economically and linguistically. If managing the social, economic and cultural heterogeneity of school populations is a challenge common to all European education systems, the policies adopted to deal with these issues vary significantly from one country to another. In some Scandinavian countries as well as in Portugal and in the Czech Republic to name but these few, admission into secondary education is automatic and takes place within a single educational system without a specific transition. In Luxembourg as in Germany, the Netherlands and in Austria, this transition depends not only on the pupil's success in primary school, but also on the decision of a so-called guidance council.

Such a guidance procedure is however rather marginal at the European level and mainly concerns countries with a Germanic educational tradition that is associated with different, often implicitly hierarchical, educational pathways. This specific policy of confronting the diversity of school populations can be seen as a part of what could be called an ideology of equal opportunities.

In Luxembourg the insistence on equal opportunities has led to differentiated teaching, the aim of which is to ensure that learning is tailor-made and adapted to pupils'/students' aptitudes.

Thus, the notion of equity implies that merit should be the only criterion for access to the so-called "noble" educational streams in secondary education. From such a point of view it is therefore vital to ensure the objectivity and validity of the assessments that decide on the success or failure of pupils/students and to disregard socio-cultural or socio-economic biases that might affect the guidance procedure.

An immediate consequence of the guidance procedure that governs the transition from primary school into secondary education in Luxembourg is that it clearly disadvantages foreign pupils. The inequalities in later educational achievement however call into question the capacity of the Luxembourg education system to really integrate the diversity of the populations it has to deal with.

The cultural bias is largely due to the predominance of a German-speaking component in the decisions of the so-called guidance councils which has the effect of excluding from most more demanding, i.e., the more academic streams of secondary education some pupils with a high potential but whose mastery of the German language is considered insufficient to succeed in the Luxembourg education system. Furthermore, pupils who have already repeated a year in primary school have almost exclusively been directed towards a less demanding stream of general secondary education. This tendency has however decreased in the last years.

The standardised tests used in the guidance procedure that takes place in the final year in primary school focus on assessing the specific competences of pupils in German, French and mathematics. As this does however hardly allow for a clear picture of the competences of the pupils, there now are some initiatives towards the creation of integrated and multidisciplinary tests which would make it possible to assess the transversal competences of pupils and thus provide the members of the guidance council with a better and more precise basis for their recommendation.

Furthermore, to remove German as the vehicular language for the evaluation of mathematics in primary school which puts pupils from a "Latin" background at a disadvantage, some officials have floated the idea of computer assisted testing, offering all pupils the possibility of choosing the language they feel most comfortable in. Such a step would considerably improve the psychometric validity of the data taken in the context of standardised tests and increase the objectivity of the decisions taken by the guidance council.

As such a move would however have little effect on wider societal inequalities, the present guidance procedure in such a culturally diverse country as Luxembourg must be questioned. Educational issues are frequently highly politicised with conflicting arguments of equality of opportunity versus equality of outcome. We are however entitled to express some serious reservations on whether a different guidance procedure might resolve the eternal debate between an education system characterised by differentiated streams such as we have in Luxembourg and which is favoured by politicians on the right of the political spectrum highlighting its ability to select the brightest pupils versus a more comprehensive education system with a common core which is promoted by politicians on the left of the political spectrum who will argue that a system with a common core has the capacity to reduce initial social inequalities. In what might be a Salomon-like decision the Minister of Education, Children and Youth has recently granted parents the final say in whether their child should go into classic secondary education or general secondary education. This measure does however not really impact any of the issues regarding the demands mentioned above the system sets on pupils and students.

With this type of guidance we are also entitled to state that some children's careers are already being decided at the end of primary school, i.e. at the age of 12 and this even if the parents now have the final say. Indeed, the pupils who "survive" this first selection round will attend classic secondary education with the others going into general secondary education. The "losers" of this first round of orientation tend to be children of foreign origin as well as Luxembourgish and foreign children from disadvantaged socio-economic backgrounds.

After 4 years in classic secondary education, a second orientation round takes place—again affecting the linguistically less gifted pupils with a shift towards French as the vehicular language in a majority of subjects. It goes without saying that such an "elitist" education system can only lead to academic failure.

Finally, within both classic secondary education and general secondary education, new constraints are being added to linguistic factors in the form of selective promotion criteria which determine not only educational success but also open or close the access to the various educational or vocational training paths. This occasionally brings about a situation where students in the third year of general secondary education—though they may have passed their year—will be refused to enter the educational or vocational training course of their choice because their grades are not good enough. This often leads to secondary school students repeating the year to get better marks. However, even if the students then get the grades required—which is the exception rather than the rule—success is frequently short-lived as quite a few of them will not be able to cope with the increasing academic demands of upper secondary education. All these considerations explain why there is actually little room for manoeuvre for guidance as strict promotion criteria determine educational avenues open to students and even predetermine their future working lives.

It is furthermore important to mention a very important and frequently ignored psychological factor in education and guidance and that is the social status of certain professions. If a lawyer has a higher social status than a bricklayer, a classic secondary education student also has a higher status than an apprentice never mind the sometimes huge gap in latter earning potential.

Finally, it is important to emphasise that there is no guidance proper for students who are going on to Higher Education. Indeed, the "Centre de Documentation et d'Information sur l'Enseignement Supérieur" (CEDIES), the Centre for Documentation and Information on Higher Education limits itself to information activities arguing that young people who want to enter Higher Education should be able to make the "right" choice by themselves. This situation still exists even though the CEDIES has now to integrate the "Maison de l'Orientation" (MO), the House of Guidance. The "Maison de l'Orientation" is a state administration that brings together in one place public players active in the field of educational and vocational guidance. The House of Guidance is aimed at any citizen looking for help in educational and vocational guidance with a view to identifying his or her abilities, skills and interests and making informed decisions on the choice of studies and training, as well as on professional projects.

Concluding we would nevertheless like to point to the fact that all the guidance services in educational settings as well as in employment agencies in Luxembourg are very well staffed and that the collaboration between the different services is excellent.

9 So, Might Luxembourg It Be the Land Where These Dreams Really Do Come True?

The simple answer to this question has to be "No" as prosperity alone is no guarantee for turning dreams into reality. With an overall score of 6.23 in the 2019 Social Justice in the EU and OECD Index Report published by the Bertelsmann Stiftung, Luxembourg ranks 19th of 41 countries. Luxembourg ranks among the top three on two of the index's six social justice dimensions: second on Health and third on Social Inclusion/Non-discrimination (cf. Fig. 1).

It is Luxembourg's demanding and selective education system that continues to pose among the greatest policy challenges. With a score of 5.73, it has improved since the first assessment ten years ago but remains among the bottom third (rank: 30). The share of the adult population without upper secondary education—21.4%—has declined in comparison to ten years but remains high comparative to many peers (rank: 30). The gap in educational attainment between women and men has nearly vanished, reaching near parity with regard to upper secondary (rank: 3). However, students from lower socio-economic households remain more disadvantaged in Luxembourg than in most of the countries in our study. The country places 35th with regard to the impact socio-economic factors have on the PISA performance of students. Among students scoring below the baseline level of proficiency on PISA, the impact of these socio-economic factors is particularly stark (rank: 39).

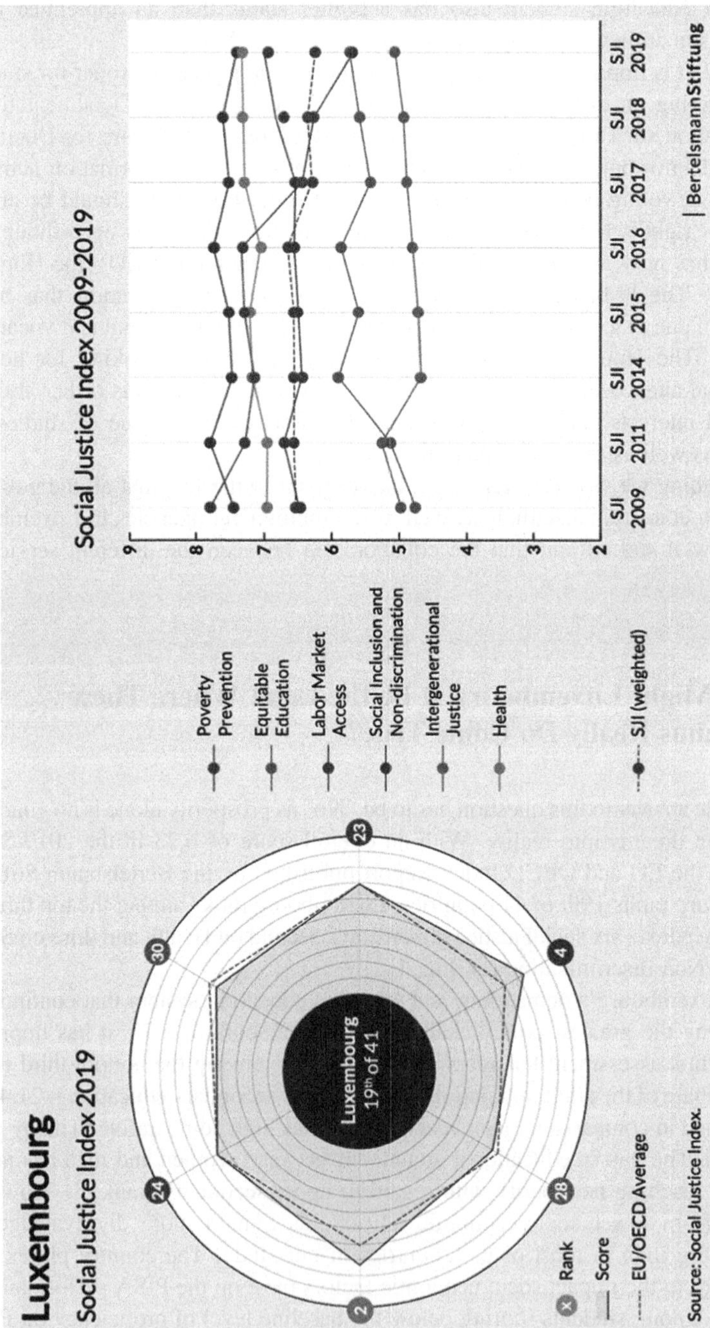

Fig. 1 Social Justice Index 2019 (Hellmann et al., 2019, p.175)

The country experts report that:

> there is a marked division between Luxembourg nationals and migrant students, as migrants (especially the Portuguese minority) generally struggle with the country's three languages and often end up in the technical track (secondaire technique), which affects their progress toward a university education. Recent studies have shown that migrant students are four times less likely to transfer to the higher-level university-oriented early school track (enseignement secondaire) than Luxembourgish nationals (Hellmann et al., 2019, p. 176).

10 Conclusion

Now that we have had to conclude that there actually does not exist *"a land where where the dreams of social justice and equity really do come true"* and where guidance and career counsellors can play a decisive part in realising these dreams, we would like to emphasise that we very much welcome innovative ideas on how to achieve greater social justice, we do not think that it would be wise to mistake our dreams for reality.

At a conference many years ago at the University of Liège in Belgium an expert from the "Institut national d'étude du travail et d'orientation professionnelle"' (INETOP), the French *"Institute for the Study of Labour and Vocational Guidance"* upsets his audience by pointing out the limitations of counselling, and foremost its total dependency on the prevailing economic conditions. Fact is that Bill Clinton's bon mot *"It is the economy, stupid"* was and still is valid.

Thankfully though, there are now at very last growing movements that challenge the orthodoxy of traditional economic theories which in term might inspire scholars in the field of guidance and career counselling to come up with more pragmatic innovative counselling approaches adapted to the new economic realities that might emerge from a break with the economic past. Our ideas on what constitutes social justice are deeply rooted in our white Caucasian European cultural background. Hence, we consider the pursuit of social justice foremost as a core philosophical value upon which counsellors should base their practices, a guiding principle but not an actual practice or a specific counselling technique.

In this context we warmly welcome any concepts and approaches advanced against prejudice regarding certain types of employment or professions not least as regards an all too often neglected factor in guidance and career counselling, i.e. the respective social status of various occupations. The perceptions children and young people have of the worlds of work and labour are bound to play a major part in their acceptance of professions. We should therefore research more closely the possible direct as well as indirect impacts the portrayal of occupations in fictional media such as books, movies and TV programmes may have through their entertainment value on the perceptions of young people of certain professions. Such investigations might lead to more nuanced information and counselling practices and more thought through career choices, but they will unfortunately not change human nature as we will never cease to compare ourselves with others. And as man's whole being is deeply rooted in his differentiation from others, *"the land where dreams of social justice and equity really do come true"* will remain just that, a land of dreams.

References

Bertelsmann Stiftung. (2019). Social justice in the EU and OECD index report.

Carroll, L. (1961). *Alice's adventures in wonderland*. The Folio Society.

EURYDICE. (2021). *Luxembourg overview*. Online-Source: https://eacea.ec.europa.eu/national-policies/eurydice/content/luxembourg_en

Frankfurt, H. G. (2015). *On inequality*. Princeton University Press.

Guerrini, J.-C. (2002). Mots. Les langages du politique 68. Les métaphores spatiales en politique Visions du temps. *Cioran analyste de la réaction, de l'utopie et du progrès*. Online-Source: http://journals.openedition.org/mots/6093

Hellmann, T., Schmidt, P., Heller, S. M. (2019). *Social Justice in the EU and OECD Index Report*, Bertelsmann Stiftung, Gütersloh. Online Source: https://www.bertelsmann-stiftung.de/fileadmin/files/BSt/Publikationen/GrauePublikationen/SJI_2019.pdf

Huxley, A. (1971). *Brave new world*. The Folio Society.

IAEVG. (2013). *Communiqué on social justice in educational and career guidance and counselling*. Montpellier, France.

Martin, R., et al. (2008). *La place de l'école dans la société luxembourgeoise de demain*. De Boeck.

Peugny, C. (2013). Le destin au berceau: Inégalités et reproduction sociale, Le Seuil.

Rawls, J. (2005). *A theory of justice*. Harvard University Press.

Sen, A. (1980). Equality of what? In *Sterling McMurrin: The Tanner lectures on human values* (Vol. 1). Salt Lake City.

Simmel, G. (2004). *Gesamtausgabe, Band 17; Miszellen, Glossen, Stellungnahmen, Umfrageantworten, Leserbriefe, Diskussionsbeiträge 1889–1918. Anonyme und pseudonyme Veröffentlichungen 1888–1920. Beiträge aus der "Jugend" 1897–1916*. Suhrkamp.

STATEC. (2021). Luxembourg in figures, Luxembourg.

UK Government. (2012). *Report on social justice*. Online Source: www.dwp.gov.uk/social-justice and www.men.public.lu

Spain: Challenges and Perspectives in Times of Inflection on Career Guidance and Counselling in Spain

Rebeca Garcia Murias

1 Introduction

The reality of European and international society in the twenty-first century, characterised by the growth of economic, cultural and technological globalisation, shapes the current model of life, facilitating people's mobility and barrier-free access to all types of information, whilst at the same time greatly accelerating the need to adapt to this ever-changing situation. In this context, the recycling of knowledge and the continuous training of workers have become indispensable factors, as discussed in the third chapter "Demographic change". Education has a key commitment to this social demand, especially guidance, which is considered to be the appropriate educational instrument to meet these needs. Effective Career Guidance and Counselling (CGC) helps individuals to make the most of their potential, economies to be more efficient and societies to be fairer. It is also essential for facilitating people's transitions in education and training, and for mobility within the labour market.

Today's labour market is increasingly complex. The second chapter "Future jobs" reflects, among other things, on how the Covid-19 pandemic has profoundly disrupted the demand for workers and accelerated patterns of automation and digital transformation that are radically changing the nature of work and increasing the risks of unemployment and precarious employment. In addition, globalisation, demographic trends and increasing efforts to create greener economies are changing the nature of the demand for skills and competencies in labour markets around the world. Career guidance has an essential role to play in economic recovery plans and in helping people of all ages and backgrounds to navigate these challenges.

R. G. Murias (✉)
University of Santiago de Compostela (USC), Santiago de Compostela, Santiago, Spain

University of Applied Labour Studies, Hochschule der Bundesagentur für Arbeit (HdBA), Mannheim, Germany
e-mail: rebeca.garcia.murias@usc.es

C. Enoch et al. (eds.), *Vocational Guidance in Europe*,
https://doi.org/10.1007/978-3-031-06592-7_9

In this context, an analysis of the existing evidence provides policy-makers with confidence that an investment in career guidance will bring economic, educational and social benefits to both individuals and society. However, international evidence shows that in too many countries, as, for example, in Spain, access to guidance is insufficient, especially for the most vulnerable, as stated in the first chapter "Counselling for migrants and refugees".

The acceleration and unpredictability of change is the constant in a time of uncertainty, movements and political, labour, educational and social transformations…, which leads us to redefine some of the key challenges of vocational guidance, to reflect on the main obstacles encountered by professionals or agents in this professional sector and to analyse the needs and realities of the European labour markets and societies.

In view of the situation described and on the basis of the different topics addressed, this chapter identifies and describes the most notable changes in the current society that affect CGC and require modifications in guidance intervention. In particular, it examines some of the challenges and perspectives for CGC in Spain, focusing mainly on counselling for migrants and refugees (Sect. 1) and the changing jobs of the future (Sect. 2) as well as demographic change and the ageing of the working population (Sect. 3).

2 Counselling for Migrants and Refugees

There is widespread concern in Europe about how best to proceed with the reception of refugees, especially in the current time of economic, humanitarian and conflict crisis, and European policies have sought to incorporate actions related to the resettlement and integration of refugees. Thus, in the countries of the European Union, there are various institutions and organisations that have been developing, with greater or lesser success, different services related to the reception system, in which guidance and counselling acquire special relevance in attending to the needs of this vulnerable group.

With the aim of finding out what the current situation is in Spain regarding this issue, the main results of a documentary study (Nogueira et al., 2018) are set out in this first chapter. The main objectives of this research were to describe how the aforementioned services are organised in Spain, as well as to find out, in general, what procedures and activities are carried out in this context. From the findings of this study it can be concluded that the reception systems in Spain are still very much focused on the needs of food, shelter and mental and physical health care. There are various career guidance services, but these do not differ in general terms from those developed for the rest of the population.

The most widely accepted conceptions of the definition of guidance, in a broad sense, understand it as a continuous and systematic process of help, aimed at all people in all its aspects, placing special emphasis on prevention and development (personal, social, vocational), which is carried out throughout life with the involvement of the different educational (tutors, guidance counsellors, teachers) and social agents (family, specialised professionals, etc.). The fact that guidance is recognised as being for all people highlights its timeliness for displaced migrant and refugee populations, among other vulnerable groups. The International Association for Educational and Vocational Guidance (IAEVG) issued a statement in this regard in 2015, calling on guidance counsellors, academics and policy-makers to increase their efforts to actively engage in providing care for the needs of displaced migrants, and to advocate services that provide educational and vocational integration in countries of settlement. Here is a summary of some of the tasks included in the statement that counsellors can carry out (IAEVG, 2015):

(a) Career counsellors have the opportunity to develop model programmes and practices to support displaced migrants in their journey to find suitable employment.
(b) Guidance and career counselling are key for the entry of migrants and refugees into the labour market and, according to experiences such as that of Sweden, labour market integration contributes significantly to social integration. "One of the main challenges refugees face when trying to integrate in their host country is finding decent work. Sweden recognizes this problem and is investing in labour market inclusion to become the driving force behind the integration of refugees" (Peromingo, 2014: 75).

However, the implementation of vocational guidance and counselling services in reception systems has not been an easy path. Some reports (Bertelsmann Foundation) show that, despite the existence of labour integration policies, refugees find it difficult to enter the world of work. The articulation of reception systems that ensure a dignified life for all asylum seekers must be guaranteed, adapting to the changing social and labour needs of the host country, as must the appropriate means to attend to people in a situation of special vulnerability or with special needs, people applying for international protection who aspire to find a job that will allow them to integrate autonomously into society and leave behind the traumatic experience that forced them to leave their country of origin (Martin et al., 2016). In order to overcome these difficulties, the need for cooperation and mutual learning between the different countries of the European Union is pointed out, with the aim of reducing the problems that refugees encounter in entering the labour market. In addition, there is a need for the intervention of local actors on an ongoing basis and thus a need to address the creation of coherent common policies, such as the intervention of governments with different levels of action at regional, local and state level.

The increase in the arrival of refugees at EU borders and the increase in the loss of life at the gates of the continent have been provoking an unprecedented public and media reaction, questioning European migration policies and forcing governments to adopt reception commitments (Díaz et al., 2016). One of the main focuses of interest has centred on the management of reception systems and their services, including guidance and counselling. So, on the basis of the research of Nogueira et al. (2018), a brief introduction to the Spanish context will be provided, presenting the configuration of the reception, hosting and counselling systems for refugees in our country.

Based on the objectives proposed in the aforementioned study and the results obtained by the authors, the following conclusions can be drawn: Spanish reception systems contemplate the development of services and activities related to guidance and counselling, mainly of a labour and professional nature, but also of an educational character. These services are part of systems run mostly by non-governmental, secular or faith-based organisations. However, specific detention and reception centres are operated by both governmental and non-governmental bodies (see the section on *Specific supportive measures to support refugees* in Spain). Although an outline of the basic tasks is given, not much information (tools/sources) was found in publicly available documentation (reports, articles, databases, news, books, statistics, papers, etc.) about professionals who carry out guidance and counselling functions in specific refugee-serving centres in the contexts explored.

2.1 Current Situation in Spain: An Overview

Based on data published by Eurydice (European Commission, 2021a) regarding migratory flows in Spain, Spain became a host country for immigrants between 2000 and 2010, but the migration balance started to be negative in 2010. This situation remained unchanged until 2016. In 2019, there were 5,036,878 foreign nationals living in Spain. In 2008, the Spanish economy experienced a period of stagnation followed by recession. Therefore, the foreign population has diminished significantly since 2010. In 2020, the percentage of the foreign population was below that of 2010: after having reached 12.22% of the total population in previous years, it dropped to 11.5%. Even so, it has shown an increase of more than 8 percentage points over 20 years. Most of the foreign population comes from countries that are members of the European Union (EU) and from Africa. Since 2010, the population coming from South America and the EU has decreased considerably.

The population migrating abroad has decreased between 2010 and 2020, except for those whose destination has been the United Kingdom, Oceania and North America.

2.2 Refugees in Spain

The seventeenth annual report from the Spanish Commission for Refugee Assistance (CEAR) (2019) analysed the situation of refugees in the world, the European Union and mainly in Spain over 2018. On 30 June 2018, according to data from UNHCR (the UN Refugee Agency), there were 70 million people who had been forcibly displaced as a result of conflicts, violence and violations of human rights. Syria, Afghanistan and South Sudan are the main countries from which refugees are fleeing. The crisis in Venezuela also exacerbated the global exodus, with tens of thousands of asylum applications officially made in the USA, Spain, Peru and Brazil.

In 2018, the Mediterranean was again the most perilous migration route on the planet. However, the response from most EU countries was to criminalise the solidarity-driven rescue work carried out by NGO boats. Once again, Europe closed its borders to refugees, with the long, complex process of building a common asylum system still gridlocked.

Spain again broke its historic record of 54,065 asylum applications to become the fourth-ranking country in the entire EU for the first time. Moreover, it was the main country for seaborne arrivals at 58,569, accounting for 51% of the total. Even so, only 575 people obtained refugee status and 2320 got subsidiary protection. There is a serious situation facing the asylum system, with long waits to formalise applications, and nearly 80,000 cases were pending a decision by the end of 2018. By February 2019, the number had risen to 93,140. Although the resources have been bolstered for humanitarian aid for people arriving by sea and for accommodation and integration, the number of arrivals has overwhelmed expectations, leading to insufficient means to attend to the migrants and asylum applicants.

2.3 *Specific Supportive Measures to Support Refugees*

There are various programmes or platforms in place to support refugees in Spain, but as mentioned previously, most services are still very much focused on shelter, food and mental and physical health care needs. As verified in the study by Nogueira et al. (2018), there are several career counselling services, but these do not differ in general terms from those developed for the rest of the population.

It is therefore necessary to open new lines of research that allow us to reach the professionals who carry out guidance tasks within the organisations explored, in order to define their profile and, if necessary, to identify training/capacity-building needs that favour not only correct job performance, but also its quality, thus having a positive impact on reception systems and fostering the socio-occupational integration of refugees, as suggested by other experiences and previous research (Peromingo, 2014).

As pointed out by Nogueira et al. (2018: 142) "In Spain, the passivity of the European authorities towards carrying out this relocation process has been denounced, as it could take up to 43 years to fulfil the commitment made to 160,000 asylum seekers in Europe in 2015. In practice, Spain received around 14,881 asylum applications in 2015. People from Syria topped the list of applications, followed by those from Ukraine and Palestine. However, only 3,200 applications were resolved, of which only 31% were accepted, a far cry from the European average of around 50% in the same year. By the end of 2015, only 18 refugees had been received in Spanish territory, a figure that had risen to 305 by the end of July 2016. The Spanish system, which is centralized in terms of its management, consists of Refugee Reception Centres (CAR), Temporary Stay Centres for Immigrants (CETI) in Ceuta and Melilla and a network of reception places in different facilities (centres and flats) managed by non-governmental organizations, the most recognized of which are the Spanish Catholic Migration Commission Association (ACCEM), the Spanish Refugee Aid Commission (CEAR) and the Spanish Red Cross (CRE), which have been joined by other organizations".

The reception procedure initiated with the resettlement process is divided into three phases: *reception*, *integration* and *autonomy*. They are oriented towards the gradual acquisition of autonomy and try to adapt to each specific situation after the individualised integration pathways have been determined. As far as possible, the aim is for the entire itinerary to take place in the same territorial administrative division. Beforehand, at the beginning of the reception stage, an assessment of needs is carried out and the specific arrangements are decided upon.

The first phase, *reception*, takes place in one of the aforementioned centres or facilities, the main objective of which is to cover the basic needs of food and accommodation, as well as to offer (Spanish Ministry of Employment and Social Security, 2016): temporary accommodation; information and legal advice on the new situation; guidance for integration into the educational, health and social system; psychological care; specialised social care and management of complementary financial aid; development of courses for language learning and basic social skills; guidance and intermediation for vocational training and labour market integration; and occupational, leisure and free time activities.

The second phase, *integration*, takes place when the families still require support after these deadlines. To this end, they receive six months of support for socio-occupational integration and financial assistance to meet basic needs. The system contemplates a third phase of *autonomy*, which takes place when the family continues to need assistance or occasional support for a further six months despite the previous interventions. The maximum length of stay in the foster care system is 18 months, unless there are circumstances of vulnerability, in which case it would be increased to 24 months (UNICEF, 2016).

In relation to guidance, information and vocational development, the Spanish reception and integration system contemplates specific actions, with activities such as (Spanish Ministry of Employment and Social Security, 2016):

- basic individual social guidance: collection of information, identification of needs and information.
- information on social, public and private services and resources.
- information on access and activities of the reception and integration system for applicants and beneficiaries of international protection.
- basic legal and administrative information (rights, duties, asylum and immigration procedures, formalities and procedures).
- referrals to other entities and general or specialised resources.
- group information and guidance sessions.
- detection and action in possible cases of human trafficking and,
- training of specialised agents.

In practice, the organisations are responsible for implementing these activities. In the case of the "Spanish Commission for Refugee Aid", it is in the area of inclusion that support is provided to people seeking international protection, refugees or migrants throughout the integration process, accompanying them and providing them with the personal and social tools that they need in order to be the protagonists of their own process. This includes, aside from the initial care of new arrivals, learning Spanish, the integration stage, mediation for access to housing, psychological care and training for employment until they enter the labour market.

It is also worth highlighting the actions developed by the "Spanish Catholic Migration Commission Association", with specific programmes focused on socio-occupational integration, as a reliable and effective approach to the social integration of migrants with numerous mechanisms aimed at achieving this end at a national, regional and local level. The methodology followed is based on the elaboration of comprehensive and individualised plans for socio-occupational integration, taking into consideration the labour market situation and the local development needs of each territory.

3 Future Jobs

For some years now, there has been talk of the impact that the introduction of certain technological innovations in companies (robotisation, artificial intelligence, 3D printing, Big Data, etc.) will have on the global economy and especially on the future of work. Numerous studies warn of the possible loss of millions of jobs in the coming years due to the transformations that digitalisation will introduce in production processes and in the very organisation of companies. A report by the consultancy firm PwC (2018) estimates that Spain will be affected by successive waves of digitalisation, the last of which, from 2030 onwards, could lead to the disappearance of 34% of existing jobs. On the other hand, there are also studies that relativise this possible loss of jobs, as it will be offset by the growing demand for new occupations linked to technology.

The Economic and Social Council has published a report (2017) that explores the effects of the "digitalization of the Spanish economy" on the different economic sectors, its impact on professional skills and qualifications and its impact on working conditions and labour relations. The report points out that Spain leads Europe in certain aspects of digitalisation, such as the deployment of fibre optics, a fact that is also highlighted in the report "The Digital Society in Spain" by the Telefónica Foundation (2017).

It should also be noted that Spain is one of the most advanced countries in the development of e-government, with a high level of electronic interaction between citizens and the government. Since 2013, Spain has had a formal strategy for developing the digital economy and society, the so-called *Digital Agenda*, which was configured as a set of all the government's actions in the field of telecommunications, information society and e-government, and constituted a roadmap both for meeting the objectives of the *Digital Agenda for Europe* in 2015 and 2020 and for achieving specific objectives for the development of the digital economy and society. The Digital Agenda actions were structured around a number of objectives, including improving e-government and digital public services, with a focus on the efficient delivery of public services, in order to move towards a more efficient and digital administration, facilitating and adapting to citizens and companies (Digital Agenda for Europe, 2021). However, in general terms, Spain is lagging behind other countries in the digitalisation process and especially in the advanced use of digital technology by companies, with this gap being even more pronounced in SMEs (small and medium-sized enterprises). The digitalisation process is facing new challenges due to its rapid dynamism and global character. In the case of Spain, these new challenges are compounded by issues such as the digital transformation of SMEs and the promotion of the digital content sector, e-government, digital security and trust, the promotion of R&D&I (research, development and innovation) in the ICT (information and communications technology) sector and the reinforcement of digital skills to improve employability.

In the field of employment, the report includes a series of proposals aimed at preparing workers for the changes that will occur in their jobs and for the automation of certain positions. It indicates that training is key to achieving professional profiles adapted to the new technologies: workers need to have training that helps them to keep their skills up to date or to re-qualify to acquire the right competencies for the future. In the field of education, it also proposes measures to promote greater development of students' scientific and technical skills and to increase the weight of degrees in technical or STEM (science, technology, engineering and mathematics) subjects.

A study by the Social Dialogue Foundation (2017) attempts to show the transformations that are taking place in employment and working conditions in companies that are already undergoing digitalisation. It analyses working hours, work-life balance, the gender gap in the ICT sector, wage regulations and the role of workers' representation in these companies. One of the study's recommendations is the need to promote an in-depth reform of the employment training system so that it adapts to the needs of the digitalisation of companies.

3.1 Promoting Digital Skills and Competencies in Education and Employment

Among the recommendations of the report of the Economic and Social Council (2017) is the need for a strategy that involves society as a whole—institutions, businesses and citizens—to comprehensively address the challenges and objectives posed by digitalisation and reduce the digital divide in society. To this end, it proposes the creation of a cross-cutting public body of appropriate rank to ensure coordination between all the agents involved.

The Spanish government has set up a task force involving nine ministries to draw up a plan to promote the "digital transformation of the Spanish economy" (Spanish Ministry of Energy, Tourism and Digital Agenda, 2018), which aims to improve business competitiveness and economic growth. The group coordinated the digital transformation initiatives of the different ministerial departments, grouped into four work areas: digital infrastructures and technologies, entrepreneurship and access to finance, security and trust and finally talent and digital skills. In the latter area, the Spanish government recognises the importance of introducing digital skills and competencies in education from primary school onwards and, in particular, encouraging vocations in science, technology and mathematics. It is also committed to promoting continuous training for workers to help them to adapt to the new digital environment as well as to supporting companies in carrying out research and experimental development projects in artificial intelligence (AI) and other digital technologies.

3.2 *Digital Competencies of Guidance Practitioners*

Guidance practitioners and policy-makers in education and employment should strive to increasingly use ICT in the traditional guidance services that they offer, i.e. to increase the use of ICT in guidance systems. The use of social networks, artificial intelligence, chatbots, interactive websites, videoconferencing, apps, virtual reality, etc., is key to making guidance more accessible to people, especially in times of Covid-19.

There is a need to reflect on the role that digital technology should play in the future of education and guidance, not only as a solution to enable continuity of services during such a pandemic, but also as a tool for personalising teaching and learning as well as guidance (Echeverría Samanes & Clares, 2018).

It is also essential to use new technologies to connect the actors involved in guidance processes: guidance counsellors with students, young people with employers, schools with companies, etc. However, in order to make better use of ICT in guidance, it is essential that guidance practitioners improve their digital competencies through continuous and quality training.

In short, it is important to analyse how CGC should be adapted to the current socio-economic, educational and employment context in order to support individuals and to find out what the new trends in guidance are as a result of the pandemic situation (e.g. the impact of the use of Big Data, apps, social media, chatbots, etc., on guidance; how guidance addresses the consequences of the digitalization and automation of work; etc.) (Zelloth et al., 2020).

3.3 *Specific Supportive Measures for the Digitalization of Guidance*

CGC has been transformed by the Covid-19 situation. The pandemic has led to changes in guidance practitioners' priorities and methodologies, as well as increasing the use of online platforms and resources to continue counselling during lockdown. The effects of the pandemic on student counselling were analysed on the basis of the research of Oliveras Bagués et al. (2020), which involved more than 230 education and guidance professionals.

The initiative shows how guidance counsellors from the educational centres have been able to make their best effort to carry out guidance in a desolate environment aggravated by Covid-19. Thus, during the lockdown, new methodologies were used to address the key moments of guidance, such as the first and second trimester of the year, when guidance becomes more evident, as these are the periods of pre-enrolment and preparation for the choice of studies.

The results of the study indicate that the digitalisation of guidance is a trend for Covid-19 that is here to stay (Oliveras Bagués et al., 2020), as it has allowed the educational community to have easier access to guidance resources, as well as to guidance experiences and meetings with professionals that have had to be carried out through webinars or video conferences. Before lockdown in Spain, 60% of guidance activities were not carried out online. Therefore, guidance counsellors had to move from mostly face-to-face guidance to fully virtual guidance in a matter of weeks. Digitalisation has created new opportunities that have allowed more sustainable strategies to be developed, which will continue to be applied when the "new normal" returns. This paradigm shift is reflected in the fact that 71.5% of guidance practitioners have used online teaching support platforms that have enabled them to organise and digitise guidance content, while 67.7% have used online guidance resources (Oliveras Bagués et al., 2020). The study also indicates that 45% of the schools surveyed in this research have carried out online guidance activities that were not initially planned, including video conferences, video tutorials, individual interviews, online vocational workshops for families, webinars and virtual education fairs. The 66.4% of guidance counsellors have had or have the need for additional training in online guidance tools, resources and content, with topics such as the use of digital platforms.

In addition to this, the study found that schools have realised that the most vulnerable families have had difficulties in accessing technological resources and Internet connection during the pandemic in order to receive distance guidance, so they have designed specific intervention strategies to offer more personalised follow-up and support to students and their families (e.g. lent computer equipment to the most vulnerable pupils, provided telephone tutorials with flexible hours, put the families in contact with local councils and social services, etc.).

Now, more than ever, guidance is needed. It should be a public good and universally accessible. Now is the time to insist on this (Hooley et al., 2020).

The Covid-19 pandemic is also an opportunity for guidance practitioners to update their knowledge and to make a greater commitment to online guidance/the digitalisation of guidance. More than ever, efforts must be made to reach out to the most vulnerable groups who have the most difficulty accessing guidance.

3.4 Other Digitalisation Initiatives in the Context of Guidance in Spain: Digitalisation of PES

The use of ICT is an area of significant development for Public Employment Services (PES), as shown by the many experiences of European countries including Spain. In this sense, the digitalisation of PES management is an indispensable process for achieving greater efficiency of the resources used in their operation, especially in the current situation of economic crisis and subsequent unemployment. The State Public Employment Service (SPES) in Spain, aware of this potential, launched several initiatives aimed at making the employment service more efficient.

Aside from other SPES digital modernisation measures (service provision, paperless office, prior appointment, etc.) with regard to new functionalities that can directly favour a greater efficiency and effectiveness of active employment policies, the *Single Employment Portal*, one of the SPES's most outstanding projects, should be highlighted, as it directly facilitates and favours intermediation. One of the main advances introduced by the SPES is the provision of information on job vacancies in public and private databases in the same web space, with the collaboration of the autonomous communities and the social partners and making use of new technologies.

Both international organisations and experts recommend, among other labour market measures, the urgent reform and enhancement of active employment policies. These policies in Spain are managed through the SPES and the autonomous regional bodies, which are responsible for the direct implementation of these actions. The performance of these public bodies has revealed shortcomings in the provision of resources and in the achievement of the objectives of the outplacement of workers, making it advisable to modernise them.

However, the context of a severe shortage of resources makes it more necessary than ever to reflect on international experience, particularly with regard to the design of active employment policies and how to articulate them, giving a central role to digitalisation processes, as a formula for reconciling the objectives of effectiveness (reduction of unemployment, improvement of training, effective intermediation, etc.) with the requirements of efficiency that condition the actions of public administrations.

On the other hand, the design and implementation of digitalisation initiatives must take into account the specific characteristics that define the unemployment problem in each country. The analysis carried out highlights the phenomenon of long-term unemployment as one of the major challenges facing European countries in general and Spain in particular. In this respect, it stresses the need to enhance the digital literacy of this group, especially when a large proportion of the unemployed are over 55 years old and their ICT skills and knowledge are, in general, more limited. Without this digital literacy, the effectiveness of new digital applications will be severely compromised.

On the other hand, the use of ICT for monitoring the performance of any large-scale programme to support the employability and re-employment of the unemployed is the best way to increase the effectiveness and efficiency of these programmes, and therefore of the institutions in charge of their implementation, the PES.

Active policy programmes, such as lifelong learning and guidance, can also take advantage of these efficiency gains by incorporating new technologies into their work. On the basis of the experience of benchmark countries, public employment systems should try to incorporate those devices and tools that improve their results.

4 Demographic Change

The population and workforce in developed countries are ageing due to declining birth rates and increasing longevity. People are living longer, but this demographic change is beginning to have consequences for employment, pension systems and working conditions and calls into question the maintenance of living standards and the sustainability of the welfare state.

By 2050, the number of people aged 55+ will grow to over 500 million in OECD countries. This is reported in the "Golden Age Index" (2015), which analyses the take-up and labour market impact of workers aged 55 and over in 34 OECD countries using a range of indicators. According to this report, increasing the employment rates of older workers would offer significant economic benefits for OECD countries. To tap the potential of these older workers, it proposes a number of measures that governments should include among their priorities: reform of pension systems and measures to encourage later retirement. At the same time, it proposes promoting more flexible forms of work and new forms of partial retirement to encourage older workers to return to or remain in the world of work. The report also highlights the important role of training in helping older workers to remain competitive and adapt to a constantly evolving working environment, especially through technological change. It shows how certain countries (Iceland, New Zealand and Sweden) have adopted policies aimed at providing education and training to older populations, which improves their employability and provides them with the skills needed for today's labour market. This adaptation to change will be particularly important in the coming years, as rapid technological progress and digitalisation threaten many existing jobs (World Economic Forum, 2016).

This demographic change is particularly affecting the countries of the European Union. The problem will become increasingly acute in the coming decades, as Europe's population will grow very slowly while ageing rapidly. By 2050, Eurostat estimates that the percentage of people over 65 will be around 28.5%. Most EU Member States have reacted to these demographic developments by, among other measures, raising the retirement age and limiting access to early retirement.

A report by four European agencies (Dubois et al., 2017) analyses the phenomenon of ageing in the EU and discusses how European policies can help to tackle this problem. Each agency focuses on a different aspect of demographic change and its implications for employment (working and health conditions, worker training) and proposes solutions to the challenges posed by ageing.

- *Cedefop*, the European Centre for the Development of Vocational Training, explores how training for employment can be used to support active ageing at work.
- *Eurofound*, the European Foundation for the Improvement of Living and Working Conditions, examines how the working conditions of workers vary according to their age and analyses the different policies of EU states to promote longer working lives and to keep older workers in work.
- *The European Agency for Safety and Health at Work* (EU-OSHA) presents examples of successful European policies to address ageing and health and safety at work, and the European Institute for Gender Equality (EIGE) provides a gender perspective on older workers and analyses the different challenges faced by men and women.

4.1 Specific Situation in Spain: Country-Specific Data

Spain's demographic situation is characterised by an ageing population. The birth rate and the increase in life expectancy are causing a progressive ageing of the population. According to data published by the National Statistical Institute (2020), the population over 65 years of age represented 19.7% of the total population in Spain (47,344,649) in 2020. To get an idea of the evolution of the phenomenon of population ageing and its impact on the population pyramid, it is sufficient to note, for example, that this percentage stood at 16.8% in 2010. Moreover, older people have an average life expectancy of 83 years, which means more than 20 years out of the labour market. This longer life expectancy adds up to a better quality of life. Once the work activity is over, there is a lot of time left that can be enjoyed to the full, but it is important to know how to face the changes. The attitude with which this stage is faced is key to making the most of it (see the section on *The role of guidance for counselling the older workforce*).

According to data published by Eurydice (European Commission, 2021b), Spain's total land area is 505,944 km^2, with a population density of 92.67 inhabitants/km^2. The proportion of the population living in urban areas is 81%. At present, the ageing of the population is the main challenge faced by the country.

In 2020, the population was 47,394,223. As for the ageing of the population:

- The average age of the population was 43.58.
- The ageing index was 125.75%, which means that, for every 100 minors under the age of 16, there were almost 126 people over the age of 64.
- The dependency ratio was 54.20%, which indicates that, for every 100 potentially active people, there were about 54 potentially inactive people.

The evolution of the population figures since 2000 in Spain shows a decrease of 8 percentage points in the 15–29 age group. There is a population growth in the age group of 45 and over.

Moreover, unemployment, one of the main social problems in Spain, which particularly affects the youngest, appears to be an important factor contributing to the population loss. Another group that is particularly affected by unemployment is that of people over the age of 45, due to difficulties in re-entering the current labour market. The unemployment rate in 2020 was 16.1%, affecting women (18.3%) more than men (14.1%).

4.2 The Role of Guidance for Counselling the Older Workforce

As noted, an important aspect is to analyse how the older workforce copes with the stage towards or in retirement and to study the role of guidance in this context. Retirement causes a number of people who are in good physical and mental condition to feel disoriented. This uncertainty highlights the need for guidance in the elderly, but it has been observed over the years in Spain that there is a lack of proposals, projects and resources aimed at this group, so we have investigated the challenges posed by guidance aimed at older people and we have brought together some of the programmes that are being carried out in our country (see the next section on *Some specific supportive measures for guidance for older people*).

In this sense, we questioned what the role of counselling for older people is and what the resulting support and development needs are from the perspective of the counsellor.

Experts highlight counselling as a key element in promoting successful ageing, which meets the psychosocial, care, competence and intellectual needs of older people.

Linked to this holistic approach, Puig and Rodríguez (2018) consider that guidance for older people should be part of a lifelong guidance project. Preparation for retirement should not be a subject to be considered only when the "dreaded" or "longed-for" moment is approaching, but should begin to be considered from the very moment we are born. If these contents were included in school curricula, we would learn from an early age to think of the post-retirement stage as a time full of possibilities, just like any other time in our lives.

4.3 *Some Specific Supportive Measures for Guidance for Older People*

As mentioned above, experts agree that there is a lack of resources, projects and guidance programmes aimed at the older people in our country. With a few exceptions, such as the training programmes carried out by some public institutions, the initiatives developed in this context are aimed at responding to specific needs.

Below are some examples of programmes:

(a) *Third Age Guidance* (guidance for older people).

The Department of Applied Economics and Economic Policy, University of Alicante (Spain) has carried out in 2004 a work project called "Third Age Guidance" (guidance for older people). The initiative was coordinated by the University of Glasgow (UK) in collaboration with fifteen partners representing 12 European countries, including Spain. Its main objective was to study career guidance models for people over 45.

According to the coordinators, such initiatives are necessary because older people are discriminated against in the labour market, where opportunities to find a new job are limited, especially if they have been out of the labour market for a long time. As for active adult workers, they are also discriminated against; they rarely receive further training or support for their professional development.

In most European countries, career guidance policies are very generous. In Spain, however, this large sector of the population is still not taken into account and actions are mostly aimed at unemployed people. If the right measures were put in place, older workers could attend self-employment training, change to a new occupation, become self-employed, change their working hours or become trainers, etc.

One of the conclusions reached in this study is that appropriate career guidance is very useful for retaining workers in the labour market, advising them in their professional development and achieving a successful return to work for older people. In the same way, it is very important to adapt guidance models to the typology of the target group.

The idea is that, based on the findings and further studies, it will contribute to the development of the necessary tools to deal with this type of career guidance.

(b) *Vocational Guidance Programme for Older People.*

The programme designed by Riart i Vendrell and Boixader i Picas (2013) is conceived as a psycho-pedagogical guidance service aimed at older people and establishes common, community and group services as well as private and personalised services, all of them through guidance intervention.

The programme with its various activities is based on a theoretical support structure that justifies and values: a concept of occupational guidance within the global vision of lifelong vocational, professional and occupational guidance; the major stages of this decision-making process for older people similar to those of the other stages of life; the importance of the multipurpose characteristics and competencies acquired in the synthesis of working life. The programme aims to provide tools for monitoring the management of ageing in order to preserve quality in the process of adding years, a process that is longer with each generation. It aims to help guide those older people who know or feel that ageing is a hypertextualised/multifaceted field and that making this path attractive, encouraging and rewarding depends on each one of them and not on a macro-social, often stereotyped view. It is a programme that helps to project a senior programme, which wants to see this stage of life as a lively, recreational stage with a clear commitment to excellence.

(c) *Council Declaration on the European Year for Active Ageing and Intergenerational Solidarity (2012): A Future Strategy.*

On 6 December 2012, in the context of the Europe 2020 Strategy, the Council of the European Union adopted the aforementioned declaration expressing its commitment to promoting active ageing and solidarity between generations and invited all the relevant actors to take this approach into account when implementing the Europe 2020 Strategy. The declaration emphasises the right of older people to a dignified life, to independence and to participate in social, economic and civic life, as well as the need for older population groups to remain active as workers, consumers, carers, volunteers and citizens.

In this "Framework for Action", the Spanish government wanted to bring together the key aspects that affect older people in the different areas of society and to implement the actions to be carried out by the different agents. The various proposals refer to: employment; participation in society; independent and healthy living; and non-discrimination, equal opportunities and attention to situations of greater vulnerability.

Based on the programmes described, we conclude that a good guidance project aimed at counselling older people should have some specific aspects that are common to other stages of life (Federation of Pensioners and Retired Persons of CCOO, 2014):

- *Self-knowledge*. This is the first step for good guidance, regardless of the age of the person being guided. After so many years of work, many people do not know themselves outside the work environment. The time has come to let personal preferences, tastes, personality, talents and motivations come to the surface.
- *Adjustment to change*. Adjustment to retirement occurs in different phases: adaptation, euphoria, disenchantment, reorientation and stability. In order to overcome them successfully, it is necessary to plan an active and productive retirement.
- *Competencies development*. This stage should not be taken as a complete break, a before and an after. The skills learnt should continue to be present at some level of intensity and probably without being a source of stress as they may have become during the working period. Therefore, deepening and acquiring new knowledge, knowing how to contextualise and apply it, doing so with positive and relaxed attitudes, perhaps seeking points of improvisation and innovation, is a competency challenge that should continue to be a priority at this stage.

- *Guidance towards training*. Training opportunities for older people are very extensive: courses at universities, municipal centres, adult schools, online training... One of the problems that affect those who leave their professional activity is the lack of information, or the lack and loss of contacts, not knowing who to turn to, or, from another point of view, the social bias that leads people to think that, at a certain age, they can no longer start courses on subjects related to new technologies, for example. The aim of the guidance counsellor is to break these taboos and to guide and advise the person so that he/she can choose the right training.

5 Conclusions and Proposals for Future Action

Technological developments, ageing populations, migratory movements, globalisation and the need to address climate-related challenges are driving massive changes in the labour market: old, traditional jobs are disappearing or changing radically, and new jobs are emerging that require a different balance of skills and competencies.

Retraining and up-skilling are increasingly being seen as an integral part of working life. More than ever, governments (and employers) expect workers to be responsible for their own education and training, yet workers depend on adequate access to the necessary information and support on which to base their career management skills (CMS) in order to make sound decisions about investments in learning, education and training. CGC enables retraining, up-skilling and mobility, which are key for older workers who need to move within the labour market, and for people who have migrated between countries and want to have their skills validated. With the restructuring of labour markets, it is essential that people in work, as well as adult jobseekers, have easy access to good quality guidance.

Labour demand is changing dramatically in all economies. Lots of jobs disappeared worldwide during the pandemic, and adult unemployment is expected to remain high in many countries, including Spain. Moreover, there is a broad consensus that the Covid-19 pandemic is accelerating changes in workplaces, such as the integration of digital technologies.

Specifically, Spain must face the social and economic consequences of the low birth rate, the accelerated ageing of its population and, among many other issues, the arrival of low-skilled immigrants. In addition, unemployment is one of the main social problems in Spain. Our country continues to record disproportionately high levels of unemployment and job insecurity, which are splitting our society in two and conditioning the prosperity of the whole country. This problem could worsen in the coming decades as a result of the demographic and technological transformations that will take place. On the one hand, if we do not increase the labour market integration of our population, ageing could lead to a fall in the number of employed people at a rate of −0.5% per year between now and 2050, compared with the 2.0% increase we experienced between 1995 and 2019. To avoid this scenario, it will be necessary to raise the employment rate of women, young people and the over-55 s;

encourage legal immigration; and boost the recovery and attraction of talent. On the other hand, the generalisation of digital technologies will give rise to a strong modernisation of our productive fabric which, in the short term, could lead to job losses and a worsening of the working conditions of certain groups. To neutralise this risk, active employment policies will have to be greatly expanded, the regulatory framework will have to be adapted and social safety nets will have to be adapted to protect people rather than jobs.

The pandemic has led to an unprecedented economic and employment crisis. The Organization for Economic Cooperation and Development (OECD) forecast that the unemployment rate in Spain would be 19.3% by the end of 2020. To address this situation, policies and mechanisms are needed to protect those most affected, as well as more investment in academic and vocational guidance and training to help them to transfer their competencies to new occupations, to retrain and to get a job.

For their part, both the Bank of Spain and the International Labour Organization (ILO) agree that it is urgent to support lifelong guidance and training for people, especially the youngest, most of whom have become unemployed by working in the sectors most affected by the crisis. In fact, Spain tops the list of unemployed young people under 25 in the EU (40.4%), according to Eurostat data from October 2020.

Against this background, it is concluded that major changes are needed in career guidance processes in order to respond to the current challenges of the labour market and societies and those posed by the new post-pandemic realities. These guidance processes should not continue to be developed as in the past. New strategies, tools, resources and ways of doing things are needed if the intention is to continue to offer users guidance services that will enable them to adapt to the new realities and needs of the labour market. And for that it is necessary to: increase investment in guidance and the monitoring of its efficiency by creating structures for a comprehensive guidance system covering all phases of human life (lifelong guidance); promote the development of guidance processes based on the needs of the organisations and the reality of the labour market; incorporate technology as a key element in all phases of the processes by segmenting users based on their digital competencies; ensure that the guidance processes are available to all citizens in a manner appropriate to their needs; develop the skills and competencies of the guidance practitioners themselves; and ensure a common legal framework that avoids or minimises diversities in contracting and conditions for all professionals in the sector (Clares & Juárez, 2011).

In light of this situation, it is concluded that CGC today has important challenges to face in a changing, complex and interconnected environment such as the one we live in, which requires a renewal of experience and competencies on the part of the CGC professionals. In this context, it is necessary to reflect on the described challenges and the actions that should be taken to better guide individuals and help them to build their own life and professional project.

References

Clares, M. P., & Juárez, M. M. (2011). La orientación en el S.XXI. [Guidance in the 21st century]. *Revista electrónica Interuniversitaria de formación del profesorado (REIFOP), 14*(1), 253–265. Retrieved August 21, 2021 from http://www.aufop.com

Council of the European Union. (2012). *Council declaration on the European year of active ageing and intergenerational solidarity: A future strategy*. Council of the European Union.

Díaz, et al. (2016). *Informe 2016: Las personas refugiadas en España y Europa. [Report 2016: Refugees in Spain and Europe]*. CEAR.

Digital Agenda for Europe. (2021). Fact sheets on the European Union. European Parliament. Retrieved on November 5, 2021, from https://www.europarl.europa.eu/factsheets/en/sheet/64/digital-agenda-for-europe.

Dubois, H., et al. (2017). *Towards age-friendly work in Europe: A life-course perspective on work and ageing from EU agencies (EU-OSHA; Cedefop; Eurofound; EIGE)*. Publications Office of the European Union.

Echeverría Samanes, B., & Clares, M. P. (2018). Revolución 4.0, competencias, educación y orientación. [Revolution 4.0, skills, education and guidance]. *Revista digital de investigación en docencia universitaria, 12*(2), 4–34.

Economic and Social Council. (2017). *La digitalización de la economía [The digitalization of the economy]. No. 03* (p. 740). Economic and Social Council Spain. Publications Department NICES.

European Commission. (2021a). *Spain. Population: Demographic situation, languages and religions*. EACEA National Policies Platform.

European Commission. (2021b). *Population: Demographic situation, languages and religions*. Eurydice network (Erasmus+ programme).

Federation of Pensioners and Retired Persons of CCOO. (2014). Social observatory of the elderly 2014. *Para un envejecimiento activo*. [For active ageing]. Madrid (Spain).

Foundation for Social Dialogue. (2017). *Economía digital: su impacto sobre las condiciones de trabajo y empleo estudio de caso sobre dos empresas de base tecnológica*. [Digital economy: its impact on working conditions and employment - a case study of two technology-based companies]. ISBN: 978-84-697-7320-8.

Hooley, T., Thomsen, R., & Sultana, R. (2020). Shaping the new normal: Practising career guidance in the time of coronavirus. *Careers Matters, 8*(2), 12–13.

IAEVG. (2015). IAEVG Press Release on *Educational and Vocational Guidance for Displaced Migrants*. Tokyo (Japan). IAEVG. Retrieved October 4, 2021, from: https://goo.gl/3bCnQV.

Martin, I., et al. (2016). *From refugees to workers: Mapping labour market integration support measures for asylum-seekers and refugees in EU member states. Volume II: Literature review and country case studies*. Bertelsmann Foundation.

National Statistical Institute. (2020). *Population of Spain over 65 years of age* (2002–2020). Madrid (Spain).

Nogueira, et al. (2018). Los servicios de orientación y asesoramiento a refugiados: el caso de Portugal y España. [Guidance and counselling services for refugees: the case of Portugal and Spain]. *Revista Lusófona de Educação, 37*(37), 131–147.

Oliveras Bagués, M., et al. (2020). *La orientación académica y profesional en tiempos del Covid-19. [Academic and vocational guidance in times of Covid-19]*. Bertelsmann Foundation, D'EP Institut & Educaweb.

Peromingo, M. (2014). El trabajo y la integración de los refugiados en Suecia. [Refugee work and integration in Sweden]. *Revista Migraciones Forzadas, 48*, 75–77.

Puig, M. & Rodríguez, G. (2018). *Programa municipal para personas mayores del Ayuntamiento de Barberá del Vallés*. [Barberá del Vallés Town Council's municipal programme for senior citizens]. Barcelona, Spain.

PwC Network. (2015). *Golden Age Index "How well are OECD economies adapting to an older workforce?"* Australian Edition. Retrieved September 6, 2021 from https://www.pwc.com.au/pdf/the-golden-age-australian-version.pdf

PwC Network. (2018). *Will robots really steal our jobs? An international analysis of the potential long term impact of automation*. Retrieved September 6, 2021, from: https://www.pwc.co.uk/economics

Riart i Vendrell, J. & Boixader i Picas, F. (2013). *Programa de Orientación Ocupacional para Personas Mayores (POOGG)*. [Programme of Occupational Guidance for the Elderly (POOGG)]. Second prize in the individual category of the Educaweb Awards 2013. Barcelona (Spain).

Spanish Commission for Refugee Assistance (CEAR) (2019). *Refugees in Spain and Europe*. Executive summary.

Spanish Ministry of Employment and Social Security. (2016). *Sistema de acogida e integración para solicitantes y beneficiarios de protección internacional. Manual de gestión.* [Reception and integration system for applicants and beneficiaries of international protection. Management handbook]. Madrid: Spain. Retrieved July 13, 2021, from: https://goo.gl/nXFSL0.

Spanish Ministry of Energy, Tourism and Digital Agenda. (2018). *Press release from the Council of Ministers Plan para la transformación digital de la economía española. [Plan for the digital transformation of the Spanish economy]*. Government of Spain.

Telefónica Foundation. (2017). *Sociedad Digital en España*. [Digital Society in Spain]. Retrieved July 12, 2021, from: http://www.sociedaddigital.fundaciontelefonica.com.

UNICEF. (2016). *El sistema de acogida y los niños refugiados en España. Análisis y propuestas desde la óptica de los derechos de la infancia. [The reception system and refugee children in Spain. Analysis and proposals from the perspective of children's rights]*. UNICEF Spanish Committee. Retrieved August 14, 2021, from https://goo.gl/MbEucZ

World Economic Forum. (2016). *The future of jobs employment, skills and workforce strategy for the fourth industrial revolution*. Global Challenge Insight Report.

Zelloth, H., Kadletz, F., & Andrei, A. (2020). *International trends and innovation in career guidance (Vol. 1, Thematic chapters & Vol. 2, Country case studies)*. European Training Foundation.

Upcoming Challenges for Vocational Guidance in Europe

Clinton Enoch, Christoph Krause, Rebeca Garcia Murias, and Jane Porath

What are main current and upcoming challenges and how can counsellors and guidance practitioners, with a focus on the transnational European perspective, master these in their respective national contexts?

The central aim of this publication was to answer the questions: which central challenges currently exist for counsellors in Europe and which will occur in the coming years and how to master these challenges with a transnational focus. In the first part, the anthology first approached this question theoretically and thus derived the necessity and project idea of the Academia+ project. There were two main objectives for the Academia+ project which should be briefly reflected upon again:

Focus on the development of training programmes to address current key challenges in labour market and counselling.

The first objective of the Academia+ project aims at current key challenges in the European context, which counsellors are/will be confronted with currently and in the near future. It turned out that especially the topics "Counselling refugees and migrants", "future work" and "demographic change" could be crystallised out of the substrate of key challenges. This was achieved methodically in two ways: On the one hand, by means of a research and literature analysis, which addresses the central

C. Enoch · C. Krause (✉) · J. Porath
University of Applied Labor Studies, Schwerin, Germany

Hochschule der Bundesagentur für Arbeit, Mannheim, Germany
e-mail: clinton.enoch@hdba.de; Christoph.krause@arbeitsagentur.de; jane.porath@hdba.de

R. G. Murias
University of Applied Labor Studies, Mannheim, Germany

University of Santiago de Compostela, Santiago, Spain
e-mail: rebeca.garcia.murias@usc.es

C. Enoch et al. (eds.), *Vocational Guidance in Europe*,
https://doi.org/10.1007/978-3-031-06592-7_10

topics of the current research landscape in the counselling sciences, but also in related professions. On the other hand, by means of qualitative expert interviews, the concrete needs of those practitioners who were/are confronted with these key challenges in their everyday counselling work could be ascertained.

This step produced a dossier with key topics that were assessed as significant key challenges for counsellors in the research landscape/literature (theory-based) as well as in the concrete practice of counsellors and in their self-assessment as significant challenges for their practical everyday work (practical-based). From these, concrete challenges for counsellors could be extracted and named, which in turn created a basis for the conception, implementation and evaluation of the training programmes. For this purpose, experts from different countries, from different professions and with different focal points were acquired to offer a programme in different didactic settings in order to meet these key challenges. This expertise and the offers to be designed from it resulted in three one-week "Counsellors' Study and Training Exchange Programme for Key Challenges of European Labour Markets and Societies" (C-STEPs).

C-Step 1: Counselling migrants and refugees focused on a highly individual and very heterogeneous target group of counselling and career guidance. Guidance for refugees and migrants is specific from various points of view, including cultural differences, recognition of foreign educational qualifications, inclusion and empowerment of migrants in their own labour market and concrete (at national level) supporting measures. According to this logic, different learning offers could be designed, which in different didactic designs should not only address the key challenges in this topic area, but at the same time offer approaches to solutions and space for reflection and exchange.

C-Step 2: The topic future jobs primarily addressed the transformation of the working world in the course of digitalisation. This transformation is an immense challenge, especially for companies, with great potential for uncertainty. There is the challenge of actively shaping digital/technological change. For this challenge, it is essential that companies also fully involve their employees in this task and train them sufficiently. The influence of Industry 4.0 on the European labour markets is just as fast-moving as the resulting challenges and opportunities for companies and their employees. Upcoming trends, such as the automation of many sectors in the national labour markets and a concomitant loss of jobs, are having an effect in two places: First, certain jobs may disappear completely. In addition, and this is the bigger key challenge, especially in connection with demographic change and the resulting shortage of skilled workers in many countries, new forms of work, work tasks and thus also new skills and fields of competence will emerge. This shift in the required skills is particularly evident in occupations where, among other things, manual production processes of employees have become replaceable by machines. The human involvement decreases. Nevertheless, only very few professions and activities will completely disappear; rather, it is becoming apparent that other/new competences are needed: agile, networked work in multigenerational and multicompetent teams, innovative and holistic thinking or a holistic process orientation.

C-Step 3: The topic of demographic change primarily dealt with the challenge of an ageing society. If fewer and fewer young people are entering national labour markets while more and more older workers are leaving, this has at least two effects: Firstly, a shortage of skilled workers in certain fields and professions emerges/ manifests. Secondly, however, a proactive and positive focus on the target group older than 50 years becomes necessary. This happens both within the company context and outside of it. Thus, in-company proactive health and ageing management is becoming more and more important in order to "wear out" employees less. This is accompanied by the need to preserve the specific competences and contexts of experience that this generation of employees has or, if necessary, to pass them on to the next generations. Otherwise invaluable knowledge will be lost. Furthermore re-employment, or more precisely retraining in old age, once again become important building blocks that also particularly influence the counselling of this target group. It does not matter whether it is digital processes that are being taught again to older employees in a retraining course or different types of working. There are significant advantages shown in the C-Step to not only enabling but encouraging multigenerational cooperation.

Support and consolidate the exchange and transnational training of counsellors in Europe.

The second objective of the Academia+ project related to the systematic development and continuation of a supportive offer for transnational exchange. This exchange adds another level of systematisation to the content perspective on the needs of the counsellors and career guidance practitioners. In the course of the conception, it was possible to abstract the above-mentioned topics from an international perspective. It turned out that the three main topics mentioned not only have a national scope, but that they fundamentally triggered an international need among the consultants. Building on the key challenges, addressed in the individual training programmes, it was possible to offer a didactic level for exchange that related these topics to the everyday practical context of the counsellors. Although the national conditions, circumstances and structures differ with regard to the three main topics of the C-STEPs, the training programmes facilitated a focused exchange and discussions to identify fundamental synergy effects.

The need and the advantages of such a multinational exchange of experiences regarding main challenges and ways to deal with them were the basis for the second part of this anthology. The country-specific approaches enable a more practical consideration of the theoretically derived and didactically elaborated thematic foci from the first part of the publication. In the following, the central outcomes of the respective countries will be briefly outlined again in order to expand the transnational exchange to include the national perspective.

1 Cyprus

Cyprus has a professional and highly qualified guidance structure that has to face two key challenges. The latter of working migrants and refugees are either underpaid or work part-time in fields different from their expertise. This means that the profitable expertise of these people in their fields is often lost, especially by highly qualified people who had to flee their home countries for various reasons. Often, they are employed in households, agriculture and construction. This frequently causes a mismatch and as a result people seek to move into other sectors with the help of skills guidance. Professional counsellors working with migrants therefore need to be particularly specialised in the VET sector at this point and at the same time not lose sight of the specific needs of their target group.

2 Finland

The authors from Finland outline a different problem in relation to counsellors and their work: the central challenge for counsellors in their everyday work are mainly the areas of re-skilling and up-skilling. There is no reliably structured or complete system of continuing education opportunities in Finland to enable lifelong learning. There is no clear system for guiding continuous learning, so guidance can take place in the workplace (as competence management) by contacting educational institutions or TE services directly. In addition, another challenge is emerging: although many counsellors in Finland are highly qualified (with degrees in psychology), they themselves are constantly challenged to adapt their skills and competences in the sense of lifelong learning and orientation towards the needs of the clients. This goes hand in hand with the need to promote continual lifelong learning measures more strongly and to link them even more closely to guidance.

3 Germany

In Germany exists a two folded problem: On the one hand, there is a defined skills shortage in various sectors and at different levels, at the same time there are many young people and graduates who have difficulties finding their way on the labour market and finding a job that suits them. This is due, among other things, to the region-specific differences in the respective sectors and occupational areas, which further exacerbate the shortage of skilled workers in some regions. One solution could be highly qualified employees from the non-EU sector, who are already being trained at various locations in Germany. The challenge is to deploy these people in a targeted and profitable way in the German economy. At the same time, Germany has enormous potential to better integrate migrants and refugees into the German education system and the German labour market.

4 Greece

With its geopolitical location, Greece is often one of the first countries of arrival for refugees and migrants fleeing to Europe. A large proportion of these people do not want to stay in Greece and emigrate to other countries in Europe. For advisors in Greece, those people who want to stay in Greece offer a key opportunity for the country. Due to an ageing workforce and a mismatch between their existing skills and those that are currently needed and will be needed in the future, especially in the digital sector, there are signs of rising long-term unemployment with a simultaneous increase in the shortage of skilled workers in Greece in the coming years. Counselling can address this at various points: It is the task of career advisors to advise and train qualified employees in Greece with regard to future job requirements. In addition, those migrants who want to live in Greece can fill this gap in the demand for skilled workers with intensive counselling and support.

5 Ireland

With regard to central challenges for counselling in Ireland, the author outlines the need for better networking and organisation of different institutions that are responsible for counselling refugees and migrants in Ireland as an example. Although counselling services have been expanded in many areas, the common professionalisation should not be lost or focused on more strongly. The development of a profession-specific common ethos of action and a common understanding on better cooperation are key challenges for the author of the chapter. Overall, this need is particularly evident in groups with a greater need for guidance, such as refugees and migrants or young people without school-leaving qualifications. The need is not only fundamentally higher for these groups, but it also encompasses several institutions and areas of responsibility, which in such a case must join forces even more.

6 Lithuania

The author of the Lithuanian contribution pointed out that there is a lack of effective vocational training and personalised guidance in Lithuanian institutions. This challenge arises above all from a profession of guidance studies that is not yet systematically anchored. Thus, there are opportunities to offer guidance in a wide variety of contexts, from schools to institutions in the field of further education and training or different institutions. Those people/institutions delivering a career education often do not have the required competencies and qualifications as each institution has its own responsibility in training those who aim to deliver this service. In addition, another key challenge for counsellors in Lithuania is the necessary focus on future working environments. What technological transformations will take place in Lithuania in the coming years? This results in a similar focus as the first key challenge: there is to a certain extent a mismatch between existing competences and those that are then needed in the situation. Programmes that deal specifically with re-skilling could thus become more of a focus for counsellors.

7 Luxembourg

The Luxembourg contribution discusses the central challenges for counsellors, especially from the perspective of social justice. This is a central task not only for Luxembourgish guidance practitioners, but rather for all guidance practitioners in Europe. Their profession and transnational orientation enable guidance practitioners in Europe to make a fundamental contribution in this regard. But at the same time, this opportunity creates an enormous task and challenge for guidance in a transnational context. Not only do guidance practitioners make a major contribution to possible social justice in their everyday work, but it is also part of their remit to think through innovative ideas in relation to improving social justice.

8 Spain

The Spanish contribution identifies two clear key challenges for counsellors in Spain. On the one hand, demographic processes such as a declining birth rate and at the same time an increasing ageing of the population are a central challenge. On the other hand, these demographic problems are complemented and at the same time intensified by the lack of qualification of young people or migrants and refugees coming to Spain. This leads to very high long-term unemployment rates and increasing uncertainty about the length of a job. In addition, there is a growing mismatch between the skills required of companies and their employees in the context of the technological transformation and the skills that have been available to employees up to now. Major change processes are on the horizon, which, according to the author of the contribution, will also have an impact on guidance. New strategies, tools and resources are urgently needed.

Summarising all country-specific contributions, it becomes clear how important the three main topics from the Academia+ project "Counselling migrants and refugees", "future jobs" and "demographic change" are. Furthermore, they all support the necessity of exchanging experiences and strategies to enable learning from each other.

With a view to the idea of a continuous exchange regarding current challenges and initial strategies to meet them, the need for a transnational perspective becomes particularly clear. This is justified by the recognition that the challenges vary in country-specific degrees, but are the same on a systemic level. In addition, it becomes clear in almost all contributions that in many cases consultants do not always have the necessary skills and qualifications needed or that there is a lack of regulated further education and training in general and with regard to the three main topics of the project in particular. Therefore, not only the exchange is important, but there is a need of structured, didactically prepared continuing education offers, which include the transnational exchange.

An idea to create a structured, theoretically sound, at the same time practice-oriented further education could be the creation and establishment of an international university for consultants. The university of applied labour studies in Germany is an example for such an institution on a national level. Further branches in other countries would be necessary, which ideally have coordinated curricula and enable regular mobility in order to gain insights into the common topics with their country-specific designs. This would lead to systematic and high standard exchange of knowledge, experience and best practice and thus enhance the competencies of career guidance practitioners and counsellors.

The manufacturer's authorised representative in the EU is Springer Nature Customer Service Centre GmbH, Europaplatz 3, 69115 Heidelberg, Germany. If you have any concerns regarding our products, please contact ProductSafety@springernature.com

Printed and bound by CPI Group (UK) Ltd, Croydon, CR0 4YY

30/09/2026

02225460-0016